W. B. YEATS

HIS POETRY AND THOUGHT

W. B. YEATS

HIS POETRY AND THOUGHT

BY

A. G. STOCK, *my Geraldine "1902-*

CAMBRIDGE
AT THE UNIVERSITY PRESS
1961

PUBLISHED BY
THE SYNDICS OF THE CAMBRIDGE UNIVERSITY PRESS
Bentley House, 200 Euston Road, London, N.W. 1
American Branch: 32 East 57th Street, New York 22, N.Y.
West African Office: P.O. Box 33, Ibadan, Nigeria

©

CAMBRIDGE UNIVERSITY PRESS
1961

Printed in Great Britain at the University Press, Cambridge
(Brooke Crutchley, University Printer)

CONTENTS

PREFACE

The main subject of this book is W. B. Yeats' poems, in their most accessible published form. I have kept in mind the reader who is interested enough to study them attentively, but may not have access to everything else he wrote. Yeats was so continuously discovering himself that his writings throw light on one another: every poem is complete in itself, but often an early poem gains in depth or a later one in clarity when they are put side by side, or beside a passage from some prose essay or letter. I have used this kind of cross-reference to throw into relief some of the continuous strands of his thought.

It may seen arbitrary to have left out nearly all the plays, except for a reference here and there, for they embody the same coherent vision as his poetry and prose. But Yeats' plays are meant to be performed, and his sense of the theatre was exact and exacting; the stage *décor*, the techniques of speech and movement, were thought out in strict relation to the words. To discuss them as plays without seeing at least some of the later ones played as he intended could be too much like talking in the air. To treat them as supplementary poetry is hardly adequate, and though it might reinforce, would not greatly change what I have found to say.

I have dwelt chiefly on the thought of the poems, with more emphasis on its fundamental cogency than on the heterodox pattern in which it took shape, because it seems to me that to ignore this cogency is to miss too much in the poetry itself. It is true that a poet's ideas cannot be detached from his words, but there is nothing wrong in taking his ideas seriously: to believe that great art does not grow out of flabby thinking is not the same thing as mistaking the 'message' for the greatness of the art. Yeats was not a flabby thinker, nor was he by any means a mere virtuoso of ideas. He sought his words arduously and corrected with pains, because they had not only to sound right, but to give precise expression to a conviction for which there was no formula other than what he could make for himself. But his thinking is disconcerting because it subverts ideas to which most of us are deeply if tacitly committed in practical life, and this makes many readers prefer to dismiss it as a regrettable oddity, or explain it away by a sort of amateur psychoanalysis—as if thoughts so unlike their own must be an aberration—rather than see it as an essential part of the poetry. We do not find it necessary to excuse Homer or Milton like this; it is possible to accept their outlook provisionally for the sake of sharing their vision. But then, Homer and even Milton have been a long time dead: it might be different if either could carry his epic sense of values into modern politics. It is harder to accord Yeats the right to his beliefs when he has not yet lost his vote, so to speak, in the world we live in.

I have also dwelt more than many readers may think necessary on his lifelong preoccupation with his Irish inheritance. In a way, it is so obvious that it escapes notice. The English and the Irish do not need to be told that their countries have different cultures, but even so Yeats' greatness as an English poet tends to make English readers overlook an eccentricity—in the literal sense of the word— that is part of its quality. On the other hand readers neither English nor Irish, especially if they approach western thought through the English language Yeats used so powerfully, are apt to mistake the difference for a mere domestic disagreement without realizing the subtle differences of tradition and temperament that lie behind it. It needs no saying that Yeats was an English poet, with debts to the Metaphysicals, to Blake and Shelley, Rossetti and William Morris, Pater and Swinburne and the companions of the Cheshire Cheese. He learnt his craft from English poets for the sufficient reason that, except for some eighteenth-century prose writers to whom he came late, he had no Irish predecessors who could teach him much about writing. He had also another tradition that was oral and Irish, and in drawing on it he believed, with grounds, that he was recovering a way of thought very deep in himself and very ancient in the mind of Europe, although it was no longer a living reality in England. This marked him out from his contemporaries, even when on the face of it his writing had the typical *fin-de-siècle* preciousness. Some of his early prose, for instance, particularly the Robartes stories, reflects an elegant nostalgia for paganism common enough in English writers of the late nineteenth century. But with them it was a literary cult; they hardly expected their sighing to raise the dead. For Yeats the country people's belief in spirits was a living thing that he respected, and when he set out to join that with Rosicrucian rites and Neoplatonic metaphysics he was after something as unlike Pater's or Swinburne's Hellenism as a live mastodon to a fossil.

He was influenced by eastern thought, but more as a borrower than a disciple: the temper of his own thinking was not eastern. From *Fergus and the Druid* to *The Statues* and *Under Ben Bulben*, what he learned from Asia was worked over and reshaped by a sense of values that he believed had come down to him from pre-Christian Europe by way of Ireland. This sense of values could transform his gleanings in theosophy, magic and spiritualism from a hotchpotch to a harmony. It is the central thing in his poetry, without which the materials it selected and used would fall to pieces.

These are the central themes of the following pages. In elaborating them I have left out much that may seem more important to a different kind of reader of Yeats. There are more ways than one of approaching most poets, and I should be sorry if the hypothetical reader mistook mine for the only one. Besides all Yeats' own writings he will find a considerable body of critical literature to choose from. If he needs to study Yeats seriously he will certainly need one or other of the two biographies, by Joseph Hone and A. N. Jeffares, from both of which I have taken indispensable information. If he wants to inquire further into Yeats' thought, he will find in F. A. C. Wilson's *W. B. Yeats and Tradition*—which I read too late to make full use of it—a much more knowledgeable discussion than mine. These and some others are listed in the bibliography at the end of this book. I have found in them the kind of stimulus that one gets from well-informed discussion, and without consciously echoing any of them must often have said the same things. If I have seldom referred to them except to disagree on some small point or other, that is only a backhanded way of expressing a much wider indebtedness. But to Mr T. R. Henn, who read the manuscript, made many suggestions now embodied in the text, and encouraged me to think the book worth submitting for publication, the debt is greater and more personal.

A. G. S.

ACKNOWLEDGEMENTS

I am obliged to the following persons and agencies for permission to quote:

To Mrs W. B. Yeats, to Macmillan and Co., London, and to the Macmillan Co. of New York, for the liberal use of W. B. Yeats' writings in prose and verse, from the following books:

Collected Poems, 1950; *Collected Plays*, 1952; *Collected Works in Verse and Prose*, 8 volumes, 1908; *Autobiographies*, 1955; *A Vision*, 1937; *The Variorum Edition*, 1957; and *Yeats, The Man and the Masks*, by Richard Ellmann.

To Rupert Hart-Davis for sundry extracts from *The Letters of W. B. Yeats*.

To the Harvard University Press for two extracts from *Letters to the New Island*, by W. B. Yeats.

To Ernest Benn, Ltd, for two extracts from *Florence Farr, Bernard Shaw, W. B. Yeats: Letters*.

To John Murray, for five extracts from *Gods and Fighting Men*, by Lady Gregory.

To Faber and Faber, Ltd, and to Messrs Christy and Moore, Ltd, for four extracts from J. B. Yeats' *Letters to His Son and Others*.

To Faber and Faber, Ltd, and to Harcourt Brace and Co., Inc., New York, for extracts from four poems by Mr T. S. Eliot.

Fuller references for these citations are given in notes to the passages where they occur.

I am also obliged to Tirthankar Bose, Lecturer in English, of Presidency College, Calcutta, for undertaking the troublesome work of checking the index.

ABBREVIATIONS

The following abbreviations are used in references:

CP   *The Collected Poems of W.B.Yeats* (Macmillan, London, 1950).

Plays   *The Collected Plays of W.B.Yeats* (Macmillan, London, 1952).

Letters   *The Letters of W. B. Yeats*, ed. Allan Wade (Rupert Hart-Davis, London, 1954).

CHAPTER I

THE BACKGROUND

A long-drawn grey evening; a ragged landscape of water and rough pasture with a line of hills in the distance; a whiff of burning peat, and a light in the window of a lonely cottage; Ireland does not look or feel like England, and the difference goes deep. The economy, the religion and tradition and ways of thought are different, but apart from these and more indefinable is something in the very essence of the country—not the human population but the earth and water. You may come from Ireland to the Weald of Kent, and feel a sort of impact from the generations who have cultivated Kent to the last ounce for centuries; as if the land had given itself to their labour and been humanized. Ireland never seems in this way to become the servant of human activities. It is true that ghosts linger there with a persistence rare in Anglo-Saxon countries. In some parts there is hardly a square mile without a face looking out of a derelict tower, or a headless coach plying round a tree-shadowed corner, or a murder re-enacting itself from time to time. The living emigrate, but the dead stay on. And yet behind this life of shadows and memories the spirit of the country remains unimpressed by civilization, preoccupied with non-human elemental things. As you walk there you feel it throwing off the print of human habitation and re-membering some supernatural past, which is not past either but only just beyond visibility. All the tribes of spirits which are not ghosts, but follow their own remote life and lay a spell now and then on chosen human beings, are an emanation from it. There is no rational way of making this statement, but I believe that it conveys something about Ireland which many people would admit they have felt.

W. B. Yeats wrote the English language: Spenser, Blake, Shelley and the pre-Raphaelites were among his masters. He was unavoidably an English poet. But by birth and temperament, by the accidents of his upbringing and no less by deliberate and studied choice, he was the poet of the Irish tradition. In a sense there was no Irish tradition, for though its elements existed no great writer had arisen to give it form. His youth in England made him sharply aware of the un-English traits in himself, of the ways of thought and threads of experience which found no immediate response among his English contemporaries. He accepted the difference and trained his genius on it. It enabled him to break away from the ruling poetic codes, not to flounder in undisciplined self-expression but to find sources of thought and imagery which both imposed their own discipline on him and led his mind forward into new ranges of poetry. Being a great artist he grew to such mastery that in his old age he was wholly his own kind of poet, but what he had done was a part of himself. In spite of a surprising change of style his latest poetry grew from his earliest, as the man himself grew, meeting new experience without renouncing his youth.

Though it may be reiterating a platitude, it is important if one wants to understand Yeats to keep on remembering that Ireland is not England. There is such a thing as an English sense of values shaped out of a national experience, and just because it is difficult to formulate completely, it is easy in reading English literature to slip into the assumption that no other values are possible. Much of what Yeats wrote will then look like mere embroideries, or a deliberate shirking of the modern world, when in fact he was true to his own experience and deeply in earnest. It is worth while, therefore, to dwell on some of the peculiarities of Ireland—not so much the Republic of Ireland of today, which may be changing in some ways, as the Ireland Yeats knew before and during the fight which began in 1916.

Towns are not Ireland's strong point. It is scarcely even a land of villages, like India; its most characteristic dwelling is the cottage standing by itself. Physically and mentally it is the least collectivized, least industrialized country in western Europe, and unlike England it has not much of a middle class. The sea-trading merchant meant something to Yeats,* but the industrial magnate and the factory-owner hardly even impinged on his consciousness, and he hated the small-town shopkeeper and all he stood for. The significant people of his world, who had stamped their likeness on Irish history and thought, were the peasants, and the landlords in the big houses.

Of the big houses Yeats writes much, with nostalgic admiration. They were diminishing even before 1916 and the remnant of their glory was finally extinguished in the civil war—not superannuated by industrialism, but burnt out in an agrarian upheaval. The peasants were the enduring element. They are not often in the foreground of Yeats' thought as they are in J. M. Synge's, but their existence in the background makes a difference. They have long traditions and their way of thinking about religion, about history, and not least about the people in the big houses, has coloured the characteristic Irish outlook.

It is not that English writers as a whole have been reconciled to industrialism, whereas the Irish have rejected it. There are things about industrialism which every artist hates, and English literature has cried out against them ever since the eighteenth century. In our own generation D. H. Lawrence, Aldous Huxley and T. S. Eliot, who are hardly members of one school, have all in one way or another shown their horror of the machine age. But they have all lived within its orbit, and had to face its torments or else run away from their own problems. Lawrence raged against it and died; Huxley seeks his answer in mysticism, but the process of discovery is traceable in the growing self-torture of his novels. Eliot has soared out of it

---

* In *Pardon, Old Fathers* (*CP*, p. 113) the
> Old merchant skipper that leaped overboard
> After a ragged hat in Biscay Bay
was Yeats' grandfather.

into religious faith, but not before dissecting it and himself with it in *The Waste Land*.

Irish writers as a whole are less concerned with the impact of industrialism, on the body or the spirit. Sean O'Casey more than most of them has felt its foot upon him and has something vivid and convincing to say about it. The young Yeats, and most of his school, had a standpoint a little outside the turmoil. Sometimes it gives their poems and stories the curious remote serenity of pastoral; often it exasperates English critics who feel that they are missing the point of the modern world. But whatever may be the crucial problems of the age, an artist's first concern is with what he himself has seen and felt and imagined. If he is to keep his integrity he can only be representative in so far as he lets these things, and not a depersonalized brain, determine who or what he shall represent. The ideal kings and country people of Yeats' early poems are folk-tale figures washed over with a pre-Raphaelite colouring, but they stand for the realities that Yeats had felt most deeply, and they fortified him against the noisier influences of contemporary London. They are thus in a direct line with the defiant social criticism of his later work.

Besides being a peasant country Ireland is Catholic. The people are Catholic, but most of the leading families were Protestant. The past tense is needed here; as a class they practically vanished in the civil war. The typical south Irish landlord felt for Catholicism an inherited contempt that was half social, half religious in origin. In general he was loyal to the Crown, though half the great leaders of Irish nationalism have been Protestant landlords by birth. But he never felt himself an Englishman, still less a poorer imitation of the English country squire (though he was poorer), and he resented nothing so much as being confused with the Ulster Protestants, whom he thought of as planters and industrialists, alien to his mental life. Perhaps of all the people he was the most conscious, and the proudest, of the distinctively Irish qualities of his heritage. And yet his Protestantism

4

kept him a little apart, and this may well have added something to Yeats' temperamental aloofness.

But the country is Catholic, and the difference between Catholic and Protestant culture goes beyond theology or politics. When Protestantism broke with the past it broke with ritual and imagery and all the concrete visible forms in which humanity expressed its sense of the unseen long before it had mastered abstract language. In its hatred of idolatry it broke, more completely than Catholicism ever had, with a thousand ancient ways of feeling which are not expressible in terms of Protestant thought.

For making a felt invisible world visible to the understanding, for giving separate identity to its regions and inhabitants, the language of imagery is an instrument far more subtle than abstract words can ever be. Its very imprecisions are capable of expressing shades and links of meaning not to be reasoned out. It is the poet's indispensable language, and if he is not born to a system of imagery he needs to adopt or invent one before he can find full freedom of utterance. In England, scholars are familiar with a grammar of imagery in Greek mythology but it is not native to the common people, and the more education tends away from fairy-tales towards actuality and the Children's Encyclopaedia, the less they can take in of its usage. In Catholic Ireland education is still unscientific; angels, devils and ghosts are serious commonplaces of popular thought. The sense of the other world being thus more expressible it is brought into closer relation with this one, and the language of poetry comes more naturally.

Moreover, Ireland is profoundly different from England in that it has never quite lost its legends. The Anglo-Saxons brought their gods with them as immigrants, and were converted to Christianity before the gods had time to be fully naturalized; and later, most of what native folk-lore managed to thrust its way upward was stamped on by Puritanism. Superstitious practices, traces of witchcraft and divination, are not, of course, extinct in England, but they have nothing august about them; they are habits merely, that no longer have power over the imagination.

The tradition in Ireland is that the gods were there before the Gaels came, that they fought for their possession of the country and at last came to terms and withdrew into the hills, leaving the surface of the land to the invaders. And before the gods there were darker powers, some of whom still survive. However that may be, the land is alive with spirits who are known and respected. Their deeds in different places are remembered; history trails away into myth and myth is projected forward into history. There are faery hills, green terraced mounds into which no farmer will drive a ploughshare. The fairies are seldom talked of, and most seldom by that name, for fear of drawing their attention to the speaker. They are the Good People, much in the way that the Greek Erinnyes were the Eumenides, or kindly ones, because disaster and madness were within their gift. But the people remember what they are—the dispossessed lords who ruled before Christ came.

The Christian Church teaches that this world is not man's true home, that he has a soul which is here to prepare for eternity. The pre-Christian faith found its eternity in nature. The gods lived on earth, but not as man lived. They were as everlasting as the elements and as immune from the ravages of experience. This is the same in Greece as in Ireland, though the names and natures of the gods may differ; and in Ireland some kind of understanding of the old faith survives in the folk imagination. The priests still have to carry on a battle against it in the Church's name. Actual, tangible daily life is confronted not only with Christian otherworldliness but with the different otherworldliness of paganism.

All these are threads in the complex web of the national mind. People for the most part live by them without explicitly thinking about them; only the student and the creative artist may realize how much they mean. Politics is a far more conscious force. In Ireland the struggle for freedom has left deep marks on the people's thoughts. Children hear stories of Oliver Cromwell's savagery, as English children hear about the Black Hole of Calcutta, and believe them as naturally; they pick up stories about Red Hugh O'Donnell, Wolfe Tone, Robert Emmett, and the Irish myth-making genius keeps the heroes vividly alive. Dean Swift himself, that tower of rationality, is a folk-tale in the cottages of Louth.* But there is more than myth and day-dream in it: there is bloodshed. Since the sixteenth century some kind of violent rebellion against England has happened in every generation but one, and from that one, 'the hungry forties', starvation left memories bitterer than bloodshed. The English, according to temperament, think these vagaries either pig-headed or picturesque; it baffles them that men will deliberately die for what they themselves can only see as a piece of attitudinizing. The average Englishman can best make sense of politics when he can reduce it all to economics:

> His resouns spak he ful solempnely
> Sownynge always thencrees of his winnynge—

he always did and probably always will. In Ireland, on the contrary, other activities tend to turn into politics. At times of crisis commerce, art, sport, in fact everything takes on a political colouring, and not even the purest artist can ignore it.

Yeats was a poet, not a politician. This, however, certainly did not mean that Irish nationalism was alien to him or that he acquiesced in the dominant outlook on politics in order to practise his art. He could remain untouched by the first world war, but felt the uprising of Easter Week, 1916, in the very pulse of his poetry. He often kept aloof from the political struggle because it seemed to him to degrade and limit the very values which gave it meaning, but never because he thought like an Englishman.

* Laracor, where Swift was rector, was in Meath, but it was on the Louth side of the border that such stories were told me by an illiterate old woman, about 1922. She asked me 'as a scholar' if I had ever heard of a man called Dean Swift and if he had really written a book; she knew him as a living legend.

With all this in his background, Yeats as a young man both was and chose to be something of an alien among the English poets with whom he was numbered. It is true that all that circle of the 1890's were dissatisfied with the values and literary codes of their time and felt themselves isolated in their own world. But whereas the others fell back on themselves, he had another reservoir, deeper and richer than his own mind could exhaust.

Not that he ever tried to be a poet of life and manners. Neither did Rabindranath Tagore; but Rabindranath could hardly have expressed his own distinctive vision if he had not summed up in himself so much of the Bengali inheritance that he was able to make the commonest and most enduring things of the life around him, effortlessly as it seemed, into a language for his spirit. Yeats recognized this in Rabindranath when he first read him, and it moved him almost to tears because it was so close to what he wanted to do himself. But his was an even lonelier mind than Rabindranath's. He wanted to revive the spirit of Ireland and to give it a voice, other than the high-pitched voice of political argument, but he wanted too to express things that were no part of the collective vision but belonged to the soul's isolation. He had two sides: he enjoyed controversy and hated it as the enemy of his genius; shunned popular applause and half envied popular leaders; took the lead in creating a national theatre, and concentrated his own dramatic art on esoteric poetic plays which studiously avoided building on collective popular emotion. He was a social man, competent in business affairs, a good intellectual fighter who enjoyed battle, and he was always founding movements and championing causes; but in the end he would turn from them and accept the loneliness essential to him as a poet rather than the comradeship within his reach as a man.

In one of his own metaphors, mankind builds up the tradition of a civilization as a bird builds a nest, to be a resting-place where the soul is nourished, whence it can take flight. But bird and soul are most truly in their element when they take off from the nest and

8

soar alone into the uncharted fields of the sky. So with Yeats. He could not be himself and cannot be understood apart from the Irish civilization which is the groundwork of his thought; but when he is most fully himself he is aloof and alone, rising out of his civilization into an emptiness of solitary experience.

Who can distinguish darkness from the soul?[1]*

* Superior figures refer to the references listed on pp. 242–7.

CHAPTER II

THE FIRST BOOK

Yeats had published several poems in Ireland before *The Wanderings of Oisin and Other Poems* came out in London in 1889. At twenty-four he had already rejected some and revised others and was finding his own distinctive voice. For the present, what he sought in poetry was a created world into which, if actual experience or intellectual argument must enter, they should be distilled into an essence indistinguishable from dream. His range of music was limited but very sure. For subject-matter, he had begun with the romantic treatment of pastoral and classical themes, the natural starting-point in those days for a devotee of Shelley and Keats, and passed through a phase when India held his imagination, but as he went on writing he turned more and more to Ireland for themes and sources of imagery. His vocabulary was eclectic because he meant to keep his poems clear of contemporary life, but he was getting rid of the 'thous' and 'doths' and other such merely verbal poeticisms which are like the finger-prints of early nineteenth-century poets on their young disciples, and his revisions tended clearly towards economy and coherence.

The Song of the Happy Shepherd[1]—in its earliest form the epilogue to an Arcadian play which he did not reprint as a whole—is notable for its explicit, rather wistful statement of a poetic creed:

> Words alone are certain good....
> The kings of the old time are dead;
> The wandering earth herself may be
> Only a sudden flaming word,
> In clanging space a moment heard,
> Troubling the endless reverie.

It is an old defence of poetry. Spenser believed in it, but as Spenser—more mature, less burdened by the adolescent's sense of isolation—put it, he made things sound a good deal less hollow and words more solid:

> For deeds doe die, how euer noblie donne,[2]
> And thoughts of men do as themselues decay,
> But wise wordes taught in numbers for to runne,
> Recorded by the Muses, liue for ay;
> Ne may with storming showers be washt away,
> Ne bitter breathing windes with harmfull blast,
> Nor age, nor enuie shall them euer wast.

The more fully the creative artist absorbs the whole man the more he must look on all heaven and earth, all knowledge and all passion, as so much material for shaping. To be wholly a poet, as Yeats fully intended to be, is in a sense to lose the common world for another shared by no living being, a world whose reality he can only know by faith until he has created it and found it good. To live in his created world and accept loneliness as his destiny was the first article of Yeats' poetic faith, and at this stage, when he was shy and awkward in human contacts, he could very well accept it. Twenty years later, writing of the long discipline of unfulfilled love, he accepted that too in the name of his poetry, acknowledging

> That every year I have cried, 'At length
> My darling understands it all,
> Because I am come into my strength
> And words obey my call';
>
> That had she done so who can say
> What would have shaken from the sieve?
> I might have thrown poor words away
> And been content to live.[3]

Then there are three poems on Indian themes. They are, no doubt, a witness to the spell of Hindu thought, cast over him by the Brahmin Mohini Chatterjee, whom he and his friends had invited to Dublin to teach them in 1886. At first sight they look as if the teaching had given him nothing beyond a vision of landscapes soaked in a languorous and sunlit peace, for the last thing he wished to make of his poems was a field of intellectual argument. But those landscapes are alive with the life of one spirit enveloping the universe, which remained an integral part of his poetry long after he had outgrown the languor and the exotic scenery. It comes out in *The Indian upon God*[4] with a clarity bordering on didacticism. The thought of God as the ideal form of each living thing is not very recondite in itself, but it is at once a denial of materialism and a glorification of life and an assertion of the individual soul—all basic elements in the philosophy which was slowly taking coherent form in his mind—and it is put simply and picturesquely in the voices of bird and beast:

> I passed a little further on, and heard a peacock say:
> 'Who made the grass and made the worms and made my feathers gay,
> He is a monstrous peacock, and He waveth all the night
> His languid tail above us, lit with myriad spots of light.'

Half a century later the thought is still a theme for his poetry, though the vigour of feeling and taut energy of expression might belong to another man:

> I, proclaiming that there is
> Among birds or beasts or men
> One that is perfect or at peace,
> Danced on Cruachan's windy plain,
> Upon Cro-Patrick sang aloud;
> All that could run or leap or swim
> Whether in wood, water or cloud,
> Acclaiming, proclaiming, declaiming Him.[5]

Not only is this defiant personal assertion instead of an impersonal report, but the idea has, so to speak, dropped its Indian nationality and been naturalized in Ireland.

There will be more to say later about the effect of Mohini Chatterjee's teaching. Yeats' own mind had an affinity with many things that he found in Indian thought, and finding them must have given him confidence. It gave an intellectual justification to much that he believed with his feelings, and helped to set in order tangled experiences which neither Christian orthodoxy nor contemporary science could deal with. Also it fortified him in a conviction, necessary for the time being, that the meaning of life was in something other than action. But the effect of all this on his poetry was indirect and became more apparent later. For the present he was right to turn away from Indian themes, for if his poetry was to grow to full expressiveness it needed an imagery more thoroughly at home in his mind.

In a group of poems about Irish country people—the old fisherman[6] and old foxhunter[7] and old priest[8]—there is more imaginative realism. They are people he has not created but found in his countryside, and he is trying by bare undecorated writing to bring to light the essential things in them, stripped clean. If the bareness does not reveal so much as it might the reason is not that he was on the wrong track; it is simply his youth. There are many old ballads whose figures are charged with greatness, when centuries of brooding imagination have filled them with meaning and a rigorously simple vocabulary has whittled them down to the bone. Yeats in his early twenties could achieve the austerity of line, and this was remarkable considering the richly coloured style of his other writings at the time, but the power to concentrate intensity of vision into it was still beyond him. *The Ballad of the Foxhunter*, for instance, does not quite bring out the noble pathos which he evidently felt in his theme, unless to a reader who has already felt like that about the same things; there is only the absence of the wrong kind of sentimentality. Whereas in his old age, in a line or two—

> Imagining a man,
> And his sun-freckled face,
> And grey Connemara cloth,
> Climbing up to a place
> Where stone is dark under froth,[9]

the man and the surroundings that have mingled with his nature are brought casually to life in a few phrases.

In a way, *Down by the Salley Gardens*[10] belongs with these poems of the living countryside. He calls it 'an extension of three lines sung to me by an old woman of Ballisodare'.[11] It is a miracle of natural-ness, recreated from the tune and a few phrases of the original song. For a literate man to write folk-song is an all but impossible feat. Yeats has not perhaps eliminated his individual mind from it as completely as the old song-makers could: the simile,

> She bid me take life easy, as the grass grows on the weirs,

contains exact, fine-drawn reflection, and is not the kind of thing that springs from the folk-mind to be passed understandingly from mouth to mouth. Yet the whole poem comes very near to that impersonal rightness which makes a folk-song wander round the world without provoking anyone to ask who wrote it. It could only have been made by one who was genuinely respectful, without pose or patronage, before the country tradition.

But in faeryland, in this early volume, he knew his way about more surely than anywhere else. He was serious about faeryland. First, he respected the ways of thought of ancient times, in which he found a surer grasp of the values he acknowledged; secondly, a deep interest in occultism and psychical research—fortified, obviously, by what he knew of Indian philosophy—had confirmed his conviction that scientific rationalism was not an inclusive account of the universe; thirdly, in Ireland he could talk to people who accepted the super-natural neither as abstraction nor as make-believe, but as part of their concrete experience. All this made it easy for him to take the faeries seriously, as possibly a physical reality and certainly a logical link in the chain of being. The way he was thinking comes out in a private note made not long after this first book was published:

The fairies are the lesser spiritual moods of that universal mind, wherein every mood is a soul and every thought a body.[12]

But it was part of his conception of poetry that it should express the fruit, not the process of his speculations. He never argues about faeryland with the reader, but uses it as his idiom.

The Madness of King Goll[13] in its final form is slight, but compact and clear. Goll was a king on whom the elemental madness fell, so that he threw away his crown in the moment of victory, and wandered in the woods, tormented and yet irresistibly drawn by the restlessness of wind and leaf. It is the war between the pride of human greatness and that lonely element in man which seeks the non-human world outside of stone walls and walls metaphysical, a conflict which haunted Yeats in many forms to the end of his life. He found it in himself but found it too, and found a language for it, in Irish legend.

Here again one may see that his technical power is only at its beginning. In *King Goll* the landscape is painted, not carelessly indeed, but in a generalized way:

> I laughed aloud and hurried on
> By rocky shore and rushy fen;
> I laughed because birds fluttered by,
> And starlight gleamed, and clouds flew high,
> And rushes waved and waters rolled.

The language is evocative without precision; it might have been, though it is not, written by one whose intimacy with nature was slight. In later years he could bring a scene much more minutely before the eyes in fewer words:

> At sudden thunder of the mounting swan
> I turned about and looked where branches break
> The glittering reaches of the flooded lake.[14]

Here, without over-emphasis, every word tells. Such mastery is won like a painter's or musician's sleight of hand by years of practice.

A better poem than *King Goll*, akin to it in theme, is *The Stolen Child*.[15] On one level it is a piece for a children's anthology; the conception, and also the verse form, owe much to *Up the Airy Mountain*, a child's song by William Allingham that belongs to the same countryside;[16] but it is none the less an exact expression of the poise of the writer's mind.

> Where the wave of moonlight glosses
> The dim grey sands with light,
> Far off by furthest Rosses
> We foot it all the night,
> Weaving olden dances,
> Mingling hands and mingling glances
> Till the moon has taken flight;
> To and fro we leap
> And chase the frothy bubbles,
> While the world is full of troubles
> And is anxious in its sleep.

These faeries are a pure incarnation of light and water, so remote from human affairs that they would be hardly more than pretty—as moonlight in a forest is pretty, looked at from the security of a roofed hearth—but for the farewell in the last verse to familiar life:

> He'll hear no more the lowing
> Of the calves on the warm hillside,
> Or the kettle on the hob
> Sing peace into his breast
> Or see the brown mice bob
> Round and round the oatmeal-chest

—where all of a sudden they are recognized for the outposts of the kingdom of shadows, and touched with faint terror.

Stories of faeries and changelings are known to country people, but they do not tell them quite like that. Ordinary humanity is firmly on the side of the singing kettle and the oatmeal-chest; and the faeries, to those who truly believe in them, are mostly more of a menace than a delight. Yet the folk-tales are full of people whom they have lured away, people who have not closed their eyes and ears in time to shut out the beauty that makes a man turn traitor to his kind, and Yeats was one such. The prevailing mood of the poem is irresponsible delight, but there is a faint undernote of foreboding: as if a child gives his hand to the elemental spirits, innocently in love with their wildness, and another presence is silently aware that their gift to their devotees is an agony of loneliness.

In *The Wind Among the Reeds* he knew more about it.

> Be you still, be you still, trembling heart;
> Remember the wisdom out of the old days:
> *Him who trembles before the flame and the flood,*
> *And the winds that blow through the starry ways,*
> *Let the starry wind and the flame and the flood*
> *Cover over and hide, for he has no part*
> *With the lonely, majestical multitude.*[17]

This is about ten years after *The Stolen Child*. The world into which he has stepped 'from a world more full of weeping than he can understand' has begun to reveal itself through the magic moonlight as a region of space-haunting elementals: to inhabit it makes demands on the spirit as high and stern as any made by the human world. But it is still his chosen place, and the only place where he can move freely.

In the course of earning a scanty income while he wrote poetry, Yeats had been researching into Irish legend and folk-lore, and poetry written in the national tradition, and had recognized his field of work there. The story of *The Wanderings of Oisin*[18] is taken from Celtic legend. He knew no Irish himself, but there were different versions translated by the Ossianic Society to be found in the British Museum, besides the mouth-to-mouth versions current among Irish country people.

Oisin or Usheen, son of Finn, who was the poet of the ancient Fianna, was loved by the faery woman Niamh. She rode away over the sea with him, and they lived for what seemed a short space of time—three days or three years maybe—in the faery eternity where nothing is real but the joy of the living moment, until some stray memory set him longing to see his friends again. He came back to the world to find that he had been away three centuries, Christianity had come to Ireland, and a race of men had sprung up to whom Finn and the Fianna were a half-forgotten hero-myth. For a while he wandered among them on his faery horse, insulated from mortality.

But when his feet touched the ground the earth asserted her claim again and his three hundred years fell upon him; he became a shrivelled old man and died with the sound of church bells ringing in his ears.

As the books tell the story, Saint Patrick baptized him and tried to save his soul by teaching him about the Christian heaven and hell. But Oisin was a bad convert; he spent his last days lamenting Finn and the Fianna for whose sake he had come back to mortality; they were gone, and instead of his ever-living bride there was nothing for him but the insubstantial Christian heaven. To Saint Patrick Niamh was a spirit of hell, but as Oisin told the story of his life with her beyond the world and of the feasting and fighting of the Fianna, he made the Christian heaven seem a bloodless, joyless eternity. The Saint listened in spite of himself; he did not exactly give way but he had no answer, and often instead of arguing he would only say, 'Tell me more'. At the end of the story Oisin declared passionately that he would rather endure the flames of hell with the Fianna for company than face the boredom of heaven among the saints.

Three worlds are brought together in the story. The first part of it may very well come down from pre-Christian days, for it is full of the interpenetration of time and eternity as pagan Ireland felt it. The world where Finn and the Fianna feast and fight and die is a good world, but it knows change and grief. Men are not free from the weight of the past and the weight of the future, and all their passion ends in death. Around them they see another life of woods that renew themselves from year to year and winds and waters everlastingly singing. This is the world of the gods, joyous and heartless; it is an eternity apart from human decay but it belongs rather to the earth than to the soul. Something in man seeks and is sought by it, and yet man cannot be other than human. He carries his grief with him, his love is touched by time's melancholy, and although the gods may claim him he comes back in the end like Oisin to his own world, only to find that it has been changing and passing.

This pagan otherworldliness is the distinctive thing which haunts the Irish legends—born, it may be, of the country itself and the weirdly beautiful lights and shadows which are always passing over and transforming it. You sail out over the western sea and you come to the Land of the Ever Young, or a hill opens, or you turn down a path you never saw before in a country you knew well, and there it is and you are lost there and time ceases to exist. It is different from the spirituality of the Christian dispensation which Saint Patrick preached. This newer teaching accepts humanity and rejects nature; salvation is won by self-suppression and the denial of nature. The shadow of it changes all the values of human life. The old gods become demons, the old warriors are men of sin, renunciation takes on meaning, life loses its self-sufficient grandeur, death becomes all-important. And the Christians assert that nature will be burnt up in the last day and the gods with it, but man's soul endures for ever in heaven or hell.

It would be possible to treat such a theme from the Christian side. De la Motte Fouqué did it in his telling of *Undine*: there the elemental powers are wildly, fiercely beautiful, but even they feel and do homage to the spirit of tender forgiveness in Christianity, though they do not share it. In the medieval legend of Tannhäuser there is in the end the same acknowledgement of the spirit by which Christianity conquered. But whatever scribe first wrote the story of Oisin was an unregenerate old heathen. The pull against each other of the Fianna and the faery world was very real to him, but as for Christ, he could see no more than Swinburne what men found in the dead limbs of gibbeted gods. His Saint Patrick is conscientious no doubt, but a rather unintelligent kill-joy who can only answer Oisin by saying that his side has won: his God is stronger than the Fianna and has locked them all in hell. For though the writer knew very well that Christianity had conquered, his own imagination remained closed to it. Indeed, the tone of the story suggests that the poets were the last defenders of the old faith; as they may well have been, seeing that they were interpreters of the courtly and aristocratic tradition, and Christianity with its mystical sharing of suffering has usually made its first headway as a gospel of the downtrodden.

This was how the tale stood, clear-cut and expressive, when Yeats found it. What did he make of it? He had no need to change the essential values, for it said exactly what he meant. His Saint Patrick is a mere shadow, even less alive than the original; Yeats took the old writer's stand, one foot in Finn's court and the other in faery-land, with only a glance of resentment for the wave of faith that had rolled over the world. His Niamh, on the other hand, is much more of an emanation from his own mind. Lady Gregory, adapting the same material in her own way, paints her in bright, clear colours which are probably nearer to the original image of grace and splendour:

And it was not long till they saw coming towards them from the west a beautiful young woman, riding on a very fast slender white horse. A queen's crown she had on her head, and a dark cloak of silk down to the ground, having stars of gold on it; and her eyes were blue and as clear as the dew on the grass, and a gold ring hanging down from every golden lock of her hair; and her cheeks redder than the rose, and her skin whiter than the swan upon the wave, and her lips as sweet as honey that is mixed through red wine.[19]

Yeats saw her otherwise, as a pre-Raphaelite goddess clothed in melancholy languor, and although she belonged to the world of joy he invested her with forebodings:

> A pearl-pale, high-born lady, who rode
> On a horse with bridle of findrinny;
> And like a sunset were her lips,
> A stormy sunset on doomed ships;
> A citron colour gloomed in her hair,[20]

in fact, more of a young man's dream than an old man's legend. And although he followed the outline of the story he filled his land-scape with mists and sunsets which are the colouring of his own mind rather than of the original. Most of the old versions told of one island of rapturous delight, but he made Oisin exhaust the power of three before his longing for the human world overcame him at last, so that without breaking the thread he might prolong his visionary descriptions. At that time the country of dreams meant more in his poetry than character, and far more than action. Indeed, the least convincing part of the poem seems to me to be the fighting on the Island of Victories, which was his own invention. Spenser was temperamentally as dreamy as Yeats, but by comparison the fights in *The Faerie Queene* are clearly drawn pictures of hard hitting and accurately directed thrusts. But there is a great difference: Spenser saw fighting as an inherent part of life, whereas Yeats was using it as an escape from the actual world.

Action is the soul of legend as it is of drama; for traditional art, being passed from mouth to mouth, must rest upon what men have in common; upon thought, not as it exists in individual minds but as it is objectified in images of action. The very dreaminess which made Yeats turn to the legends for a refuge prevented him from being true to the spirit in which they were conceived and handed down. All the same there was a man of action latent in him, who emerged later under the influence of love and friendship and the Irish theatre and the fight for freedom. The maturer Yeats still found in the legends an interpretation of life, a definition of greatness and a starting-point for thought. He never grew out of them; they were rather the point from or round which he grew. In his preface to Lady Gregory's *Gods and Fighting Men*, written about 1904, one may see how their significance had widened and deepened for him since *The Wanderings of Oisin*. He saw them now not as a refuge from the world but as a concrete expression of the love of life and of the heroic virtues which bind men together; their distinguishing mark he saw as a lordly comradeship.

It is one of the ailments of our life that thought, when it is not the planning of something, or the doing of something or some memory of a plain circumstance, separates us from one another because it makes us always more unlike, and because no thought passes through another's ear

21

unchanged. Companionship can only be perfect when it is founded on things, for things are always the same under the hand.[21]

He saw the part they had played, by giving a clear outline to the people's imagination, in making successive generations of immigrant overlords conform to one ideal of greatness.

Surely these old stories, whether of Finn or Cuchulain, helped to sing the old Irish and the old Norman-Irish aristocracy to their end. They heard their hereditary poets and story-tellers, and they took to horse and died fighting against Elizabeth or against Cromwell; and when an English-speaking aristocracy had their place, it listened to no poetry indeed, but it felt about it in the popular mind an exacting and ancient tribunal, and began a play that had for spectators men and women that loved the high wasteful virtues.[22]

He saw too, more explicitly than he had been able to state in the early poem, that in the broken memories of those old gods and heroes there lingered the remains of a view of life which may once have been profound, and had been deliberately suppressed by Christianity. He tried to trace something of its reality in what survives:

They have no asceticism, but they are more visionary than any ascetic, and their invisible life is but the life about them made more perfect and more lasting, and the invisible people are their own images in the water. Their gods may have been much besides this, for we know them from fragments of mythology picked out with trouble from a fantastic history running backward to Adam and Eve, and many things that may have seemed wicked to the monks who imagined that history, may have been altered or left out; but this they must have been essentially, for the old stories are confirmed by apparitions among the country people today.... These gods are indeed more wise and beautiful than men; but men, when they are great men, are stronger than they are, for men are, as it were, the foaming tide-line of their sea. One remembers the Druid who answered when someone asked him who made the world, 'The Druids made it'. All was indeed but one life flowing everywhere, and taking one quality here, another there. It sometimes seems to one as if there is a kind of day and night of religion, and that a period when the influences are those that shape the world is followed by a period when the greater power is in influences that would lure the soul out of the world, out of the body. When Oisin is speaking with St Patrick of the friends and the life he has outlived, he can but cry out constantly against a religion that has no meaning for him. He laments, and the country people have remembered his words for centuries: 'I will cry my fill, but not for God, but because Finn and the Fianna are not living.'[23]

One remembers that druid again, more than twenty years later, in *The Tower*:

> Death and life were not
> Till man made up the whole,
> Made lock, stock and barrel
> Out of his bitter soul,
> Aye, sun and moon and star, all,
> And further add to that
> That, being dead, we rise,
> Dream and so create
> Translunar Paradise.[24]

The first fascination which the druids and ancient gods exercised over him was a gateway into a world of philosophic musings which became the stuff of his poetry as time went on.

If a modern reader took up this first book without knowing anything of the later Yeats, he might be excused for thinking that here was a poet with a marvellous gift of word-magic but a somewhat finicky and precious imagination bent on enclosing itself in dreams. Yeats noticed it himself: when he had sent off his MS. to press he wrote to his friend Katherine Tynan:

I have noticed some things about my poetry I did not know before, in this process of correction; for instance, that it is almost all a flight into fairy-land from the real world, and a summons to that flight. The Chorus to the 'Stolen Child' sums it up—that it is not the poetry of insight and knowledge, but of longing and complaint—the cry of the heart against necessity. I hope some day to alter that and write poetry of insight and knowledge.[25]

But immature though the book may be, underneath the decorative imagery and remote themes it is full of mental adventure. Trains of thought that are latent in it kept on recurring with widening significance to the end of his life. They were in his mind, but when he read the legends or listened to the country talk he found them reflected back to him, reappearing with something changed or added, so that he became aware that he was not speaking for himself alone but for a tradition which existed outside, though it had been almost silenced, as well as inside himself. Later, as his reading and experience extended, he found similar ideas in other ancient literatures, outlines of a conformation of life that had been submerged, first by Christian ideology and then by the values of urban democracy. In the dream-pictures of that early volume the outline is already faintly discernible, and although much was added to it later it was never lost. The world of action did not satisfy him, the values of modern life were antipathetic to him, Christian mysticism he could respect without desiring it for himself; but

> The half-read wisdom of daemonic images,
> Suffice the ageing man as once the growing boy.[26]

CHAPTER III

THE FIRST PLAYS

Yeats' achievements in drama are a large topic, and I do not intend
to discuss them more than is necessary in writing about Yeats the
poet. But poems and plays cannot be altogether separated: from the
beginning, and long before he had any objective sense of the stage,
dramatic poetry had been one way of working out his conceptions,
and parts of his early plays were revised and preserved as separate
poems. *The Countess Cathleen*,[1] written in 1891, was the first that
he retained as a stageable dramatic whole; it was also the next considerable landmark in his verse after *The Wanderings of Oisin*.
It was partly prompted by love of Maud Gonne, but also it fitted in
with a vast, rather vague plan to regenerate the soul of Ireland with a
cycle of works about successive phases of its history.* *Oisin* was his
rendering of pagan Ireland: *The Countess Cathleen* was to be Christian.

It was a west-of-Ireland folk-tale, in a version he had found
retold in French, about a famine, and a woman who sold her soul to
the devil to save her tenants from starvation and to win back for
heaven their own souls which they had bartered for food. The people
were saved but so was Cathleen, for charity can never commit the
soul to damnation.   The Light of Lights
        Looks always on the motive, not the deed,
        The Shadow of Shadows on the deed alone
is the verdict spoken at the end by an angel.

In the Saint Patrick of *The Wanderings of Oisin* Christianity was
crude and forbidding; in Cathleen, whom compassion has impelled
to perfect renunciation, it is gentle and full of charity and conquers

* Cp. *Estrangement* (*Autobiographies*, p. 493): 'When I was twenty-five or twenty-six
I planned a *Légende des Siècles* of Ireland that was to set out with my *Wanderings of
Oisin*, and show something of every century.'

in its own right. She has transcended her own soul's salvation; in her sacrifice is seen the one thing in Christianity for which paganism can find no answer—the selfless sharing of the world's sufferings which is Christ. She is in a world apart from her friends, who can only look on helplessly while angels and devils battle for her soul. So here for once the sympathy of the story is where the ordinary tale-teller would put it, with the orthodox faith.

This at least is where it ought to be. But although superficially the story is simple, beautiful and clear-cut, and although in its final form* Yeats has worked it out scene by scene with fine stagecraft, in poetry which is never irrelevant to character and action, never too diffuse or too obscure for stage utterance, the main action does not spring into tense dramatic life. There is no conflict in Cathleen's decision; her renunciation is the fulfilment of a love which possesses her whole soul, and her choice of Hell has no effect on her other than the external, spiritually unimportant effect of death. It is all very well for Aleel to tell us that

> Angels and devils clash in the middle air,
> And brazen swords clang upon brazen helms

but to the spectators Cathleen's ultimate entry into Heaven cannot at any point seem doubtful. In old age Yeats wrote of it:

It was not, nor is it now [i.e. after many revisions] more than a piece of tapestry. The Countess sells her soul, but she is not transformed. If I were to think out that scene today, she would, the moment her hand has signed, burst into loud laughter, mock at all she has held holy, horrify the peasants in the midst of their temptations.[2]

Damnation would thus be represented directly as a state of soul instead of symbolically as a place, and the horror of evil as well as the beauty of goodness would be focused in Cathleen herself. It would be a different, altogether more powerful play. But though the

---

* The play was much revised, and I have quoted only from the final version in *Plays*. In *Autobiographies* (p. 290) he speaks of 'its first meagre version'; in *Dramatis Personae* (*Autobiographies*, pp. 416-17) he says of the first acted version: 'The play itself was ill-constructed, the dialogue turning aside at the lure of word or metaphor, very different, I hope, from the play as it is today after many alterations.'

peasants might well be thus shocked back into a state of grace, it is difficult to see how Cathleen herself could be saved. In fact, Yeats' mind had not come to grips with the idea of damnation, and the picturesque convention he was using held it at a distance.

And yet to call the play a piece of tapestry is over-harsh. Aleel brings it to life. He is there because he is necessary, not to the story (he does not come into the French version which is Yeats' source) but to Yeats' imagination. Through Aleel he brought in that third world he loved and was at home in, of moonlight and the dancing elemental powers, neither good nor evil in Christian terms, and linked human passion with that world rather than with Heaven. In the play the real opposition dividing the soul is not between Heaven and Hell, but between Heaven as the peace of perfect renunciation and the wild joy of the old gods,

> Who wander about the world to waken the heart—
> The passionate, proud heart—that all the angels,
> Leaving nine heavens empty, would rock to sleep.

For they too are beautiful and enthroned deep in the imagination of man, but this is not their day. Thus the real theme is still the same triple conflict of the earlier poems.

Between *The Wanderings of Oisin* and *The Countess Cathleen* Yeats had been editing and interpreting William Blake; he had also continued his occult studies with passionate intensity. Ideas about good and evil and the nature of reality were sorting themselves in his mind, and are reflected in the play. There is a war between good and evil, but the reality of evil and its nature are uncertainly defined. Cathleen herself, a few moments before she resolves to sell her soul, is absolutely sure of God's universal forgiveness:

> There is no soul
> But it's unlike all others in the world,
> Nor one but lifts a strangeness to God's love
> Till that's grown infinite, and therefore none
> Whose loss were less than irremediable
> Although it were the wickedest in the world.

The idea of Hell is inconsistent with her Platonic view of evil as a kind of mistake, an obstinate clumsiness of matter under God's hand:

> For surely He does not forsake the world,
> But stands before it modelling in the clay
> And moulding there His image. Age by age
> The clay wars with His fingers and pleads hard
> For its old, heavy, dull and shapeless ease;
> But sometimes—though His hand is on it still—
> It moves awry and demon hordes are born.

And the simple peasant woman Mary, equally sure of the impermanence of evil, cries out to the demon merchants:

> Destroyers of souls, God will destroy you quickly.
> You shall at last dry like dry leaves and hang
> Nailed like dead vermin to the doors of God.

A little while before, the first merchant had spoken very positively of himself as no illusion:

> For there is nothing on the ridge of the world
> That's more substantial than the merchants are
> That buy and sell you—

but he does not deny Mary's assertion: instead, he answers with the humility and confidence of perfect faith:

> Though we're but vermin that our Master sent
> To overrun the world, he at the end
> Shall pull apart the pale ribs of the moon
> And quench the stars in the ancestral night.

Behind his nothingness is a vaster, more powerful negation which is Satan, and the end of the world is to be Satan's victory, not God's: the eternal reality behind matter is—nothing. This is the faith of devils, and it seems that to sell one's soul to them is to accept this nothing; it is to cease to have a soul. Teigue and Shemus, feeling a good deal more comfortable without theirs, refuse to let Cathleen buy them back:

> For souls, if there are souls,
> But keep the flesh out of its merriment.
> I shall be drunk and merry.

There is a passage in the third scene where Aleel, charged with a vision from the god Aengus, comes to Cathleen to bid her cease troubling herself about God's business

> And live in the hills,
> Among the sound of music and the light
> Of waters, till the evil days are done.

Is there any difference except in the degree of refinement between this invitation and Shemus's preference for being drunk and merry? Christianity which sees no distinction between the old gods and the powers of Hell would say there is none; for the Christian there is no gateway into the world of the spirit except through denial of the self. The old nurse Oona in her jealousy accused Aleel of being unbaptized and of filling Cathleen's head with fantasies unfit for a Christian ear, and by her standards she was right. All the same Aleel belongs to the world of the spirit and not to that other world which is the negation of everything except the flesh. Whatever he may be he is no part of Satan's kingdom, and the merchants, who vaguely fear him, cannot touch his soul when he throws it at them. He is as sure as Mary that their dominion is not final:

> men yet shall hear
> The archangels rolling Satan's empty skull
> Over the mountain-tops

and in the last scene when the unseen powers do battle for Cathleen's soul, the battle is shown to Aleel in his vision as the same that raged between the powers of light and darkness long before Christianity came to Ireland. He recognizes one after another of the dark powers as the ancient enemies of his own De Danaan gods, and the name he gives their king is neither Satan nor Beelzebub but Balor of the Evil Eye. Yet at the end it is none of the Danaan gods but an angel in visible form who is seized by him and reports the issue of the fight:

> The light beats down; the gates of pearl are wide;
> And she is passing to the floor of peace,

And Mary of the seven times wounded heart
Has kissed her lips, and the long blessed hair
Has fallen on her face.

So Cathleen is received into the Christian heaven where she belongs. Earlier in the play she had said firmly that Aleel's gods were 'not angelical', but at least it is clear that they and the angels share the same enemies.

Rewriting the last scene for easier stage presentation,[3] Yeats changed the language of Aleel's vision because, as he said, the Dublin audience knew too little about ancient Irish mythology. Instead of the names of the Fomor—the dark prehistoric powers whom the Danaan gods had conquered when they first possessed Ireland—he put in Asmodeus and Belial, gods out of Asia, whom a Christian audience might accept as in some sense real, because they have a significant place in the Bible, and as demonic because they were enemies of the God of Israel. Superficially this simplifies the pattern—and of course Yeats knew that gods have many names in different countries—but the effect is to do some violence to Aleel's nature and to obscure rather than clarify the tangled mythology in the background. The Old Testament, monotheistically indifferent to conflicts within the ranks of the pagan gods, lumps them all together as idols of the heathen; but in Irish legend the memory of their wars with one another is as clear as that of Christ's wars with the survivors. There is a dream-like confusion in the way the powers who speak through Aleel seem now to oppose, now to replace, and again to become merged in the power to which Cathleen has dedicated herself.

Possibly at this time Yeats himself could not have explained the tangle more clearly than he did; his symbols carried meanings vaster and more obscure than he could unravel and he knew it, but had faith in their validity. In the preface to the 1899 edition[4] of his poems he wrote:

I must leave my myths and images to explain themselves as the years go by and one poem lights up another...I would, if I could, add to that majestic heraldry of the poets, that great and complicated inheritance of images which written literature has substituted for the greater and more complex inheritance of the spoken tradition, some new heraldic images gathered from the lips of the common people. Christianity and the old nature faiths have lain down side by side in the cottages, and I would proclaim that peace as loudly as I can among the kingdoms of poetry, where there is no peace that is not joyous, no battle that does not give life instead of death;

and he goes on to speak of

a subtlety of desire, an emotion of sacrifice, a delight in order, that are perhaps Christian, and myths and images that mirror the energy of woods and streams, and of their wild creatures,[5]

and to ask

Has any part of that majestic heraldry of the poets had a very different fountain? Is it not the ritual of the marriage of heaven and earth?

This passage shows that Yeats was deeply serious about his mythological imagery, though he might not yet be able to give a clear account of its meaning. He was not merely playing with decorative language; the powers which he calls 'the energies of woods and streams, and of their wild creatures' meant enough for him to set them up beside Christianity as a starting-point for an alternative interpretation of life. It was only a starting-point, for then and always he was too wise a poet to write down more doctrine than he could vitalize with poetry distilled from his inward experience, but if Aleel's visions and the sympathy between him and Cathleen are any guide, he had in mind some remote reconciliation between the two ways of thought.

It may be questioned whether it is worth while, or even fair to the poet, to analyse so slight a play. For when all is said *The Countess Cathleen* is not a monumental work. Not only was Yeats hampered by a too-decorative poetic convention, but he was still too much wrapped up in dreams to treat his theme with full dramatic intensity. To interpret life through myth one must find life as significant as myth. To many critics the play is interesting only in so far as it

originated in his worship of Maud Gonne, his desire to write a part
for her, and his disapproval of the waste, as he felt it to be, of her
beauty and energy in famine relief and arid political propaganda.

This is part but not the whole of the truth. He had met Maud
Gonne soon after the publication of his first book and had fallen
headlong in love with her, and all his poetry for years to come was
directly or indirectly about her. Her energy and generosity fascinated
him as well as her beauty, but from the beginning he was troubled by
the violence of that energy, the recklessness of the generosity which
absorbed her in wild action as if action were a good in itself. He was
torn between adoration and criticism, and in the figure of Cathleen
he seems to be dramatizing and transfiguring something unacceptable to him in Maud Gonne. Cathleen was no likeness of Maud, not
even Yeats could have taken her for one, yet Maud, haggard and
spent after weeks of famine relief work, may have suggested her. It
was she who tormented his mind with the question, 'Can a soul be
lost through its own generosity?'—and the play is at the same time
an attempt to deny it and to reconcile himself, in Aleel, to his own
premonition that he must lose her.

Such questions are for the psychoanalyst, whose main interest
is in noting how the poet is like other men, in that there are personal
emotional drives behind his actions. But if the poet begins where
all of us begin he ends where most of us do not, in the creation of a
world, and the poetry is in the created world rather than in its source.
To Yeats himself, critical though he was of it, *The Countess Cathleen*
was a work of some importance; he showed this in his persistent
revisions of the original version and the frequency of his references
to it in later writings. In a diary kept in 1909[6] it was still associated
in his mind chiefly with thoughts about Christianity:

In Christianity what was philosophy in Eastern Asia became life, biography
and drama. A play passes through the same process in being written.
At first, if it has psychological depth, there is a bundle of ideas, something
that can be stated in philosophical terms; my *Countess Cathleen*, for

instance, was once the moral question, may a soul sacrifice itself for a good end? but gradually philosophy is eliminated until at last the only philosophy audible, if there is even that, is the mere expression of one character or another. When it is completely life it seems to the hasty reader a mere story. Was the *Bhagavad Gita* the 'scenario' from which the Gospels were made?

Years later in *The Circus Animals' Desertion*,[7] he wrote of its genesis in an emotional storm:

> And then a counter-truth filled out its play,
> *The Countess Cathleen* was the name I gave it;
> She, pity-crazed, had given her soul away,
> But masterful Heaven had intervened to save it.
> I thought my dear must her own soul destroy,
> So did fanaticism and hate enslave it,
> And this brought forth a dream and soon enough
> The dream itself had all my thought and love.

The thought which brought forth the dream is not the dream itself; it is only a lever which raises images from some deep in the poet's mind, groups them and sets them moving; and to Yeats as a poet the images matter more than their source. A few lines further on in the poem he writes as if they had a pre-ordained form independent of his will, only needing his mind as a seed needs sunlight to grow in:

> Those masterful images because complete
> Grew in pure mind.

They may begin from the heart, but once they are called into being the imagination must govern them with its own laws, make them speak its own truth. And although the play has a starting-point in his life it leads him back to that country whither everything draws him, where myth clashes with myth and the forms of the old gods are dimly visible through the mists in which a new faith has sought to obliterate them.

In *The Land of Heart's Desire*,[8] written four years later, the conflicting forces are the same but the pattern has shifted, God's heaven is in alliance with the world of human society; together they form an orb of peace enclosed against the wildness of the elemental world.

It is May Eve, the night when the faeries' power is strongest, and the little woodland cottage is an island of human security protected by the crucifix—God's blessing—that hangs within, and the quicken branch hanging outside to invoke the faeries' blessing. On such a night it is dangerous to speak of supernatural powers, but the newly married bride, who feels the security of life's routine closing round her like a prison, not only speaks of them but calls them by their names, to her mother-in-law's terror and the disapproval of the priest. And step by step they gain power over the house from this invitation, till they have stolen away her soul.

Love, piety and safety on one side; on the other the joy of the storm. Father Hart is very clear that the powers of whom Mary is dreaming are God's enemies, the rebel angels, and that their gaiety is the other side of despair. Mary Bruin's uncoordinated mind has room for both God and the faeries: to her the faeries are the wild loveliness of the world which religion and duty have shut out. But when she suggests that God may open his door to them at the end of time she is firmly told:

> Did but the lawless angels see that door
> They would fall, slain by everlasting peace;
> And when such angels knock upon our doors,
> Who goes with them must drive through the same storm.

The soul's choice is absolute. The faery child who comes for Mary gives her the same warning in different terms:

> But clinging mortal hope must fall from you,
> For we who ride the winds, run on the waves,
> And dance upon the mountains are more light
> Than dewdrops on the banner of the dawn.

She reveals herself as a form of the ancient earth-spirit:

> When winter sleep is abroad my hair grows thin,
> My feet unsteady. When the leaves awaken

34

> My mother carries me in her golden arms.
> I'll soon put on my womanhood and marry
> The spirits of wood and water, but who can tell
> When I was born for the first time?

When Mary's call had given her a footing in the house every person there, except Shawn the lover, felt an impulse to submit to her. Even the priest was cajoled into taking down the crucifix with his own hands; he did not recognize, till too late, the lawless angels in a child's unearthly beauty. Now he is powerless to stop her, he can only warn Mary to

> Think of this house and of your duties in it

and remind her in cold uncoloured language of the saints and of Christ crucified. On faery lips

> their Land of Heart's Desire,
> Where beauty has no ebb, decay no flood,
> But joy is wisdom, time an endless song

is a thousand times more alluring than these names. Heaven is in retreat and leaves the battle to its ally, human love. There is more to hold Mary in Shawn's arms than in the hope of heaven, but even there is a captivity from which she has already recoiled. She would stay and she would go; her heart is torn between the earthly love and the more than earthly loveliness, and she dies; and the air is full of the faery chorus, exultant and sad, joyous and heartless:

> The wind blows out of the gates of the day,
> The wind blows over the lonely of heart,
> And the lonely of heart is withered away.

The priest points the moral as a man of God should see it:

> Thus do the spirits of evil snatch their prey
> Almost out of the very hand of God;
> And day by day their power is more and more,
> And men and women leave old paths, for pride
> Comes knocking with thin knuckles on the heart.

But Yeats' imagination is wholly on the faeries' side; the logic of his poetry evokes a secret joy in the reawakening of pride and the return of the old gods to power over the heart. There is a beauty of storm as well as a beauty of peace: there is an ecstasy which is another kind of peace in the wild race of a sea wave or a dead leaf in the wind, and it is this element, thrust out by religion, that triumphs in the whole poetic movement of the play.

It is a slight piece, and in later days Yeats disliked it for the sentimental prettiness which had made it popular. The woodland setting is too idyllic, the verse too limpidly sweet, the characters too simplified, with all the ferocity of human and elemental life left out. The war of supernatural forces is etherealized till sensitive school-children can act it adequately, and this is not what is demanded by the latent thought and the breath of terror blowing through it. All the same, slight though it is there is a hint of poignant personal significance in the changed alignment of forces. The faeries now belong unequivocally to the outer darkness; the choice is clear and absolute between the path of consummated love and the soul's salvation, and the lonely path of poetry.

CHAPTER IV

THE WORLD OF DREAM

There were two more books of poems before the end of the century: the lyrics published in 1891 along with *The Countess Cathleen*, and later gathered in 'The Rose' section of his collected volume, and *The Wind Among the Reeds*, published in 1899, four years after *The Land of Heart's Desire*. The second book brought a certain kind of writing, which he had practised from the beginning, to such elaborate and self-contained perfection that readers must have wondered what there was left for him to do except repeat himself. If he had died then it would have been easy to believe of Yeats what some have thought of Keats, that he had exhausted his genius.

These two books contain the most widely loved and most commonly anthologized of his poems. They please, and will perhaps always please, most readers who want no more than to accept self-evident beauty. But in later life he himself grew impatient of his early style, and critics have tended to agree with him. It is not because of these that he is counted among the greatest poets of our time; they are overshadowed by his later work which has fewer readers but evokes deeper admiration.

Probably the idea that our age, or any age, has a uniform outlook is largely an illusion. Within the same generation experience fails differently upon different people, but for one reason or another certain views of it become more vocal. Contemporary critics tend to distrust dreaming for the dream's sake, and turn away from obvious beauty which carries no visible traces of agony. They demand that poetry should light up sharp psychological or social conflicts. 'Sweetest Shakespeare, fancy's child' whom Milton loved appeals to them less than the author of *Troilus and Cressida*.

37

Yeats in these poems deliberately turned his back on the actual. Outside his poetry, as the next chapter will show, he was thinking with the utmost excitement about politics, philosophy and art, and was more and more actively concerned with all three, but you would hardly guess it from a mere reading of the poems. He seldom expressed a thought till it was so inextricably fused with music and imagery that it had ceased to be distinguishable as thought. And although he was deeply in love and the emotion of his love is felt throughout his writing, he did not sing in simple lyric ecstasy nor did he, like Donne or Shakespeare in the Sonnets, make poetry out of love's self-questioning. What then did he write about? It was contrary to his idea of poetry at the time that it should appear to be 'about' any part of tangible experience. He set out from the belief that there is that in a man which underlies all experience. Poetry is a discovery of that inner soul, which emerges when all outward preoccupations are stilled, like a shy ghost, to possess the deserted landscape. His early poems, therefore, have not received a great deal of critical attention; and yet they are not only beautiful in themselves, but in many ways relevant to the more powerful work of later years.

The rhythms to which his mind moved were quiet and delicately precise. It has been said that Yeats had no ear. This may be true in the sense that he could not sing in tune nor catch the sound of his own voice speaking, but an ear for the cadence of verse is different, and this he certainly had. His rhythms are formal, not mechanical; they hesitate often, like a mind feeling its way to exactitude rather than asserting a dogma, but they never lose their music. The lines are not cluttered with thick consonants where they should slide easily, nor do they ask the voice to dwell on a short sound too light to bear its weight of meaning. He is at ease with a slow, chanting, heroic measure, full of long monosyllables that ring like a ceremonial invocation:

> *Turn if you may from battles never done,*
> I call, as they go by me one by one,

Danger no refuge holds, and war no peace,
For him who hears love sing and never cease,
Beside her clean-swept hearth, her quiet shade:[1]

or:

Thy great leaves enfold
The ancient beards, the helms of ruby and gold
Of the crowned Magi; and the king whose eyes
Saw the Pierced Hands and Rood of elder rise
In Druid vapour and make the torches dim;
Till vain frenzy awoke and he died.[2]

He is solemn but never clumsy-footed and can easily break into a dance; there is dance in the light-hearted movement of *The Fiddler of Dooney*, where for once the pace is swift, as if he had thrown off the burden of himself, and in the grave but light-footed measure of

Out-worn heart, in a time out-worn,
Come clear of the nets of wrong and right;
Laugh, heart, again in the grey twilight,
Sigh, heart, again in the dew of the morn.[3]

Very often, especially in *The Wind Among the Reeds*, he is experimenting with a longer flexible line, with room in it for hesitations and changes of mood. It varies from the stumbling movement of

A man with a hazel wand came without sound;
He changed me suddenly; I was looking another way;
And now my calling is but the calling of a hound;[4]

in which the stresses and pauses are almost prosaic, to the solemn incantation of

We who still labour by the cromlech on the shore,
The grey cairn on the hill, when day sinks drowned in dew,
Being weary of the world's empires, bow down to you,
Master of the still stars and of the flaming door.[5]

A poet's characteristic rhythms are an expression of the frame of mind in which poetry comes to him. Pope, for whom poetry is a heightened form of social conversation, uses the neat antithetical balance of couplets to point his phrases, so that his most trivial thoughts sound like witticisms and his profoundest like casual repartees. Shelley's innumerable lyric tunes are, almost every one of them, single emotions heightened to ecstasy, the expression of a unique moment. Swinburne's rhythm is hypnotic, drowning thought in a monotonous tide of feeling generated by the sound of words. T. S. Eliot, and some other modern poets, commonly use rhythm less to induce emotion than to discourage it by a calculated flat anticlimax, as if to snub the expansiveness of the natural man. Yeats' rhythms at this stage of his work are half entranced, like a man walking alone lost in a train of visionary thought, or incantatory, as if he thought of poetry as a priestly vocation.

In his imagery he creates a world to reflect his spirit. It is a limited world connected somewhat remotely with the common world of men, compounded of a few simple and enduring elements. His landscape is bare; there are woods and pools and lonely hills but neither cities nor cultivated fields. The 'pavement grey' in *The Lake Isle of Innisfree** is the most positively urban thing in the whole book; it is a vague and fleeting intrusion of the actual world upon the dream. His world is seen, not in full sunlight or the clear neutrality of a grey day, but in starlight and twilight and the unearthly cold light of dawn, and under visionary fires. The human figures are few and belong to ancient times, or to all times. There is a hermit or two, and an old priest, and the Fiddler of Dooney, and an occasional cottage-dweller is hinted at in the background; there are Druids and heroes out of old legends, and vaguely medieval queens. But it is thickly populated by supernatural beings, faeries who have not forgotten their divinity, flaming angelic presences, and vaguely distinct voices which are emanations from the poet but are not the voice of the whole flesh-and-blood man; and everywhere it is pervaded by the symbolic Rose, more a spirit than a flower.

When he meditates his thoughts take the form of a train of images

---

* Innisfree was an actual island; he was standing on an actual London pavement when a jet of water in a chemist's shop set him dreaming of it nostalgically (see Jeffares, *W. B. Yeats, Man and Poet*, p. 64).

succeeding each other with a logic of their own. He developed this technique in his later work with a wider sweep of thought and greater concentration of power, and to read him with understanding one must learn to follow his mind's flight from image to image. At this stage he is more concerned to communicate the images themselves than the thoughts behind them; but many poems repay close study, for as one image evokes another they light up other poems and the pattern of his mind grows clear.

The dedicatory lines *To Some I Have Talked with by the Fire* condense a philosophy into a kind of pictorial shorthand:

> While I wrought out these fitful Danaan rhymes,
> My heart would brim with dreams about the times
> When we bent down above the fading coals
> And talked of the dark folk who live in souls
> Of passionate men, like bats in the dead trees;
> And of the wayward twilight companies
> Who sigh with mingled sorrow and content,
> Because their blossoming dreams have never bent
> Under the fruit of evil and of good;
> And of the embattled flaming multitude
> Who rise, wing above wing, flame above flame,
> And, like a storm, cry the Ineffable Name,
> And with the clashing of their sword-blades make
> A rapturous music, till the morning break
> And the white hush end all but the loud beat
> Of their long wings, the flash of their white feet.[6]

The scene is the human soul; not only the 'dark folk' but all the figures are Shelleyan presences who 'wander, like a day-appearing dream, through the dim wildernesses of the mind'. His vision moves from darkness through the half-light into the white radiance of eternity. The bat-like powers of unillumined passionate action are such, perhaps, as possessed the heroes of late Elizabethan tragedy. Then come the aloof 'twilight companies' of dream, with whom Yeats was most at home; we find them in *The Man Who Dreamed of Faeryland*, isolating him from all action and all human desire. Beyond them are other brighter companies whose life is battle and exultation. Their sword-blades clash; if I read the image rightly they are fighting one against the other, but all are radiant and all cry out the ineffable Name. For as he said in the preface to *The Countess Cathleen*, in the kingdom of poetry 'there is no battle that does not give life instead of death'. But they are not the end: beyond their battle he sees

> the morning break
> And the white hush end all but the loud beat
> Of their long wings, the flash of their white feet.

It is a glimpse of angelic hosts disappearing into the dawn of eternity, the flashing feet of a multitudinous ascension. One might not be altogether sure of this but for the poem called *To Ireland in the Coming Times*, where it is more explicitly put:

> —we, our singing and our love,
> The mariners of night above,
> And all the wizard things that go
> About my table to and fro,
> Are passing on to where may be
> In truth's consuming ecstasy,
> No place for love and dream at all,
> For God goes by with white footfall.*

---

* See *Poems* (1899). This earlier version should be compared with that of the definitive edition. In the latter the lines beginning

> For in the world's first blossoming age

have become:

> When Time began to rant and rage
> The measure of her flying feet
> Made Ireland's heart begin to beat;
> And Time bade all his candles flare
> To light a measure here and there;
> And may the thoughts of Ireland brood
> Upon a measured quietude.

A few lines further on

> Yet he who treads in austere ways
> May surely meet their ancient gaze

becomes:

> Yet he who treads in measured ways
> May surely barter gaze for gaze

From this it seems that all things supernatural as well as natural
have their day, and are merged at last in God.

This poem too deserves scrutiny. It is a considered statement of
faith, more directly expressed than most of the others, in which he
defines the relation of the outside world to his world of dream. It
begins like an answer to some accusation, from Maud Gonne perhaps
or John O'Leary, of turning away from Ireland's battle for freedom
to lose himself in visions. He declares that he is a true patriot poet;
his vision is of that which gives meaning to the soul of Ireland and
therefore to the battle itself:

> Nor be I any less of them,
> Because the red-rose-bordered hem
> Of her, whose history began
> Before God made the angelic clan,
> Trails all about the written page.
> For in the world's first blossoming age
> The light fall of her flying feet
> Made Ireland's heart begin to beat;
> And still the starry candles flare
> To help her light foot here and there,
> And still the thoughts of Ireland brood
> Upon her holy quietude.

Then he affirms his faith in elemental beings, older and wiser
than man but fellow-travellers with him in the world of time and
moved by the same vision:

> In flood, in fire, in clay, and wind,
> They huddle from man's pondering mind,
> Yet he who treads in austere ways
> May surely meet their ancient gaze.
> Man ever journeys on with them
> After the red-rose-bordered hem.

(Yeats having renounced the asceticism of his youth). And throughout the poem the
idea of 'measure' has become the keynote. This brings it into line with the thought
of *The Statues* and with 'Measurement began our might' in *Under Ben Bulben*. Yeats
would hardly have doctored it with so much care had he not regarded it as an important
but imperfect statement of his belief.

Then comes the passage already quoted about 'truth's consuming ecstasy'. An eastern mystic might have ended here, looking with open eyes at the vast engulfing absolute. Yeats has looked, and finds that passion is still passion and that his craving for song is not yet quenched in that white eternity.

> I cast my heart into my rhymes,
> That you, in the dim coming times,
> May know how my heart went with them.
> After the red-rose-bordered hem.

Beginning from a relatively superficial conflict between the life of action and the life of dream, the poem itself has carried him forward into a deeper opposition: on the one side are all things natural and supernatural, on the other the awful negation of 'truth's consuming ecstasy'. He has seen eternity and chooses to live in time while he may. On the whole he held to the choice throughout life, but the argument was never altogether closed; it reappears again and again in the poems of his old age, with fiercer intensity and greater directness of statement. In the *Dialogue of Self and Soul*,[7] the Self, summoned by the Soul to turn away from temporal experience, retorts finally:

> I am content to live it all again

—and in *The Man and the Echo*,[8] written at the end of his life, the dialogue is even more trenchant:

> 'Lie down and die.'
>   'That were to shirk
> The spiritual intellect's great work.'

For the spirit is responsible for making its life in time an embodiment of something from eternity.

She of the red-rose-bordered hem here symbolizes that embodiment. She is not Ireland though she is Ireland's meaning: Yeats served his country for a vision's sake but did not confuse two worlds by identifying them. In this poem she is unmistakably related to 'that lady Beauty' of Rossetti's sonnet:

44

> long known to thee
> By flying hair and fluttering hem, the beat
> Following her daily of thy heart and feet,
> How passionately and irretrievably,
> With what fond hope, how many days and ways!

But it is kinship, not plagiarism; she is Yeats' direct and complex apprehension of the Rose of medieval and occult symbolism. She is the Rose who fills the earlier volume, reappears once or twice in *The Wind Among the Reeds*, and fades from his writing as other symbols emerged and faded later. While she stays with him her image focuses the diverse elements of his mind and harmonizes them into an apparent unity. She is the Rose of Peace whose beauty has power to reconcile heaven with hell,[9] and at the same time she is the insatiate Rose of the World for whose red lips

> with all their mournful pride,
> Mournful that no new wonder may betide,
> Troy passed away in one high funeral gleam,
> And Usna's children died.[10]

She belongs to eternity and was before men and angels, yet in another sense she is an emanation of earthly sorrow:

> Beauty grown sad with its eternity
> Made you of us, and of the dim grey sea.[11]

And again she is the Rose upon the Rood of Time—Beauty crucified in the deeds and sufferings of the world; and while her image shines in all remote legendary things he prays also to find her near him, entangled in common life, lest he lose touch altogether with humanity. She is eternity embodied in things temporal, and she has the face of Maud Gonne. The Rose poems are at once a lover's homage to his mistress and a condensation of Yeats' philosophy, for to him all worship was one worship and all beauty the embodiment of a single idea.

He conceived the created universe as an act of worship, and therefore in the utter adoration of one woman he became himself a living symbol of the truth. The question of reward did not arise; the sun does not ask a wage for shining nor a man for worshipping the divine. That is so in the earlier volume at least, for below the surface melancholy of many poems a deep serenity shines through the whole of it. But that is not the whole truth about life in the world. In *The Wind Among the Reeds* the strain of unrequited love had gone on too long; some of its poems are stormy and many are full of the knowledge of desolation:

> I became a man, a hater of the wind,
> Knowing one, out of all things, alone, that his head
> May not lie on the breast nor his lips on the hair
> Of the woman that he loves, until he dies.[12]

And now that the coherence of his pattern has broken down, the Rose is no longer the all-inclusive symbol it had been in the earlier book. In *The Wind Among the Reeds* it appears thrice, only once directly signifying love. *The Lover Tells of the Rose in His Heart* is a sigh of partial discontentment; for the first time in his poetry it seems to trouble him that the outside world is not perfectly in accord with a lover's vision, and

All things uncomely and broken, all things worn out and old...
Are wronging your image that blossoms a rose in the deeps of my heart.[13]

In the other two passages he seems deliberately to seek elsewhere than in love for the ecstasy of attainment of the Rose. In *The Blessed* it is in drunkenness; Cumhal asks Dathi the saint which is the blessedest soul in the world, and is answered:

> 'O blessedness comes in the night and the day
> And whither the wise heart knows;
> And one has seen in the redness of wine
> The Incorruptible Rose.[14]

In *The Secret Rose* it is found

> where those
> Who sought thee in the Holy Sepulchre,
> Or in the wine-vat, dwell beyond the stir
> And tumult of defeated dreams[15]

and only as an afterthought in the beauty of woman. The god of the Cross and of the Grape: either of them may bestow the illumination of reality.

Yeats' biographers have pointed out that between *The Countess Cathleen* and *The Wind Among the Reeds* he gave up the austere celibacy which love and idealism had imposed on him and tried to temper his hopeless passion for Maud Gonne by living with another woman, and that a few of the poems in the latter book were written of this second love. It did not, immediately at least, have the kind of effect on his love poetry that a naïve psychologist would think proper; for certainly *The Wind Among the Reeds* is not a more satisfied book than *The Countess Cathleen* lyrics. His whole conception of love was something other than a rationalization of frustrated sex and was too deeply part of himself to be renounced as easily in thought as in action. A close student may decide that the poems into which some physical experience enters bear traces of it, but also, as it seems to me, they are more laboured in their expression. The imagery tends to lose its way. In *He Bids his Beloved be at Peace*, for instance, I doubt whether the elaborate symbolism of the four quarters of heaven does much to the movement of the thought from

> I hear the Shadowy Horses, their long manes a-shake

to

> Beloved, let your eyes half close, and your heart beat
> Over my heart.[16]

But the sense of eternity seeking embodiment in time and time overshadowed by eternity is unchanged:*

> And when you sigh from kiss to kiss
> I hear white Beauty sighing, too,
> For hours when all must fade like dew,

---

* To measure the distance Yeats travelled, cp. *The Lady's Third Song* in the *Three Bushes* sequence (*CP*, p. 345):

> That I may hear if we should kiss
> A contrapuntal serpent hiss,
> You, should hand explore a thigh,
> All the labouring heavens sigh.

But flame on flame, and deep on deep,
Throne over throne where in half sleep,
Their swords upon their iron knees,
Brood her high lonely mysteries.[17]

Ultimately, to renounce his virginity was to begin letting in the outer world upon his inner dream, and this made all the difference to the strength of his poetry, which became not less visionary but more actual. To the end of his life he had things to say which could only be spoken in symbols, but as time went on he learnt to use the actual world symbolically. In *The Wind Among the Reeds* he was not trying to do this, but the experience which his poetry had to master was breaking through forms that used to be enough for it. His symbolism became more intricate and elaborate. He was studying it for its own sake, learning it as one learns a language and makes it express increasing depth and subtlety of meaning.

One learns a language not only to speak it but to be initiated into a culture and a tradition of thought. Yeats' prose essays* of the period make it clear that he recognized symbolism as a way of thought coming down from the remote beginning of history, expressing concepts which modern thought has no terms for, and he did not believe that men had grown wiser in abandoning it.

There is a poem cumbrously named *He Mourns for the Change Which Has Come upon Him and His Beloved and Longs for the End of the World*,[18] which talks about a hound and a deer without horns and a boar without bristles. It is not one of his most memorable; it has the obscurity of a riddle more than of a profound mystery, but for that very reason it shows his mind at work, bringing together his experience and his understanding of mythology. Essentially it is a cry of longing and despair. It records, possibly, the desolating discovery that his relation with another woman ('I was looking another way'), instead of calming his worship of Maud Gonne had

* See particularly *The Celtic Element in Literature* (1897), *The Symbolism of Poetry* (1900) and *Magic* (1901), all in vol. VI of the 1908 *Collected Works*. For a fuller discussion of his beliefs cp. below, chap. V.

48

changed it to an implacable craving for possession of her; but it is not written out of a desire to make that plain. In some deliberately cryptic notes[19] he drew attention to the kinship between the hounds of his desire and the hounds that flicker through the ancient legends of the world, and themselves are related to the voice of the night wind and to the hounds that hunt the souls of the dead in primitive belief. The enchanted deer, in many a legend from India to Ireland, has led the hero away from his friends to meet some unknown peril of the wilderness. The boar without bristles is one with the boar who brought down Attis and Adonis and Diarmuid, and symbolizes darkness and death. All this belongs, so to speak, to the alphabet of symbolism; through the image thought ignites thought more rapidly and in more directions than a psychoanalyst can follow it. But the very multiplicity of meaning expresses a kind of wild helplessness as of a boat sliding down a cataract. The change in him and his beloved is the work of 'somebody', of 'a man with a hazel wand', which is a symbol of divinity; that is, there is no escape because the passions that grip them are immortal powers, not generated in the minds of individuals but descending on them and living through them.

That the passions have their own dynamic life, that human beings are caught up by them as instruments, is in fact a very ancient pagan way of thought: it is thus, for instance, that Euripides saw Phaedra and Hippolytus, though a modern man can translate their story into different terms. It was very real to Yeats, and perhaps one of the chief things he sought in symbolism was a language to express it and explore its implications. In *The Symbolism of Poetry* he wrote:

All sounds, all colours, all forms, either because of their pre-ordained energies or because of long association, evoke indefinite and yet precise emotions, *or, as I prefer to think, call down among us certain disembodied powers, whose footsteps over our hearts we call emotions....*Because an emotion does not exist, or does not become perceptible and active among us, till it has found its expression, in colour or in sound or in form or in all of these, and because no two modulations or arrangements of these evoke the same emotion, poets and painters and musicians, and in a less degree because their effects are momentary, day and night and cloud and shadow, are continually making and unmaking mankind.[20]

The phrase which I have italicized makes no difference to Yeats' argument in the essay: from a practical point of view it is all one whether disembodied powers exist or not, if they are not operative till they are embodied in tangible expression. But it is a confession of faith, and it makes a very significant difference to the poet's or the priest's view of his vocation, whether he regards himself as manipulating men's hearts and minds by irresponsible invention, or as perceiving supernatural realities and calling them down to earth.

The same thought underlies the short and beautiful poem, *The Moods*:

> Time drops in decay,
> Like a candle burnt out,
> And the mountains and woods
> Have their day, have their day;
> What one in the rout
> Of the fire-born moods
> Has fallen away?[21]

—and as so often with ideas that are basic in his mind, it reappears in his old age, so much more powerfully phrased and more closely integrated with human life that it has become a different idea. Ribh declares in *Supernatural Songs*:

> Eternity is passion, girl or boy
> Cry at the onset of their sexual joy
> 'For ever and for ever'; then awake
> Ignorant what Dramatis Personae spake.[22]

In *The Wind Among the Reeds* there is nothing like the concentrated energy of this whole poem, but the view of reality is the same.

It may be that Maud Gonne would have been easier to attain if Yeats had not made her an image of the unattainable. I doubt it, since there are two persons in a love affair, and the difference between them was not a mere self-delusion of his own. She held her view of life as firmly as he, and was no more capable of changing into a serene pre-Raphaelite goddess for the sake of an overwhelming passion than he was of letting his art drag in the wake of political violence. It is true, however, that as a poet, if not as a man, fate did well by him in setting her before him. Love concentrated all his emotions on a single image; it made him adept in the use of symbolism to weave together the diverse strands of his mind; above all, the long discipline of love balked fitted him to accept loneliness as his destiny.

Loneliness is his theme as much as love. It was not a mere refuge from failure in love: something in Yeats was committed to it from the beginning and could not grow in schools or coteries. It kept on recalling him from his incense-laden shrines to the woods and the wilderness, where a man sheds his surface personality and becomes the human spirit itself in converse with other elementals.

> And no more turn aside and brood
> Upon love's bitter mystery;
> For Fergus rules the brazen cars,
> And rules the shadows of the wood,
> And the white breast of the dim sea
> And all dishevelled wandering stars.[23]

This is quietly and lightly said in a slight lyric, but often the truths that will govern a lifetime slip into the mind in just this unobtrusive way. There is more poignancy in a poem of *The Wind Among the Reeds*:

> I wander by the edge
> Of this desolate lake
> Where wind cries in the sedge:
> *Until the axle break*
> *That keeps the stars in their round,*
> *And hands hurl in the deep*
> *The banners of East and West,*
> *And the girdle of light is unbound,*
> *Your breast will not lie by the breast*
> *Of your beloved in sleep.*[24]

Against the heart's contentment are set the splendour of desolation, the sheer immensity of time and space and the everlasting estrangement of light from darkness. But to write of them thus he must have chosen these things and accepted the cost.

He was inclined, as he himself commented later, to over-use some purely evocative adjectives, more to proclaim a mood than to define a picture. 'Lonely' is one that recurs most often, and always with a kind of exaltation of spirit. It belongs to the Eternal Rose:

> Under the passing stars, foam of the sky,
> Lives on this lonely face [25]

of whose sadness in another poem

> stars, grown old
> In dancing silver-sandalled on the sea,
> Sing in their high and lonely melody. [26]

It is never a state of misery as it could be with Shelley, but a high condition to which none but the fearless may attain:

> Him who trembles before the flame and the flood,
> And the winds that blow through the starry ways,
> Let the starry winds and the flame and the flood
> Cover over and hide, for he has no part
> With the lonely, majestical multitude. [27]

And he summons his heart to come where

> the mystical brotherhood
> Of sun and moon and hollow and wood
> And river and stream work out their will;
> And God stands winding His lonely horn,
> And time and the world are ever in flight. [28]

The elemental powers are lonely, and when a man has risen to the full height of his spirit and stands among them as an equal, loneliness is his achievement and his reward. This is a consciousness faintly present in *The Stolen Child* and much more explicitly in the poems just quoted. It gives an arrogant, rock-like strength to his maturer poems and is the substance of the epitaph he made for himself at last:

> Cast a cold eye
> On life, on death.
> Horseman, pass by![29]

The sheer beauty of these poems of Yeats' early manhood is generally acknowledged, though to some readers it seems a rather meaningless beauty. But it is not superficial, though it shines on the surface. They are the work of a mind at once delighting in loveliness and austere in the rejection of all triviality, a mind which, having brooded closely and passionately over high philosophy, can no more help knowing its way among transcendental images than a scholar can help knowing his accidence.

For all that, they are not poetry of the greatest kind: too much of human life is deliberately excluded from them. It is not the mythological themes themselves that hinder him; half the world's great poets have said their say through myth. But he is using them to exclude the world, which means excluding a part of himself, and for the greatest art a man's whole self must be thrown recklessly into the theme, with all his powers focused. Then the greatness is limited only by the quality of that self and by his power over the meaning and music of words.

Looking back at his youth in 1933, Yeats wrote:

My isolation from ordinary men and women was increased by an asceticism destructive of mind and body, combined with an adoration of physical beauty that made it meaningless. Sometimes the barrier between myself and other people filled me with terror...I had in an extreme degree the shyness—I know no better word—that keeps a man from speaking his own thought. Burning with adoration and hatred I wrote verse that expressed emotions common to every sentimental boy and girl, and that may be the reason why the poems upon which my popularity has depended until a few years ago were written before I was twenty-seven. Gradually I overcame my shyness a little, though I am still struggling with it and cannot free myself from the belief that it comes from lack of courage, that the problem is not artistic but moral. I remember saying as a boy to some fellow student in the Dublin art schools, 'The difference between a good draughtsman and a bad is one of courage'.[30]

Obviously he is less than just to himself, or to his readers, for these early poems endure by virtue of what is in them, not what is missing. But he is right in that the difference between them and the greatest poetry of his old age is the difference between a man withdrawn in his dreams, sheltering behind them, and one who has dared to come out dreams and all, and live in the world without capitulation. It is much more than a change of technique.

It was necessary, however, that he should begin by building a kingdom of poetry remote from common life. His poetry was founded in the soul: it is empty without the assumption that a man brings something into the world which he has not first drawn from it. The world must give him his forms of expression, but they are a clothing or an embodiment. The great religions have their several ways of expressing this, but Yeats had no orthodoxy, only faith in the assumption itself; and the mental climate around him, both religious and sceptical, was alien to his sense of values. He had to find images which would define the shape of his soul, to disentangle its essence from the experience of the senses and the rationalizing of the intellect, and the way to do this was to dream.

While he was writing his world of dreams he was coming to grips with the outer world in thought and action, testing his convictions and gaining the courage of them. For the time being he kept his intellectual adventures carefully apart from his poetry, but they had a powerful effect on it later and something must be said of them in the next chapter.

CHAPTER V

'HAMMER YOUR THOUGHTS
INTO UNITY'

Besides writing poetry, Yeats in his twenties and early thirties was meeting people, engaging in diverse activities, dealing fairly success-fully with the world in most things with the two large exceptions of love and money. He was also thinking his way furiously towards intellectual coherence. In a late, reminiscent essay he wrote:

One day when I was twenty-three or twenty-four, this sentence seemed to form in my mind without my willing it, much as sentences form when we are half-asleep. 'Hammer your thoughts into unity.' For days I could think of nothing else, and for years I tested all I did by that sentence. I had three interests, interest in a form of literature, in a form of philosophy, and a belief in nationality. None of these seemed to have anything to do with the other, but gradually my love of literature and my belief in nationality came together. Then for years I said to myself that these two had nothing to do with my form of philosophy, but that I had only to be sincere and to keep from constraining one by the other, and they would become one interest. Now all these three are, I think, one, or rather all are the discrete expressions of a single conviction. I think that each has behind it my whole character, and has gained thereby a certain newness—for is not every man's character peculiar to himself—and that I have become a cultivated man.[1]

His memory may have over-dramatized the past; I doubt, for instance, whether within his consciousness the cleavage between occult studies and his other interests was ever quite so sharp as he represents it here, though it was sharp in action; but it was the integration of the three that brought his poetry to its full strength at last, and his letters and diaries and prose essays help to elucidate the process. This chapter will trace something of its early stages.

First, since it came first with him, the 'form of literature', the conception of poetry in his mind. Its original outline certainly came from his father, J. B. Yeats the portrait painter. Few poets can have been luckier in fathers. J. B. Yeats, a fine artist himself, served his art to the disregard of worldly prudence and found it natural for his family to do likewise. He had a gift for friendship which included his children and drew to his house, whether in Dublin or London, a company of artists and men of letters whose talk must have been nearly as good as his own. He read poetry to his son in childhood and discussed it with him as he grew older, and when he saw in the boy the makings of a poet of some kind neither drove nor discouraged him, but sent him to the Dublin School of Art as a rather desultory student, to give him a breathing-space to find himself. If Yeats outgrew his father's influence slowly, it was chiefly because he was not greatly cramped by it; the family home was a good place for a poet to flourish. Of course, they disagreed; of course, like almost every youth growing up, he discovered himself largely by emphasizing his difference from his father; but fundamentally they had too much in common, and the father was at once too tolerant of ideas and too appreciative of personality, to make understanding difficult.

For J. B. Yeats personality was the supreme value and art was its fullest expression. He did not despise thought, but to have value for him it had to spring from energy of feeling. Thus he wrote in 1869 to his friend Edward Dowden:

It seems to me that the intellect of man *as man*, and therefore of an artist, the most human of all, should obey no voice except that of emotion, but I would have a man know all emotions. Shame, anger, love, pity, contempt, admiration, hatred, and whatever other feelings there be, to have all these roused to their utmost strength, and to have *all* of them roused, (two things you observe), is the aim, as I take it, of the only right education.... Art has to do with the sustaining and invigorating of the Personality. To be strong is to be happy. Art by expressing our feelings makes us strong and therefore happy. When I spoke of emotions as the first thing and last in education, I did not mean excitement. In the completely emotional man the least awakening of feeling is a harmony, in which every chord of every feeling vibrates. Excitement is the feature of an insufficiently emotional nature, the harsh discourse of the vibrating of but one or two chords.[2]

This is very like the idea of 'unity of being' which the poet worked out later, though unlike his son J. B. Yeats did not try to found it on a transcendental philosophy. Personality as he knew it in the living world was enough for him; one might say that his ideal was to be a person worth being in a world of people worth knowing. But this means loving the uniqueness of individual men, not the common face imposed on them by their times and their views. 'Poetry is the voice of the Solitary Spirit, prose the language of the sociable-minded', was one of his sayings. What he meant by it is made clear in remarks scattered through letters to his son at a later time.

Art is solitary man, the man as he is behind the innermost, the utmost veils. That is why with the true poet we do not care what are his persuasions, opinions, ideas, religions, moralities—through all these we can pierce to the voice of the essential man if we have the discerning senses. These are no more than the leafy wood out of which the nightingale sings.[3]

It was not the solitude of the hermitage he had in mind: art needs to be rooted in the world:

All art is *reaction from life* but never, when it is vital and great, *an escape*.[4]

But there is a depth where every man is alone, and great poetry springs from there, not from the enthusiasms and arguments generated in society.

If he cannot do his best without having someone to assail or cajole or persuade then he is of the prose writers—and only incidentally a poet. The true poet is all the time a visionary and whether with friends or not, as much alone as a man on his death-bed.[5]

Of all poetry he loved drama best because the dramatist, disappearing into his creations, is most completely freed from his theorizing self; and he loved the later Elizabethans best of the dramatists. He loved them, indeed, for the very reason that makes Mr T. S. Eliot distrust while he admires them: because their art ranges the gamut of their emotional possibilities, not ordered or restrained by any coherently formulated philosophy. To Mr Eliot and many modern critics the chief sin of Romanticism is just this glorification of self-expression as the end of art. To J. B. Yeats it was precisely here that the Romantic poets fell short. They talked too much in the first person, which is only that aspect of the self the world has already outlined; they argued and philosophized when they should have been creating. These preferences were passed on to his son in his schooldays:

at breakfast he read passages from the poets, and always from the play or poem at its most passionate moment. He never read me a passage because of its speculative interest, and indeed did not care at all for poetry where there was generalization or abstraction however impassioned. He would read out the first speeches of the *Prometheus Unbound*, but never the ecstatic lyricism of that famous fourth act; and another day the scene where Coriolanus comes to the house of Aufidius and tells the impudent servants that his home is under the canopy....He did not care even for a fine lyric passage unless he felt some actual man behind its elaboration of beauty, and he was always looking for the lineaments of some desirable, familiar life.[6]

They were unorthodox ideas in his generation. In the mid-nineteenth century there was a marked tendency to interpret art in terms of its moral or philosophical 'message' and morality as the constraining of the personality by a code. Ruskin, great art critic as he was, often seemed surer that he knew right from wrong than good art from bad, and tried to establish his criticism on his ethics. In his respect for the individual vision J. B. Yeats was nearer to Pater and to those young Nineties poets who were his son's associates in London, but he had not their faint life-weariness and his writings never seem, as theirs often do, to be striving for a poise which topples over into a pose. His letters to his son dance with life, and he puts his ideas in terms not of art as an abstraction but of the artist working and thinking, so that they have an air of coming hot from a lifetime of eager experience. And yet art itself was his experience; he cared little for the world of action outside it.

He certainly turned his son's thoughts to poetic drama and to narrative, which has nearly the same liberating objectivity. Yeats seems to have written his early lyrics almost in spite of himself, because the gift was in him. They were not objectively dramatic, like Browning's, for he was interested in no one's processes of thought but his own; but he thought of them as the utterances of characters dramatically conceived, who were nevertheless at least as truly himself as the man who wore out his shoes in saving bus fares to the British Museum. While he wrote them he was dreaming of tempestuous, improbable cycles of epic and drama. It was against his father's disapproval—and therefore with the clarity of a man originating a heresy—that he discovered that he could be stirred by a poem expressing the passionate feeling of an actual moment, and that what stirred him was not the language but the actuality.

I began idly reading verses describing the shores of Ireland as seen by a returning, dying emigrant. My eyes filled with tears and yet I knew the verses were badly written—vague, abstract words such as one finds in a newspaper. I looked at the end and saw the name of some political exile who had died but a few days after his return to Ireland. They had moved me because they contained the actual thoughts of a man at a passionate moment of life, and when I met my father I was full of the discovery. We should write out our own thoughts in as nearly as possible the language we thought them in, as though in a letter to an intimate friend. We should not disguise them in any way; for our lives give them force as the lives of people in plays give force to their words. Personal utterance, which had almost ceased in English literature, could be as fine an escape from rhetoric and abstraction as drama itself. But my father would hear of nothing but drama; personal utterance was only egotism. I knew it was not, but as yet did not know how to explain the difference...'If I can be sincere and make my language natural, and without becoming discursive, like a novelist, and so indiscreet and prosaic,' I said to myself, 'I shall, if good luck or bad luck make my life interesting, be a great poet; for it will no longer be a matter of literature at all.' Yet when I re-read those early

59

poems which gave me so much trouble, I find little but romantic convention, unconscious drama. It is so many years before one can believe enough
in what one feels even to know what the feeling is.[7]

It was a prophetic discovery, though its effect was long delayed.

J. B. Yeats insisted on the need to escape from abstraction; this
passage shows how fully his son had accepted it. It was good doctrine
to accept even if it hampered the fluency of his early writings.
Abstractions are the currency of communication; they define just
so much of a thought as can be understood by everyone in common
and express only that, whereas images rightly used are the instrument of self-discovery and the natural language of that solitary
spirit whose voice is poetry. Yeats moved in a world of ideas and
eager controversies, and by his own account he had a turn for
generalization, and was afraid of it. It was capable of confusing the
deep intuitive convictions which were the only truths fit for poetry,
or relevant to sincere action.

Even in practical life I only very gradually began to use generalizations,
that have since become the foundation of all I have done, or shall do, in
Ireland. For all I know all men may have been so timid, for I am per-
suaded that our intellects at twenty contain all the truths we shall ever
find, but as yet we do not know truths that belong to us from opinions
caught up in casual irritation or momentary fantasy. As life goes on we
discover that certain thoughts sustain us in defeat, or give us victory,
whether over ourselves or others, and it is these thoughts, tested by
passion, that we call convictions.[8]

He says that this fear of abstract thought sentimentalized his
early poetry. Perhaps it did: but since the thought of his early
twenties had not been sifted and tested by passion like that which
formed the backbone of his greatest work, it was a wise caution that
restrained it.

Above all, his upbringing impressed on him that an artist lives
to create, letting neither creed nor comradeship distort his creative
imagination. It is perhaps easier for a painter to keep this clear than
for a poet, since words are also the medium of speculative thought

and controversy. It was easier, as Yeats felt keenly, for a poet in pre-Reformation Europe, when because there was one inclusive ideal of life there was no need to argue about it; he had only to create images for his vision, for all men to understand in proportion to their capacity. When men begin to argue about ideologies there is a pressure on the poet to turn his images into the troops of a propaganda war, to manipulate them so that they embody a disputed ideal. To renounce the world is no way out; it may be the path to a saint's mystical insight but a poet must nourish his dreams on human life and passion. But in an embattled world to love and hate and believe, and still in the thick of battle to preserve the spiritual solitude of the deathbed, is an austere test of his devotion to his calling. And unlike his father, who was a natural lover of his kind and never seems to have found sincerity in social relations difficult, Yeats as a young man was shy and self-conscious. When he discovered his ability to mix with people, it meant so much to him that he was all the more acutely aware of the danger of selling his soul for it.

It is perhaps because Nature made me a gregarious man, going hither and thither looking for conversation, and ready to deny from fear or favour his dearest conviction, that I love proud and lonely things.[9]

This was where the two interests in literature and in nationality were in danger of constraining each other. Yeats was an Irishman and a nationalist hardly less passionately than a poet, and the woman he loved and the friends whose approval he most coveted were nationalist and Irish too. Patriotism called him into a world of action, poetry to single-hearted devotion to itself.

He belonged to the Irish Republican Brotherhood, a semi-underground organization which inherited the Fenian tradition and talked, though rather vaguely, in terms of an armed uprising. Most Englishmen would certainly have looked on this as empty-headed romanticism. But in Ireland, since Tudor times, a tradition of armed action had been passed from generation to generation. Yeats believed that those who carried it on would train the heroic qualities in themselves and set the stage for a regenerated national life. It is true that later on his judgement rejected it as impracticable for the men and the times—and then the times changed and 1916 brought it to pass without him, and to his shattering surprise. But for the moment I am speaking of his thoughts some twenty years earlier.

For political manœuvres his imagination had no sympathy. The parliamentary lobbying and backstairs bargaining, the small-town political committees where great ideas are twisted to the ends of small men—such means could only bring the wrong men forward and destroy the very values that made liberty worth winning. Yeats did not idealize all his countrymen but claimed that they had a better tradition of life than the English and wanted them to live by it. Nor did economic arguments mean much to him: he himself had never found poverty degrading and did not think wealth necessarily ennobling, nor that men would fight better for small savings of rent and property than for an idea which possessed their souls. He worshipped Parnell as a leader, but that was because of a proud, cold quality in the man who could use politics and economics as weapons without subduing his spirit to them. People did not follow Parnell because he promised them votes or incomes, but because he was a man who put the spirit of greatness into the fight he led— the kind of man for whom stars fall at his funeral.[10] When Parnell was gone the heroism went out of politics. Yeats' mind turned naturally to a literary and artistic revival, which was as necessary to his vision of Ireland as political freedom itself. He needed no leader here; out of his own intuition he prophesied what must come and did much to bring it about.

Though a poet's and not a statistician's, his vision of Ireland was not entirely a subjective fantasy. No doubt there is always a subjective element in patriotism; men at the same time inherit values from their country and credit it with those that nourish their self-respect. But Yeats lived both in England and Ireland and judged what he experienced. As a boy, when his father lived in London, he had gone to an English day-school; then the family returned to Dublin and he was an art-student there, and conversed with patriots and mystics and sat at the feet of Mohini Chatterjee; then again they were in London and he lived in his father's house, writing literary gossip for two Irish-American papers to earn a thin living without putting Ireland out of his thoughts. He was meeting English men of letters and beginning to be known as a poet. But always he spent part of the year at his uncle's home in Sligo and always the atmosphere of his father's house was Irish, so that although he had his name to make in the London literary world it was never the whole world of his mind; he half-belonged to a life quite unlike it.

Working and thinking in London, he saw much that repelled him. The spirit that depends for its strength on public approval, judges each thing by its practical success, worships sheer size as if it were intrinsically glorious—this spirit may be widespread else-where than in England, but he found it neither in his father's house nor in the remote corner of Sligo where he spent his holidays nor yet among the old Fenians and young mystics he knew in Dublin. It was hostile to great art, and in spite of Ruskin whom he admired and Morris whom he adored, it had seeped into every corner of English life. As most people accept their own environment, the English around him accepted it as the norm, and even when they hated it as he did felt that they hated an inescapable fact. He saw it as the expression of a vulgar materialism inherent in English culture, which made poverty disgusting and wealth stupidly complacent. He saw Ireland as a country, alone perhaps among western nations, still inwardly uncorrupted by it, and he dreamed of Ireland, freed from the humiliation of alien rule, regenerating humanity by restoring an older tradition, more visionary in thought and more heroic in action.

It would make no sense to argue that he was right or wrong from an absolute standpoint, since an absolute standpoint is unattainable and would be irrelevant to poetry anyway. My point is that his devotion to Ireland was not blind sentiment, but an assessment of his own experience in the light of his values. Had it not been so it must either have faded as time went on or have vitiated his poetry, whereas in fact it stood up to disillusionment, and exasperation sharpened its edge without destroying it. He had seen with his eyes that the peasants of the west could live on a bare subsistence without making gain their sole preoccupation, and could retain an imaginative joy in living, a dignity and freedom of manners, different from anything in industrial England. And he met a few individuals, particularly the old Fenian John O'Leary, in whom he saw his ideal of heroism incarnate. O'Leary had the beauty of an ancient carving and the moral grandeur of an ancient sage; he was a man who could risk death and suffer imprisonment for a cause and still value fine personality in friend or foe above any cause, a simple man who said great things without noticing them, because they grew naturally from his life.

Once when I was defending an Irish politician who had made a great outcry because he was treated as a common felon, by showing that he did it for the cause's sake, he said: 'There are things that a man must not do to save a nation.' He would speak a sentence like that in ignorance of its passionate value, and would forget it the moment after.[11]

In O'Leary he saw that greatness of spirit such as the ancient poets conceived could walk the earth in his own time. Although such men might be few, he saw that it was not life itself, but only the dominant way of life, that was at war with all the values of the poetic imagination, and thus his faith was increased. In his early youth when he lived withdrawn in his own dreams active life seemed unreal compared with poetry. The perception that life itself might equal the poet's vision of it, that the two were joined at the source, gradually brought the scattered elements of his mind together.

In working with the nationalist movement he was among people who were not primarily artists, and was compelled to bring his own beliefs into relation with the life of action. Moral passion was the unifying force. At a centenary celebration of Wolfe Tone (in 1898) he said:

We hated at first the ideals and ambitions of England, the materialisms of England, because they were hers, but we have come to hate them with a nobler hatred. We hate them now because they are evil. We have suffered too long from them, not to understand, that hurry to become rich, that delight in mere bigness, that insolence to the weak are evil and vulgar things....We are building up a nation which shall be moved by noble purposes and to noble ends.[12]

Oratory for the occasion, certainly; but no one familiar with the whole trend of Yeats' thought can doubt that it was utterly sincere. Six years later, before a different kind of gathering in New York, he was putting the same thing in literary rather than ethical terms:

We wish to preserve an ancient ideal of life. Wherever its customs prevail, there you will find the folk song, the folk tale, the proverb and the charming manners that come from ancient culture. In England you will find a few thousands of perfectly cultivated people, but you will find the mass of the people singing songs of the music hall....In Ireland alone among the nations that I know you will find, away on the western seaboard, under broken roofs, a race of gentlemen keep alive the ideals of a great time when men sang the heroic life with drawn swords in their hands.[13]

When he said that J. M. Synge, who had gone to the Aran Islands at his suggestion, was just beginning to recreate that life in his art. Synge's genius is his own, his response to the life of the western seaboard unlike anything that Yeats could have written; and yet without the clarity of Yeats' prevision *The Playboy of the Western World* might never have come into being.

That his poetry should reawaken the soul of Ireland was an obvious ambition. At first he thought the way was by the resurrection of myth. There had been ages when the consciousness of Europe was integrated; all men could draw on a collective understanding because all understood the same images, though not at the same depth. It was abstract, analytical thinking which had pulled that consciousness apart in the last two or three centuries. He thought the synthesis would be restored for Ireland if poets gazed on its legends and ancient history intently, without abstract thought, till the meaning passed into them and they created images so clear, so firmly rooted in enduring life, that they brought to light the hidden energies of a people's soul. In 1897 he declared

that literature dwindles to a mere chronicle of circumstance, or passionless phantasies, and passionless meditations, unless it is constantly flooded with the passions and beliefs of ancient times, and that of all the fountains of the passions and beliefs of ancient times in Europe, the Sclavonic, the Finnish, the Scandinavian, and the Celtic, the Celtic alone has been for centuries close to the main river of European literature.[14]

Active work crystallized the notion into a more precise programme of cultural unity:

Have not all nations had their first unity from a mythology that marries them to rock and hill? We had in Ireland imaginative stories, which the uneducated classes knew and even sang, and might we not make those stories current among the educated classes, rediscovering for the work's sake what I have called 'the applied arts of literature', the association of literature, that is, with music, speech and dance; and at last, it might be, so deepen the political passion of the nation that all, artist and poet, craftsman and day-labourer would accept a common design?[15]

In this way the two streams of passion had begun to flow together. At least the freedom of Ireland was necessary to preserve a way of life fit for poetry, and poetry was necessary if the fight for freedom was not to degenerate into an angry squabble over nothing worth dying for. 'Neither religion nor politics', he wrote, 'can of itself create minds with enough receptivity to become wise, or just and generous enough to make a nation.'[16]

The spirit that responds naturally to folk-song and ballad was still, as he said, visibly alive among the common people; it survived somewhere even in the minds of the educated, but English had so long been the national language that the overshadowing greatness of English literature had choked its expression. A writer of talent turned naturally to England both for his public and his models. Yeats' idea of Ireland required a national literature. He wanted Irish writers to be conscious of a past; he wanted the native legends and folk-lore to be widely enough known to be the medium of that image-thinking which is the wisdom of poetry and the language of a national mind. With this for a background he wanted to see contemporary poetry and novels come into being, national not in mere showmanship and propaganda but in genuine love and understanding of their native land. He wanted a native drama—of which, incidentally, ancient Irish tradition has no trace—creating out of Irish life images of character and action to awaken and sharpen the discernment of a whole people.

For a young man in his twenties with no special influence this sounds an unmanageable programme, since it could not in its nature be carried out single-handed. Was Yeats a magician or a seer, that it should have been more or less fulfilled? He himself might have said that all men are fountain-jets of a world soul, channels through which creative life wells up, and that creation is a name we give to discovery. At all events there was insight in his thinking, and he seemed to watch over the Irish literary awakening at the end of the century with uncanny perceptiveness, much like a necromancer watching his evocations come to life.

He was not in fact working single-handed; there were already Standish O'Grady, Kuno Meyer, John Eglinton and other scholars and folk-lorists and historians, many of them much his seniors, busy bringing the past of Ireland to light. But the inclusive vision was his, and he did much to point out the significance of their work to the Irish, both in Ireland and America, whom it chiefly concerned. His weekly articles in *The Boston Pilot* and *The Providence Sunday Journal* were used mainly for talking about Irish literature. In 1890 he wrote in the former:

The first thing needful if an Irish literature more elaborate and intense than our fine but primitive ballads and novels is to come into being is that readers and writers alike should really know the imaginative periods of Irish history. It is not needful that they should understand them with scholars' accuracy, but they should know them with the heart, so as not to be repelled by what is strange and *outré* in poems or plays or stories taken therefrom.[17]

By about the turn of the century old stories such as the Children of Lir and the Doom of the Sons of Usna, hitherto known to a few scholars, were circulating in English versions retold for children. Deirdre took her place with Helen and Guinevere and Cleopatra in the western world's dream of fair women. By 1916 Pearse, leading the rising whose failure was the foundation of Irish freedom, could invoke Cuchulain with certainty that the people's imagination would respond to the name.

The poets and novelists who began to create a literature of the Irish countryside existed actually or potentially before Yeats invoked them. They were not all his imitators. But he did much disinterested work to call attention to them, fostering in their Irish readers a critical sense worth writing for, and reiterating his belief: 'There can be no great literature without nationality, no great nationality without literature.'

In the past there had been Irish writers of genuine talent. One of them, Maria Edgeworth, observed her own class honestly and seriously from her own point of view; but mostly, like Thomas Moore or the novelist Charles Lever, they were content to exploit their knowledge of Irish life and sentiment to gratify the English reader's taste for the picturesque. Others of a later time, better patriots than artists, mistook patriotic feeling for good writing and were read by a public like themselves, who valued them according to their fervour. And because nationalism was intensely self-conscious all its judgements were distorted to reinforce national self-esteem.

If one examined some country love-song, one discovered that it was not written by a man in love, but by a patriot who wanted to prove that we did indeed possess, in the words of Daniel O'Connell, 'the finest peasantry upon earth.' Yet one well-known anthology was introduced by the assertion that such love-poetry was superior to 'affected and artificial' English love-songs like *Drink to me only with thine eyes*.[18]

Yeats founded literary societies in London and Dublin, to set up standards of criticism and to free Irish literary taste from its entanglement with false propaganda values. Already (in 1891) his reputation was high enough for journalists and writers whose names counted to come forward in support of him; and for a time the movement grew fast. Still, the going was not easy: it is never easy to persuade men preoccupied with other matters to keep an open mind for what is true in art. Many members thought it treachery to admit within earshot of an Englishman that the Irish could be anything short of angels; others assumed that the only proper function for literature was to inculcate Catholic doctrine; Dublin was jealous of the country towns, the older generation was suspicious of the younger; and so forth. In time the movement fell to bits, but not before Yeats himself had learnt a good deal about committees and public speaking and the technique of making colleagues work together. As for achieving his aims, he did not change Dublin into a modern Periclean Athens, but he got further than cynics would have thought possible. Looking back with the detachment of old age, he thought the movement had at least shaken Dublin's complacency enough to prepare an audience capable, fourteen years later, of listening to J. M. Synge.

Then, with Lady Gregory, Edward Martyn and George Moore, he began the dramatic movement which brought the Abbey Theatre into being. The writing of his own plays was not the main part of his work in the Abbey; it was founded for purposes far wider. Though there had been great dramatists who were Irish there was no distinctively Irish drama; Yeats was convinced that there could be, and it was essential to his plans for Ireland that there should be. His eagerness more than any other person's got together a small band of actors and inspired them to work for the art's sake alone, on a small stage before a small audience, with a style of production and acting designed to make the words of the play the chief thing; his unmistakable disinterestedness convinced an English patron, Miss Horniman, that the scheme was worth financing. It was thanks to him that Lady Gregory discovered her talent for writing comedy, and later he risked the life of the theatre to get a hearing for J. M. Synge, whom he regarded as a greater dramatist than himself; and besides these he enabled other writers to find their chance at the Abbey whose work, less congenial to him personally, had the integrity and artistic sincerity that he required. He saw the Abbey develop a life of its own and produce realistic comedies and social problem plays very unlike what he had pictured as the image of Ireland's soul. No matter; he held it together through its early troubles, let it live in its own way, and at last was content to hand on the management to others. The very fact that it turned out otherwise than he had imagined it goes to prove that he was right in thinking that Ireland, and not merely himself, needed a theatre. He liberated other men's genius, a different thing from gathering a school of imitators round himself, and a greater achievement.

In all this work Yeats acted as if he had faith in an objective reality that he was labouring to bring to life. If he had been trying, out of some inward need of followers, to impose the reflection of his ego on a nation, he could hardly have shown so much detached insight. He showed himself an able man in public life, capable of judgement and responsible action; he could work with colleagues, handle business, deal with committees and command the confidence which, up to a point, would get rival factions to work together. The result was that he did in fact, by sheer single-minded work, colour the awakening Irish literary movement with his own personality.

Had he not been a poet of acknowledged distinction he might have been less readily accepted as the leader of a movement, but what made him a good leader was practical judgement, humour, disinterestedness and ability to work with people. None of this, except the disinterestedness, had much to do with the poetry he was writing at the time; for whatever his theories, his genius had its own will. There is an inevitable antagonism between the solitary spirit whose voice is poetry and the spirit of the committee room, even when both are aspects of the spirit of Ireland, and in the 1890's while he was meditating his vast heroic cycles, the poems and prose sketches he actually wrote grew more and more subjective behind their veil of symbolism, more and more esoteric and aloof. In 1897 he evidently felt that his prose romance *The Secret Rose* needed justification before his patriot friends, for he wrote to John O'Leary:

It is at any rate an honest attempt towards that aristocratic esoteric Irish literature, which has been my chief ambition. We have a literature for the people but nothing yet for the few.[19]

The dedication of the same story to A. E. said:

So far, however, as the book is visionary it is Irish; for Ireland, which is still predominantly Gaelic, has preserved with some less excellent things a gift of vision, which has died out among the more hurried and more successful nations.

The visionary, the esoteric and the aristocratic were already linked in his mind. The 'vision' he meant is in the Irish legends with their ever-present sense of a spirit world made visible, in the fireside talk of peasants, in the general acceptance of the supernatural, in the conscious or unconscious recognition of imagination as one side of reality. It is also in 'all that delirium of the brave' which was the life of certain historic leaders of rebellion and of men like O'Leary, who lived by a natural greatness that disregarded success. It amounts to a living belief in the soul and vanishes when men surrender utterly to the outside world. But the soul is a lonely essence; because it cannot tell its meaning in ordinary language its wisdom is esoteric; and it is aristocratic because it cannot hold itself accountable to men, but only to its own vision. It may accept comradeship but may not seek it as an end; and the language of all others that it cannot master is that of the constitutions of committees.

It took years of labour to convince Yeats that there was no

collective experience for his images to express. The disintegrating
process of the times had gone too far; his consciousness and that of
every thinking man were islanded in oceans of their separate thoughts.
The slow discovery shaped and hardened his mature poetry, which
is made out of a loneliness more immense than his father could have
pictured. Later, when this was fully clear to him, he wrote:

When I was twenty-five or twenty-six I planned a *Légende des Siècles* of
Ireland that was to set out with my *Wanderings of Oisin*, and show something of every century...and I did not see, until Synge began to write,
that we must renounce the deliberate creation of a kind of Holy City in
the imagination, and express the individual. The Irish people were not
educated enough to accept images more profound, more true to human
nature, than the schoolboy thoughts of Young Ireland. You can only
create a model of a race to inspire the action of that race as a whole, apart
from exceptional individuals, when you and it share the same simple
moral understanding of life....Having no understanding of life that we
can teach to others, we must not seek to create a school.[20]

At the time he wrote this, the younger English poets were straining
to be 'contemporary' and to interpret a collective consciousness:
Yeats had so far gone on his own way that he was not even referring
to them.

But in his youth, more than his poems suggest on a first reading,
he felt the strong pull of human comradeship against the loneliness
he had chosen. It was both a delight and a danger, and he thought
Irish poets yielded too easily to the delight and paid for it with the
sacrifice of vision. In an essay written about 1895 on *Modern Irish
Poetry* he says:

For the most part, the Irishman of our times loves so deeply those arts
which build up a gallant personality, rapid writing, ready talking, effective
speaking to crowds, that he has no thought for the arts which consume
the personality in solitude. He loves the mortal arts which have given
him a lure to take the hearts of men, and shrinks from the immortal
which could but divide him from his fellows.[21]

Besides being a tactful rebuke to shallow writers the words relate
to a conflict in his own mind. It took form years later in *The Grey*

Rock,[22] which reveals the lure those mortal arts had for himself. It is the story of a man loved by a goddess, who deserts her to die with his comrades. The man is not presented unsympathetically. In giving him her love the goddess had laid an obligation on him which he did not seek and chose not to fulfil; and to her complaint of his ingratitude:

> Why must the lasting love what passes,
> Why are the gods by men betrayed?

—to that complaint the story she tells of him is an answer good enough for human listeners, for to be generous and brave and careless of one's fate is a good life. Besides, for all her clamour, what can it matter to her? How does a man's indifference hurt the immortal whose favour he rejects? The other gods merely drench her with the wine of immortality and she forgets her betrayer and resumes the joy of the ever-living. All the same Yeats sides with the injured goddess against the hero.* At the end of the poem, he speaks in his own person to the fellow-poets, 'companions of the Cheshire Cheese' in whose memory he wrote it:

> I have kept my faith, though faith was tried,
> To that rock-born, rock-wandering foot,
> And the world's altered since you died,
> And I am in no good repute
> With the loud host before the sea,
> That think sword-strokes were better meant
> Than lovers' music—let that be,
> So that the wandering foot's content.

For himself he had accepted both gift and burden and kept faith; still there is an undertone of wistfulness for a lost world of comrade-

---

* In *Towards a Mythology* (p. 32), Mr Peter Ure says of this poem: 'The theme is the rejection of the inhuman spiritual in favour of that in human life which is heroical and passionate, and which, it is implied, because conditional upon death and time is only to be found in a human context.' It seems to me, as I hope the general drift of this book makes clear, that Yeats seeks in heroic and passionate life the utmost embodiment, rather than the rejection, of the 'inhuman spiritual', and that this is the dominant theme of his poetry. In this poem, however, having faced himself with a choice by setting the two ideas in dramatic opposition, he is pledging his faith to the *inhuman*: a necessary decision if there were to be anything to embody.

ship. But the logic of the decision was yet to be worked out. In 1916, a famous man, with youth behind him, he found that his faithfulness to poetry had separated him from the insurrection and the civil war where men well known to him, some of them his old friends of the Republican Brotherhood, some whom he had even come to despise, died for Ireland.* He stood by his choice, but the burden of isolation remained heavy on him:

> I turn away and shut the door, and on the stair
> Wonder how many times I could have proved my worth
> In something that all others understand or share;
> But O! ambitious heart, had such a proof drawn forth
> A company of friends, a conscience set at ease,
> It had but made us pine the more.[23]

The same battle is fought and re-fought and, like Oisin's in the Island of Victories, it remains as hard as ever, though the issue is never in doubt. It is fought first in impersonal reasoning and criticism of others, then in the verse tale with a kind of imaginative prescience, and at last in the immediate facts of history; and each time as the experience comes nearer home it is put in words more simple and forthright.

The Grey Rock was addressed to his friends of the Rhymers' Club, the London poets who used to meet in the 1890's at 'The Cheshire Cheese' and read their verses to each other. Most of them were dead when he wrote it, but in dedicating it to them he acknowledged the moral support their integrity had given him, before he had altogether outgrown the need for it.

> You had to face your ends when young—
> 'Twas wine or women, or some curse—
> But never made a poorer song
> That you might have a heavier purse,
> Nor gave loud service to a cause
> That you might have a troop of friends.
> You kept the Muses' sterner laws,
> And unrepenting faced your ends.

* For the complexity of Yeats' reaction to Easter Week, 1916, see below, chap. x.

It is possible that he might have become more of a demagogue and less of a poet but for these friends who admitted no counter-claims to the service of poetry.

That group of Nineties men felt the oppression of a great burden of views, social, moral, political or whatever else, which the weight of the times imposed on them, and all wanted to clear them out of art. To them it was a man's own affair whether he found poetry in brothels or music-halls or the Catholic Church; he was justified by the poetry he found, and poetry needed no justification. In their presence Yeats' own turn for theories and arguments made him feel, as he said, not quite well-born—for a man no more formulates the code his breeding has ingrained in him than he calculates the geometry of his walking. When he ventured to put forward a theory there was a gentlemanly silence which brought him back, reproved, to the concrete poem.

It was probably a healthy discipline, and their influence would be strengthened by the fact that they were better poets, more perceptive and more learned in their craft, than his argumentative Irish friends. If he came to 'The Cheshire Cheese' from a function like the Wolfe Tone centenary meeting and took his place there with his own elo- quence ringing in his ears, one can easily imagine him wondering in inward perplexity which of his two selves was real. But between himself and them there was the difference between young Ireland and *fin-de-siècle* England. For them life and poetry were two things so widely severed that it was impossible to be serious about both at once. The world they lived in was a huge going concern with fixed values; nothing they thought or said could shake it; at the most they could keep their art uncontaminated by its vulgar judgements, and that was much. Yeats lived in a more malleable world. A little experience soon convinced him that the Ireland he believed in was hardly less a kingdom of the imagination than the poetry he wrote; but he did believe in it to the point of labouring to make it actual, so that for him life had as much reality as creative art. 'Reality' for every man is the meeting-point where the life that springs from within him encounters a life without. It is perhaps the characteristic disease of the modern West that the two are cut apart; a man may have limitless activity if he lays aside his dreams and does as the world prescribes, or limitless dreams so long as he does not presume to live them.

I well remember [Yeats wrote about the Rhymers' Club] the irritated silence that fell upon a noted gathering of the younger English imaginative writers once, when I tried to explain a philosophy of poetry in which I was profoundly interested, and to show the dependence, as I conceived it, of all great art and literature upon conviction and upon heroic life. To them literature had ceased to be the handmaid of humanity, and become instead a terrible queen, in whose service the stars rose and set, and for whose pleasure life stumbles along in the darkness.[24]

To Davidson, Dowson and Lionel Johnson, with their disordered private lives from which poetry was a refuge, this philosophy of literature must have been even more irritating than Yeats could guess, for at the time he knew them only as fellow-artists. By 'humanity' he certainly did not mean the common or regulation man of the nineteenth or any other century, a figure whom he never in his life acknowledged as a fit arbiter for poetry. But if a man is to write greatly he must believe that greatness is real, or realizable, outside his writing. Such belief rings in Homer and Dante and Shakespeare and Milton; it sounds in Spenser, perhaps more faintly; it is not audible in Tennyson. It was in Yeats, uncertainly at first, but it grew in strength as he lived more actively in the world; whereas the world these fellow-poets lived in gave them little ground for holding it.

In *The Tragic Generation*, Yeats wondered why it was that so many of these friends from whom he had learnt so much ended their lives in suicide or insanity. He found no full answer, but it is possible that the answer, so far as it is general, lies here: that for each of them either circumstances or temperament or both made too deep a gulf between the creative spirit in him and the life he lived, and this left him nothing to believe in, so that poetry withered and life became meaningless.

The third of Yeats' preoccupations, his 'form of philosophy', was concerned with supernaturalism and the occult. More than the other two it took him away from the beaten paths of contemporary thought; perhaps therefore he kept quieter about it; but it was quite as serious and as significant to his poetry.

Throughout Europe until about two hundred years ago belief in magic was reputable, even though the practice of it was condemned. Nowadays the climate of thought has changed. A man well educated in the European tradition may respect the contemplative who withdraws from the world altogether, seeking to merge his mind with absolute mind, as sincerely as he respects the scientist who seeks to comprehend matter by self-abnegating study of its inherent laws. But if he is religious enough to believe that supernatural power controls the physical world he usually regards Christian prayer and submission as the only permissible approach; if he is not, he thinks of any such belief as a kind of intellectual atavism. Either way a serious interest in magic, otherwise than as a branch of anthropology, strikes him as sinister or foolish or both. Yeats' early writings, however, are transparently innocent and intellectually coherent. His interest was so serious that at twenty-seven he wrote to John O'Leary that he had long ago decided to make magic his chief preoccupation after poetry, and that if he had not, he could neither have edited Blake nor written *The Countess Cathleen*.

It was a religious interest. Because his father was an agnostic Yeats had never been asked to accept Christianity as literal truth, nor did he find in its values an expression of emotional truth; but the supernatural and miraculous elements of Christianity gave him no difficulty. Had he been born a Catholic he might perhaps have remained one, for he was religious by nature and needed symbols and rituals to express his deep awareness of a reality behind, and embodied in, the phenomenal world. Yet it is hard to picture him an obedient son of the Church: he was outside the fold and unregenerate in the sense that he loved heroic pride and the fulfilment

77

of passionate life more than humility and pity and renunciation. At the same time he hated the scientific realists whose outlook turned all things of the spirit into an insignificant by-product of material forces. Huxley, Tyndall, Carolus-Durien, Bastien-Lepage: the names honoured among his father's friends are repeated in the early books of *Autobiographies* in an impatient, derisive refrain.[25] There was a youthful phase when he thought himself a Darwinian because he was not a Christian. But it appears that what he saw in the concept of evolution was not the mechanical determinism that so appalled the young Bernard Shaw; it was rather a confirmation of his own vision of a great memory, part of a great mind, that lives through individuals —and this was also the foundation of his faith in magic.* From the very beginning he was looking not so much for a faith as for the formulation of a faith born in him.

The first influence which gave to his own tentative formulations the reassurance of a wider background was Hindu thought. While he was still a Dublin Art School student he and some friends invited a young Brahmin, Mohini Chatterjee, to come and teach them the philosophy of the east. According to Joseph Hone,[26] Mohini Chatterjee

taught that everything we perceive, including so-called apparitions, exist in the external world; that this is a stream which flows on, out of human control; that we are nothing but a mirror, and that deliverance consists in turning the mirror away so that it reflects nothing.

Yeats himself did not remember the teaching precisely like this, though he admits that, looking back, he could no longer distinguish what he learnt then from what came to him from other sources. But he certainly learnt from the Brahmin that desire was in its nature evil, and action unimportant:

* Cp. *Letters*, p. 31 (he is finding fault with George Eliot): 'She understands only the conscious nature of man. His intellect, his morals—she knows nothing at all of the dim unconscious nature, the world of instinct, which (if there is any truth in Darwin) is the accumulated wisdom of all living things from monera to man, while the other is at the very most the wisdom gathered during four score years and ten.'

Not only did he think that the imaginative arts were the only things that were quite sinless, but he spent more than half a day proving, by many subtle and elaborate arguments, that art for art's sake was the only sinless doctrine, for any other would hide the shadow of the world as it exists in the mind of God by shadows of the accidents and illusions of life, and was but Sadducean blasphemy. Religion existed also for its own sake; and every soul quivered between two emotions, the desire to possess things, to make them a portion of its own egotism, and a delight in just and beautiful things for their own sake—and all religions were a doctrinal or symbolical crying aloud of this delight. . . . I am certain that he taught us by what seemed an invincible logic that those who die, in as far as they have imagined beauty or justice, are made a part of beauty and justice, and move through the minds of living men, as Shelley believed; and that mind overshadows mind even among the living, and by pathways that lie beyond the senses; and that he measured labour by this measure, and put the hermit above all other labourers, because, being the most hidden, he lived nearer to the Eternal Powers, and showed their mastery of the world. . . . And I am certain that we, seeking as youth will for some unknown deed and thought, all dreamed that but to listen to this man who threw the enchantment of power about silent and gentle things, and at last to think as he did, was the one thing worth doing and thinking; and that all action and all words that led to action were a little vulgar, a little trivial. Ah, how many years it has taken me to awaken out of that dream.[27]

For he awakened out of it in the end. He belonged to the western world which has Homer in its blood and drama at the heart of its imagination, and could not have excluded action from his philosophy. But action, like art, has meaning when it gives form to something that emerges through the imagination. What Yeats sought and retained from the Brahmin's teaching was a clearer understanding of what he already believed by instinct—that the world of the imagination was no less real than the world of matter, that art and action and the physical world are all in some sense the incarnation of a thought, the body of a spirit.

Broadly, I think his view might be stated thus: There is mind or spirit (in this context the term is unimportant so long as it is not taken to mean analytical reason), and its external forms are the

79

phenomenal world. A man's body is the form of his mind, which in turn is an idea of the divine mind, as also are rocks and trees and water. Since all things are aspects of the one mind and mental life is continuous, not only may mind communicate with mind, but physical objects may retain in themselves the impress of thoughts and passions that have gathered about them, so that the universe is alive with memory.

If once the fluid universal mind is granted it becomes almost meaningless to ask whether gods and faeries and demons, or for that matter stone and water, are its primal thoughts or a sublimate of the collective thoughts of men. All things must be thought in order to take form; and the human imagination is one mode, possibly (as in later years Yeats seems to have held) the ultimate mode of the divine thinking.

This is neither science nor Christianity, but Yeats saw in it the outline of an older world-view ignored by both. He expounded its practical implications in an essay on *Magic* written in 1901:

I believe in the practice and philosophy of what we have agreed to call magic, in what I must call the evocation of spirits, though I do not know what they are, in the power of creating magical illusions, in the visions of truth in the depth of the mind when the eyes are closed; and I believe in three doctrines, which have, as I think, been handed down from early times, and been the foundation of nearly all magical practices. These doctrines are:

(1) That the borders of our minds are ever shifting, and that many minds can flow into one another, as it were, and create or reveal a single mind, a single energy.

(2) That the borders of our memories are shifting, and that our memories are a part of one great memory, the memory of Nature herself.

(3) That this great mind and great memory can be evoked by symbols.[28]

At first, he says, he thought that the evocative power of symbols came from the minds of those who used them, by focusing and as it were objectifying their intention. Later, after many experiments, he came to believe that it was inherent in the symbols themselves independently of the individual mind. 'They act because the great memory associates them with certain events and moods and persons.' For he held his faith confidently enough to test it and examine the results critically.

Much of the search for occult wisdom is told in his *Autobiographies*, much more in unpublished notes.* He attended spiritualist seances, became for a while a disciple of Madame Blavatsky, studied Rosicrucianism, and joined secret orders for the study and practice of magic. He used symbols and incantations to put himself in a state of trance in which visions, perhaps coming from beyond his individual mind, would rise before him. He was of course well aware that a vision might be merely the projection of one's own wishes and fears; nevertheless, because he believed in the great memory and the existence of disembodied intelligences, he recognized that it might also be the key to a storehouse of forgotten wisdom.

An idea latent in his two first plays and much of his prose is that Christianity does not contain the whole of supernatural revelation. Buried under fifteen hundred years of it an older understanding survived in Ireland, which linked men's sense of the eternal with the past of the race and with the hills and rivers around them. By evoking images from the great memory he hoped to build a kind of synthesis to give full expression to it all and thereby restore to the soul its supremacy in the material world.

Perhaps, too, it would be possible to find in that new philosophy of spiritism coming to a seeming climax in the work of Ernest Myers, and in the investigations of uncounted obscure persons, what would change the country spiritism into a reasoned belief that would put its might into all the rest. A new belief seemed coming that could be so simple and demonstrable and above all so mixed into the common scenery of the world, that it would set the whole man on fire and liberate him from a thousand obediences and complexities. We were to forge in Ireland a new sword on our old traditional anvil that must in the end re-establish the old, confident, joyous world.[29]

* Many of these are given at length by Ellmann, *Yeats, The Man and the Masks*, and by Virginia Moore in *The Unicorn*.

'The old, confident, joyous world' is not the Brahmin's vision of deliverance; but if there is one enduring faith that runs through Yeats' work from first to last, it is this poetic joy in the world and in the very act of living; to deny it would be denying God. In *The Wanderings of Oisin*, overcast as it is with a brooding adolescent melancholy, the Danaans sing

> 'God is joy and joy is God,
> And things that have grown sad are wicked,
> And things that fear the dawn of the morrow
> Or the grey wandering osprey Sorrow.'

In 1936 he excluded most of the poets of World War I from his *Oxford Book of Modern Verse* because, as he said in the preface,

passive suffering is not a theme for poetry. In all the great tragedies, tragedy is a joy to the man who dies.

And in *The Gyres*, one of his last poems, he wrote:

> Out of cavern comes a voice,
> And all it knows is that one word 'Rejoice!'

Symbols and the visions they evoked were his constant pre-occupation. But he had no positive inherited creed to invest particular visions with authority and prohibit others: he was at large in a dim hinterland of thought, where every myth was a potential expression of truth and his own recognition of it as true the main criterion of its value. Such a liberal philosophy might leave a man at the mercy of his own unconscious impulses, starting up in the dress of gods to beckon him this way and that. Indeed, this was one of the difficulties Yeats encountered in the occult orders where he sought wisdom and companionship. In a note to *The Trembling of the Veil* (*Autobiographies*) he remarks:

My connection with the 'Hermetic Students' ended amid quarrels caused by men, otherwise worthy, who claimed a Rosicrucian sanction for their own phantasies.

Some such maze is that 'Hodos Chameliontos' against which he says that 'some ancient poet' has warned us:*

Stoop not down to the darkly splendid world wherein lieth continually a faithless depth and Hades wrapped in cloud, delighting in unintelligible images.[30]

For a while he wandered there, evoking his images, experimenting with strange approaches to the spirit world, trusting to unknown powers to put in order for him the ancient wisdom he hoped to recover for mankind. Before everything, however, Yeats was a poet, and in all his labyrinths poetry gave him a sense of direction to make up for the lack of a creed. Poetry is the commonsense of the soul: it distinguishes greatness from triviality, mere fancifulness from beauty that lights up the deeps of thought. Though he listened hopefully to messages from his evocations he was never their humble slave. They only got into his poetry when they made good poetic sense.

He tested philosophy by poetry, not vice versa. A poem is not great because of the belief it expounds, but when it convinces us of its greatness we know that it cannot have been made from false or trivial thoughts. The images in his poems had to impress by their own poetic rightness. What they symbolized was of no importance to the reader till their own power carried it home to him, but it mattered immensely to himself. He could not even imagine them

* Yeats says that his friend, McGregor Mathers, showed him in a cabbalistic MS. these words 'which antiquity has attributed to Zoroaster, but modern scholarship to some Alexandrian poet'. They appear to me to originate from a passage in Plotinus, Ennead I, 6, vii–viii, thus translated by Stephen MacKenna:

'For if anyone pursue what is like a beautiful shape playing over water and clutch at it as something true—there is a myth somewhere, I think, that tells of such a one, how he sank into the depths of the current and was not seen again. So, too, one that possesses himself of beautiful material things and will not let them go, *shall be carried down, not in body but in soul, to the dark depths loathed of Intelligence where, blind, in Hades also he shall have converse with shadows, there as here*' (my italics).

Plotinus, obviously, is distinguishing the beauty of sensible things from the Idea of Beauty imaged in them. At the time he wrote *The Trembling of the Veil*, Yeats may not have known the passage in Plotinus: he could well have come across the words detached from their context in some esoteric manual, and applied them in his own way, just as Plotinus took over the myth to apply in his own way.

with the necessary intensity except by labouring to make them express his deepest sense of the truth.

In his mature poetry, having learnt to rely more confidently on his own thought, Yeats took his visionary images less solemnly. It must have been about 1906 that he wrote in an undated letter to his friend Florence Farr, who was studying Vedantic philosophy:

I once cared only for images about whose necks I could cast 'chains of office' as it were. They were so many aldermen of the ideal, whom I wished to master the city of the soul. Now I do not want images at all, or chains of office, being content with an unruly soul.

But he held to his faith in the world of life as the proper sphere of the soul's activity. The letter ends:

I have myself by the by begun meditations of your sort, but with the object of trying to lay hands on some dynamic and substantialising force as distinct from the eastern quiescent and supersensualizing state of the soul—a movement downward upon life, not upwards out of life.[31]

This is a long way from that young disciple of the Brahmin who thought that all action and all words that led to action were a little vulgar. Yeats' very perceptive father had always told him that he was far too much in love with the world to find truth, as mystics do, by detaching himself from it. Oriental philosophy had liberated him from what was uncongenial in his age, but he took from it only what suited his inherent genius.

It should be evident from this account that on the intellectual plane there is no deep discord between Yeats' 'three interests'. His poetry is visionary; it rests on the faith that there is a transcendental reality of which the actual world is a garbled copy, and that the creative imagination unfettered by the actual can draw from the model direct. It is a faith that goes back through Plotinus to Plato, and has been held in more recent times by Sidney, Spenser, Blake and Shelley among others; it is not in keeping with modern scientific materialism, but is perfectly compatible both with Yeats' half-mystical nationalism and his belief in a mind partially embodied in the universe. The sense of an incoherence to be overcome came to him chiefly from practical life. Each of the interests led him into action in different company, since not all revolutionary nationalists are poets and occult philosophers need not be one or the other; yet each to him was one aspect of an indivisible truth and had his whole loyalty; thus he was always alone among allies. However, a man who means something consistent and can express it makes his own field of action in the end. Yeats' love of literature and his belief in nationality 'came together', as he put it, without much difficulty, because both poetry and nationalism can be explained in terms that make sense to the modern mind. A religion so remote from the accepted tracks of thought as his occultism is much less amenable. In one breath to reject science for refusing to recognize the supernatural and Christianity for disparaging earthly life is cutting across too many preconceptions to win a hearing. Those who were impressed either by the excellence of his poetry or by his selfless work for an Irish literary renaissance would not follow him equally readily into resurrecting old gods and reinstating folk superstitions; but Yeats himself was firmly convinced that all these things belonged together. He saw mankind on the brink of a revelation and counted the signs and tokens. First in Ireland, then in the world, the imagination was to reawaken and men return to a perception as old as the hills, only despised and denied by the modern rationalizing intellect, that the whole earth was alive with spiritual energy.

But the very fact that he was dreaming of a world movement held back his poetry, for he wanted to convince, and to do so must use his readers' terms of thought when his own were too strange.* As his father had realized, it is impossible for an artist at the same time to

---

* Sometimes he deliberately construes from one to the other. Cp. *Symbolism in Poetry*: 'All sounds, all colours, all forms,...evoke indefinable and yet precise emotions, *or, as I prefer to think, call down among us certain disembodied powers, whose footsteps over our hearts we call emotions.*'

In a poem, the words I have italicized might be passed over by a negligent reader as 'nothing but' a figure of speech. By using them here, Yeats asserts the literal meaning, and at the same time gives an equivalent in what can be accepted as rational language.

be himself and to be telling others what they should be. Until he had given up that dream and recognized his essential loneliness his full meaning would not come into his words.

At last, when he had ceased to expect it and by a channel he had not thought of, his visions did speak clearly, and set in order for him his understanding of this and all other worlds. *A Vision* will be discussed in later chapters,* but its continuity with these earlier thoughts is plain to see: it draws together the ideas I have been tracing here, and many more, in a pattern of great complexity. But when he wrote it he was bent not so much on enlightening the world as on explaining himself to himself. It was something like the liberation for himself that he had dreamed of for the world, for his most powerful and concentrated poetry was written after he had assimilated its bizarre cosmology. Then, with his thoughts at last hammered into unity, he became what before he had only been able to imagine. In his early prose, for instance, he described how a man ought to waken into eternity without leaving the body:

I am orthodox and pray for a resurrection of the body, and am certain that a man should find his Holy Land where he first crept upon the floor, and that familiar woods and rivers should fade into a symbol with so gradual a change that he never discover, no, not even in ecstasy itself, that he is beyond space, and that Time alone keeps him from Primum Mobile, the Supernatural Eden, and the White Rose over all.[32]

In his early poetry, this prayer remains incompletely answered: the rhythm, the imagery, the carefully chosen vocabulary all betray his awareness that he has left the actual world to inhabit a world of vision. But in *The Tower*,[33] when he looks out on the landscape, mind and place, the visionary and the actual, have become indistinguishably one.

This is going far beyond the stretch of years I have been considering here. It has seemed necessary to be discursive, since Yeats' thought makes itself clear, not by falling into line in an argument

* See below, chaps VIII, IX.

but by reappearing with a connotation that widens and deepens. But the main theme of this chapter has been a sketch, somewhat over-simplified, of the ideas working in his mind, and mostly kept below the surface, while he wrote his early poetry. One need not know them to read the poetry, but when they are known his early poetry is seen to have closer bearing on his later than at first appears. The thread which wove the pattern was his certainty that man and nature, action and vision, are alike the utterance of a reality which transcends appearances and yet speaks itself for ever in concrete forms. This was inborn in him; it was the man himself. The warp and woof of the pattern were the service of Ireland, which defined his life in the world of action, and the service of poetry which held him apart in the world of vision.

CHAPTER VI

MATURITY

I have forgot awhile
Tara uprooted, and new commonness
Upon the throne and crying about the streets
And hanging its paper flowers from post to post
Because it is alone of all things happy.

The lines are from the title poem of *In the Seven Woods* (1904). They were written in 1902 of the coronation festivities of Edward VII. Yeats, in retreat from them, is walking in the woods of Coole Park, Lady Augusta Gregory's country house. It is as if the dreamer of *The Wind Among the Reeds* has opened his eyes for a moment on the contemporary world rollicking around him and turned away from it in distaste.

A reader of the early Yeats might be less surprised that he had forgotten the paper flowers on the lamp-posts than that he had deigned to remember them at all. The descent into an actual time and place is a new departure in his poetry; and in this thin book of fourteen poems there is a good deal that is new.

He still has the key to a world of visions and speaks familiarly of beings like the wood-woman whose lover was changed to a blue-eyed hawk. But something has gone wrong with its relation to his own life.

I have no happiness in dreaming of Brycelinde[1]

he cries, and

No boughs have withered because of the wintry wind;
The boughs have withered because I have told them my dreams.[2]

And yet in *The Happy Townland*—a favourite of his own in later days—a fresh, salt wind with the tang of common life in it has

88

blown upon his visions, blown away the awestricken hush and blown
in a sparkle of gaiety. Compare the solemnity of

> flame on flame, and deep on deep,
> Throne over throne where in half sleep,
> Their swords upon their iron knees,
> Brood her high lonely mysteries[3]

with

> Michael will unhook his trumpet
> From a bough overhead,
> And blow a little noise
> When the supper has been spread.
> Gabriel will come from the water
> With a fish-tail,* and talk
> Of wonders that have happened
> On wet roads where men walk,
> And lift up an old horn
> Of hammered silver, and drink
> Till he has fallen asleep
> Upon the starry brink.[4]

The writer is no longer a reverent postulant but is on easy terms
with the lonely majestical multitude.

His subject-matter has widened: it has begun to include themes
picked up from the activities of his prose self. *The Players Ask for
a Blessing on the Psalteries and on Themselves*,[5] written for recitation
by the Abbey Players, rings with his sense of the eternal brooding
over the temporal. So does *Red Hanrahan's Song About Ireland*,[6]
which for the first time acknowledges some real and hard experience
of political factiousness. The language is poetic but the feeling less
idyllic than that of the prose play *Cathleen ni Houlihan*, written about
the same time:

> The wind has bundled up the clouds high over Knock-na-Rea,
> And thrown the thunder on the stones for all that Maeve can say.
> Angers that are like noisy clouds have set our hearts abeat,
> But we have all bent low and low and kissed the quiet feet
> Of Cathleen, the daughter of Houlihan.

---

* How Yeats discovered that Gabriel ruled the waters is told in *Autobiographies*,
pp. 268–9.

Even the climate of his mind has changed: the landscape of this poem is not made of glimmering half-lights but of wind and cloud and floodwater and naked thorntrees, in a world altogether more bracing to the spirit.

Most of his writing is still about love, but the tone has changed. For the first time there is something like an individualized portrait of Maud Gonne; she is no longer a symbol obscured in a haze and blaze of worship but a woman at whom a man may look and note that she is

> Tall and noble but with face and bosom
> Delicate in colour as apple blossom[7]

—or more precisely that she has been like this and that her beauty has both lost and gained with the years.

In the earlier poems moments of actual life were never more than a springboard from which he floated up into poetry. Maud, tired after a long walk, sat on the grass to rest, and Yeats finished *The Rose of the World*:

> Bow down, archangels, in your dim abode:
> Before you were, or any hearts to beat,
> Weary and kind one lingered by His seat;
> He made the world to be a grassy road
> Before her wandering feet.[8]

Now the actual moment and the actual words get into the poem:

> One that is ever kind said yesterday:
> 'Your well-belovèd's hair has threads of grey.'[9]

The most elaborate poem in this new style is *Adam's Curse*,[10] which has for theme the twin passions of poetry and love. They are talking of both, and like a symbol of beauty's laboured perfection there appears in the sky

> A moon, worn as if it had been a shell
> Washed by time's waters as they rose and fell
> About the stars and broke in days and years

—and then, as instantly and quietly as a blinking of the eyes of thought, the symbol turns its other face as he remembers how the long labour of love

> had all seemed happy, and yet we'd grown
> As weary-hearted as that hollow moon.

It was love, not poetry, which had grown weary-hearted. This poem was written before the day in 1903 when a telegram, handed to him as he was about to begin a lecture, told him that Maud had married Sean McBride. The news was so stunning that he gave the lecture as if he had not received it; but *Adam's Curse* shows that in his heart he knew already what the marriage could only confirm. His love was irrevocable, its object unattainable, his youth gone.

However deeply the heart may have grasped such a reality, to see it accomplished in fact and stated with the cold finality of a telegram sets up a new relation between the inner and the outer world. Yeats began to write with a hard detachment which is exactly what was missing from the incense-clouded visions of *The Wind Among the Reeds*. There, he had wailed for a sorrow diffused over the universe:

> Until the axle break
> That keeps the stars in their round,
> And hands hurl in the deep
> The banners of East and West,
> And the girdle of light is unbound,
> Your breast will not lie by the breast
> Of your beloved in sleep.[11]

Now he puts it to a lilting tune in phrases as bare as the language of Lear's fool:

> Sweetheart, do not love too long:
> I loved long and long,
> And grew to be out of fashion
> Like an old song.[12]

In those years about the turn of the century, however, other things besides defeat in love were changing the temper of his poetry. He first met Lady Gregory in 1896; she invited him to Coole Park, and

presently he was spending a part of every year there. He was worn
out between London and poverty and frustration; she gave him back
health and a quiet mind. Many years later he wrote his gratitude:

> because her hand
> Had strength that could unbind
> What none can understand,
> What none can have and thrive,
> Youth's dreamy load, till she
> So changed me that I live
> Labouring in ecstasy.[13]

Coole Park with its woods and waters sank gradually into his mind
and poetry, but that was a little later. Lady Gregory herself immediately became a powerful ally, at once patron, disciple and friend. She
lived among the country people and could speak the local dialect as
Yeats could not: to give him a fresh interest she took him with her
from cottage to cottage gathering reminiscences and old stories, so
that as he listened their turns of thought and phrase became familiar
to him. She shared his dream of an Irish theatre; without her he
might never have set out to make it come true. Incidentally, in
working with him she discovered her own talent for writing comedy
truer to the speech and spirit of the countryside than anything till
J. M. Synge came forward. She even livened up his own rather
solemn muse to write that light-hearted prose comedy *The Pot of
Broth*.

From 1898 till about 1911 he was steadily at work on the Irish
theatre, coping with its problems of organization and finance and
with temperamental players and playwrights, and working out techniques of speech and movement for the kind of plays he had set his
heart on. He half enjoyed, half rebelled against the work; in any
case it was necessary to his plans for Ireland and necessary to himself,
to bring down his poetry to a world of practical realities. Staging
a play in Dublin was not by any means dull. An outsider might
think *The Countess Cathleen* a harmless entertainment. But when it

was produced, there was first an outcry from the Catholics that it was heretical to say that a soul could be sold to the Devil and escape damnation, and then from some patriots that it was an insult to Irish womanhood to represent the Countess as doing such a thing anyway, and then Arthur Griffith, who at the time was a young anticlerical journalist, offered to bring along a fighting audience from the docks, ready to applaud whatever the Church objected to. Yeats, determined to defend the freedom of creative art, had to avoid a theological riot by staging the play under the ignominious protection of the imperial government's police.

Defending the detachment of art was exciting, but Yeats did not feel that it absolved him as man and patriot from facing straight issues outside his art. The years before the turn of the century were the most violently coloured in all his political life. The year 1897 was Queen Victoria's Jubilee, 1898 the centenary of Wolfe Tone: both occasions stirred Irish anti-imperialism to fevered activity, and the Boer War kept the temperature high. Yeats, with a moderately cool head, was up to his eyes in it, and Maud Gonne was carried away on a tide of reckless exploits. The next year he was helping her out of a wild political scrape, and between them they had the utmost difficulty in persuading still more excitable comrades from assassinating the enemy who had got her into it. This was the year of *The Wind Among the Reeds*, from which he remarked later that his thinking had been too completely excluded. It was so, but one can see that the gap between Aedh wishing for the cloths of heaven to spread at his lady's feet, and the riotous mobs and dashing conspiracies on which, because the lady was entangled with them, his thinking had to be focused, was too wide to be bridged by the kind of poetry he had yet learnt to write. Yet the very width of it, and the intensity with which each side of him was engaged, made it necessary for him to make his way to a synthesis.

Without knowing it [he says in *The Tree of Life*], I had come to care for nothing but impersonal beauty. I had set out on life with the thought of putting my very self into poetry, and had understood this as an attempt to cut away the non-essential....Then one day I understood, quite suddenly, as the way is, that I was seeking something unchangeable and unmixed and always outside myself, a Stone or an Elixir that was always out of reach, and that I myself was the floating thing that held out its hand ....To put it otherwise, we should ascend out of common life, the thoughts of the newspapers, of the market place, of men, of science, but only so far as we can carry the normal, passionate, reasoning self, the personality as a whole.[14]

William Morris, absorbed in socialism and handicrafts, wrote poetry as he wove tapestry, to take a holiday from fighting the world. 'You write my sort of poetry' he had told Yeats[15] when *The Wanderings of Oisin* came out, and left his comment unfinished because he was distracted to fury by the atrocious design of a street lamp. It was never the whole truth. Though Yeats also created a world he, unlike Morris, took it more seriously than the one he moved about in; it was a cloudy citadel where he could discover his true self. Now he was coming down to earth, and the poetic conventions of pre-Raphaelitism and the Cheshire Cheese were no longer wide enough. In middle life he set himself to learn a new vocabulary, new techniques, new themes, to take in wider circles of the outer world without letting them slip from the control of poetry.

He began to react violently against his 'Hodos Chameliontos' and the style that went with it. He wrote to A. E. in 1904:

This region of shadows is full of false images of the spirit and of the body. I have come to feel towards it...even a little as some of my own stupidest critics feel. As so often happens with a thing one has been tempted by and is still a little tempted by, I am roused by it to a kind of frenzied hatred which is quite out of my control.[16]*

He began to dislike the word 'Celtic' with all it had come to stand for—largely through his own influence on lesser writers—of vague yearnings and misty sentiment, and to strip his language of poeticisms

---

* In this letter Yeats was at the same time apologizing for the harshness of his criticism of some of A. E.'s own poetry, and defending in carefully measured terms the grounds of his objection to it.

and evocative words like 'haunted' and 'dim', to rely more on the stark essence of a thought; his rhythms too lost their invocational ring and came closer to the composed speech of normal life. The measure of the change can be taken by setting a few lines from *The Secret Rose* (in *The Wind Among the Reeds*) beside a few from *Adam's Curse*. Here is the earlier style:

> Far-off, most secret, and inviolate Rose,
> Enfold me in my hour of hours; where those
> Who sought thee in the Holy Sepulchre,
> Or in the wine-vat, dwell beyond the stir
> And tumult of defeated dreams; and deep
> Among pale eyelids, heavy with the sleep
> Men have named beauty

—and against it this:

> Better go down upon your marrow-bones
> And scrub a kitchen pavement, or break stones
> Like an old pauper, in all kinds of weather;
> For to articulate sweet sounds together
> Is to work harder than all these, and yet
> Be thought an idler by the noisy set
> Of bankers, schoolmasters, and clergymen
> The martyrs call the world.

Both are in decasyllabic couplets. The first gets resonance from its slow pace, its echoing vowel-sounds and lingering rhymes; the second runs along almost like a prose conversation accidentally falling into rhyme and metre. But even more obviously, the second is as crowded with mundane objects as the first with the furniture of the kingdom of dreams.

The transformation was not a movement away from symbolism. From beginning to end, nothing in life or art had meaning for his poetry until it became the symbol of some transcendental reality. If he wrote more about actual life, less of faery women and the golden apples of the sun, it was that he had begun to see in actual life a partial embodiment of the truth he sought to realize. The elements

95

of the world, physical, social and political, are taken into his poetry as they become charged with significance reaching out beyond themselves.

In this direction *The Green Helmet*, published six years later, is an advance on any earlier book. If one looked only at the poems in it and not at the plays he had been writing at the same time, it would seem that his gift of vision had fallen asleep. Only the first poem *His Dream* has that echo of the supernatural that filled all his earlier work, and this as it happens is a transcript of a sleeping dream, not a waking one. The rest of the book is more like a record of thoughts arising from the day's encounters. It carries out his newly discovered aim: to ascend out of common life, but only so far as he can take with him 'the normal, passionate, reasoning self'.

The most striking impression is that the book is essentially Maud Gonne's. Seven of the poems are for her, and it is here that she first shines on the page with a peculiarly living, individualized quality.

Many poets have boasted that they will immortalize the beauty of a woman. Of most, all that we remember now is that there was beauty and that the poet was moved by it: the women themselves are shadows. The darkness of Shakespeare's mistress, Stella's black eyes framed in golden hair, the roses of innumerable cheeks— what do they all amount to, and what difference would it make beyond the turn of a sonnet if the lady had been of a different colour? A painter could have told us better. But if every painting of Maud Gonne vanished something of her would remain credible in Yeats' verses. He painted her as words can, dynamically, seeing her body as the projection of a quality of spirit which stirred him:

> With beauty like a tightened bow, a kind
> That is not natural in an age like this,
> Being high and solitary and most stern.[17]

Now that hope was gone he could assess the gain and the loss of loving her. It had lifted him irrevocably to the plane where life and legend meet:

For she had fiery blood
When I was young,
And trod so sweetly proud
As 'twere upon a cloud,
A woman Homer sung,
That life and letters seem
But an heroic dream.[18]

But still she had gone out of his reach; she had become a Catholic and accepted her own wrecked marriage as final. In *A King and No King* he wrote:

And I that have not your faith, how shall I know
That in the blinding light beyond the grave
We'll find so good a thing as we have lost?
The hourly kindness, the day's common speech,
The habitual content of each with each
When neither soul nor body has been crossed.[19]

There is poignancy in the deliberate ordinariness of the words. When he was young he wrapped up common life in metaphor and prayed to

find under the boughs of love and hate,
In all poor foolish things that live a day,
Eternal beauty wandering on her way[20]

—with a touch of condescension that made the prayer unlikely to be answered. Now that common happiness was out of his reach he stopped condescending and described it clearly.

Love and dream are not his only themes. In *The Green Helmet* he suddenly drops his aloofness and becomes a man of the world, a satirist and a thinker with clear-cut, unpopular views. In two poems, *The Mask* and *Brown Penny*, he celebrates the discovery of casual love, a discovery which gathered significance in the poems of his old age. In two others he is absorbed in theatre business, sardonically observing his own and other men's follies. He is growing famous, and his contempt for popular judgement makes him impatient of fame; he turns his satire against himself and the public and points it with arrogance. Asked to encourage the school of his imitators who are doing well out of the Celtic Revival, he retorts:

> But was there ever dog that praised his fleas?[21]

—and in a fit of disgust at the inertia of his own muse, he blasts love in one line and political passion in the next:

> All things can tempt me from this craft of verse:
> One time it was a woman's face, or worse—
> The seeming needs of my fool-driven land.[22]

This, from the dramatist who had focused centuries of idealism in the simple and moving image of Cathleen ni Houlihan. The suppressed thinker is taking his revenge.

As a whole they are prickly poems. His plays at the time were romantic and poetic, and in all the business that belonged to producing them he was exposing his inward vision to a modern democratic public. The climate was not congenial and this sardonic attitude was a mode of defying it. He neither vulgarized his writing nor retreated from experience, but put on a mask of haughty self-sufficiency and met the world on his own terms.

It made him sigh for a courtly age when men of action had been men of culture too, so that the poet had a public worthy of the highest imagination: the world that Raleigh and Spenser had known, that grew old and died before the French Revolution. Several poems celebrate the proud virtues of aristocracy. *Upon a House Shaken by the Land Agitation* is an attack on the mounting spirit of social equality.

> How should the world be luckier if this house,
> Where passion and precision have been one
> Time out of mind, became too ruinous
> To breed the lidless eye that loves the sun?[23]

This may not be the whole truth about hereditary landlords, but it is a better defence than Burke's famous phrase about vice losing half its evil in losing all its grossness.

There is a new courage of his convictions, a new consciousness of friends and enemies, a new respect for the fighting will and its weapon the analytic intellect. All this is closely related to the welcome he had found at Coole Park. The place itself was an old family house maintained with pride, and house and family stood for a tradition of public-spirited aristocracy. Their life was open to ideas, yet rooted in the country round them and ordered by conventions which guarded the comfort of the body and the privacy of the mind. It was an ideal place for Yeats to think and write in peace. Not only this, but it crystallized into a concrete image his notion of the aristo- cratic way of life. It was his luck, or his talent, to dream of fine things and then wake and discover them—to conceive heroic simplicity and make a friend of John O'Leary; legendary beauty and find Maud Gonne at his door; a tradition of nobility, and be made at home in Coole Park. That O'Leary suffered defeat and imprisonment, that Maud Gonne's political passion made her throw herself away, that Coole Park belonged to an order visibly fading from the world, did not destroy their reality; but it defined his attitude to the modern world and gave substance to his hatred of the materialism which he saw as an export from England.

Ireland missed the industrial revolution and with it some of Victorian England's prosperous smugness, for it never grew a sub- stantial middle class. Its 'big house' tradition, derived straight from the eighteenth century, retained something of the careless extrava- gance and assurance of that age, and preferred a dash of recklessness and the courage of eccentricity to the more sober English virtues. The eighteenth century was its flowering-time, the century of Swift and Goldsmith, of Berkeley, Burke and Grattan, when courage of the intellect and the imagination had distinguished it. Yeats, who hitherto had cared only for the romantic ages of history, now began to see in the eighteenth century a mental liberation of his own Protes- tant Ireland, corresponding somewhat to the Elizabethan age of England. He began to learn from it: from Swift especially and from Berkeley, whose metaphysics he liked, he learnt the fighting virtues of language—conciseness, clarity and precision of statement, and the naked style which relies on the intensity of a thought and the compactness of its expression.

Louis MacNeice has said[24] that a contemporary reviewer, reading *In the Seven Woods* and *The Green Helmet*, might easily have thought that Yeats' power was failing. Certainly their strongest qualities were both unfamiliar to the age and unlike his earlier work; it must have been hard to assess them then, as it is hard now not to read them in the light of what came after. Yet there was plenty to make the reviewer cautious. A failing poet repeats patterns of thought and expression already mastered; he does not teach himself a new idiom and a new range of feeling. And whatever else he overlooked, a critic might have been startled into alertness by the condensed force of *The Coming of Wisdom with Time*:

> Though leaves are many, the root is one.
> Through all the lying days of my youth
> I swayed my leaves and flowers in the sun;
> Now I may wither into the truth.[25]

CHAPTER VII

ART AND ARISTOCRACY

Yeats' ideas about politics and society are as unpopular as his pre-occupation with magic. Many of his admirers find them even more annoying, because in active life beliefs about heroes and aristocrats have more disconcerting social consequences than beliefs about spirits, and are therefore less easy to laugh off as idiosyncrasies. Yet they, like his magic, are part of an intricate, coherent design of thought, which throughout his life he seemed to be not so much constructing as discovering. He never put his thoughts into poetry till they had ceased to be mere abstract hypotheses; he had to feel them in the heat of action or the glow of vision as convictions irrevocably valid for himself. Fragments of them jutted out at first, disconnected and uncompromising, like island peaks indicating the contours of a submerged mountain range. It was only when *A Vision* had been written that the whole mass was laid bare even before his own eyes, and afterwards he could move with a new assurance from point to point.

The Green Helmet is pervaded with a haughty contempt for democracy, a feeling for traditionally heroic and aristocratic virtues, more positive than anything in the dreamy aloofness of the earlier books. The love poems are full of it. Maud Gonne, who

> would of late
> Have taught to ignorant men most violent ways,
> Or hurled the little streets upon the great,
> Had they but courage equal to desire

is pardoned because she is most unlike the rabble she stirs up:

> with a mind
> That nobleness made simple as a fire,
> With beauty like a tightened bow, a kind
> That is not natural in an age like this,
> Being high and solitary and most stern.[1]

It is in all his references to the theatre, for work at the Abbey showed him that a playwright cannot ignore public opinion; he must yield or fight: but it is strongest and plainest in all that touches Coole Park. Coole Park showed him, first of all, that a privileged aristocracy which took its freedom for granted could shelter the artist against the vulgarity of popular demands. It might have been an Elizabethan who cried out against the levelling modern spirit:

> The weak lay hand on what the strong has done,
> Till that be tumbled that was lifted high
> And discord follow upon unison,
> And all things at one common level lie.[2]

But this was too general. In *Upon a House Shaken by the Land Agitation* he detailed the virtues of the 'big house' tradition which would not flower again in democracy:

> Although
> Mean roof-trees were the sturdier for its fall,
> How should their luck run high enough to reach
> The gifts that govern men, and after these
> To gradual Time's last gift, a written speech
> Wrought of high laughter, loveliness and ease?[3]

There is a certain stiltedness in the last line which falls short still of being 'written speech', but it shows how his new ideal of art is linked with his feeling for aristocracy.

Coole Park was a living image for his imagined world. He found there something like the poet-honouring courts of ancient legend, or the Urbino that Castiglione celebrated, and found no servility in his position there, since he admired Lady Gregory's outlook on life no less than she admired his poetry. A world beyond literature was necessary to him as it probably is to any great writer; he could not have remained satisfied with the over-specialized literary coteries of London. When he told the disapproving Rhymers' Club that great poetry depended on conviction and on heroic living he was asking for hearers who took him seriously, who recognized the excellence pictured in art as an image of the excellence they tried for in life, in everything from ruling kingdoms to building houses. He was right. Epics were made when the poet sang of greatness that his hearers believed in, and in the great age of Greek tragedy dramatist and audience must have shared the same profound and simple conception of man's fate. Poetry withers when it finally gives up hope of the living world.

From Demodocus singing at a Phaeaecian banquet or the Athenian crowd hanging on a chorus in *Oedipus* it seems a long way to a Galway race meeting. But Yeats was thoroughly Irish about horses. Watching the crowd that watched them he saw in their eyes the breathless, discriminating attention that once, when men of action were men of understanding, must have been given to poets too; and for a moment it brought him a vision of those vast cycles of time which were to haunt the poetry of his old age:

> We, too, had good attendance once,
> Hearers and hearteners of the work;
> Aye, horsemen for companions,
>
> .   .   .   .
>
> Sing on: somewhere at some new moon,
> We'll learn that sleeping is not death,
> Hearing the whole earth change its tune,
> Its flesh being wild, and it again
> Crying aloud as the racecourse is,
> And we find hearteners among men
> That ride upon horses.[4]

By 1914, the year of *Responsibilities*, he had changed from defence to attack. Not only was aristocracy the necessary guardian of art, but on the honour of art civilization itself depended. Again it was Coole Park that led him into battle, in the storm over Sir Hugh Lane's collection of pictures.

Sir Hugh Lane, Lady Gregory's nephew, had a magnificent collection of French Impressionist paintings which he offered to the City of Dublin, provided that the Corporation built a suitable gallery to house them. After a good deal of argument the Corporation refused. Neither did they feel justified in building the gallery at public expense, nor would the wealthy citizens who might have afforded it subscribe enough.

Though the sequel belongs to later history it is worth a digression. Embittered by Dublin's indifference to his generosity, Sir Hugh lent the pictures to the London National Gallery, which was slightly more interested, and then left them to it in his will. But in 1915—by which time Dublin had an art gallery and he was its Director—he made a codicil, carefully prepared and signed but never witnessed, revoking this and leaving them to Dublin. He went down in the *Lusitania* that same year. The National Gallery Trustees refused to return the pictures: they claimed, not that the codicil was legally invalid, but that if Sir Hugh had lived he would have approved of their place in the Tate Gallery, where they have remained on view.*

It seems possible that the 1916 rebellion influenced the judges' decision to some extent. After all Sir Hugh had made his will and died before there was talk of Easter Week, and presumably thought of himself as a British citizen. Dublin had given him no special reason for loyalty, and in fact he had wavered between Dublin and London. Probably most Englishmen see grounds for the judgement, probably most Irishmen think it typical of the English blindness to the reality of feelings not shared in England. At any rate, when the question changed from the intrinsic worth of the gift to the rights of Ireland, Dublin awoke to its loss and protested. For more than forty years, by way of asserting its right to the collection, it kept one room in the Municipal Gallery empty. At last, on 12 November 1959, an agreement was made between the Commissioner of Public Works in Dublin and the Trustees of the National Gallery in London. The Lane Collection is divided in half: for four successive periods of five years each, first one half and then the other is to be lent to Dublin for

* For Yeats' considered view of the question, see his letter to the *Observer* of 12 January 1917. For further information, see the Editor's note to this letter, in *Letters*, pp. 616–24.

public exhibition. At the end of twenty years the parties may make a new agreement if they choose. And there for the present the matter rests.

But in 1913 the question was still whether Dublin thought it worth the cost of accepting. This, even had it not been Lady Gregory's cause, was just the question to rouse Yeats' fighting spirit. Reading about it one gathers that Sir Hugh was not a graceful benefactor. He was as proud as Coriolanus; he knew the pictures were a priceless treasure and could not endure that more ignorant people should doubt his word for it. The Dublin Corporation was prepared to vote about £2000 a year, but it was not enough. Sir Hugh could have paid for the gallery himself, but thought that half a dozen wealthy people ought to pay up, and this they would not do.[5] In private Yeats tried to calm his anger and persuade him to overlook the failure of the half dozen, but the central issue was clear. Here was a passionate and generous man, offering for all generations to come such a gift as,

> had they only known,
> Had given their children's children loftier thought,
> Sweeter emotion, working in their veins
> Like gentle blood[6]

—and the democratic set-up of the age hampered his freedom and gave ready excuses to those who should have helped him. Some of the rich argued that they ought not to subscribe, unless there was evidence that the people really wanted his gift—an impeccably democratic appeal to the common man which can, and does, reduce all taste to the lowest common denominator. Yeats asked where Italy would be, if the great renaissance dukes had deferred to public opinion in their planning and building, and urged them to

> Look up in the sun's eye and give
> What the exultant heart calls good
> That some new age may breed the best
> Because you gave, not what they would,
> But the right twigs for an eagle's nest![7]

He had never written so topically nor so violently: he gave himself up joyfully to a cause where the friends he admired and the ideals he served were ranged on the same side. Years later he wrote in prose of the 'vision of evil', meaning that a man must define what his soul hates in order to realize fully what he is; later still, as was so often his way in old age, he reduced it all to simpler terms in the racy testament called *Under Ben Bulben*:[8]

> You that Mitchel's prayer have heard,
> 'Send war in our time, O Lord!'
> Know that when all words are said
> And a man is fighting mad,
> Something drops from eyes long blind,
> He completes his partial mind.

Straightaway, as if the idea of battle was inseparable from the war for art, the poem goes on:

> Poet and sculptor, do the work,
> Nor let the modish painter shirk
> What his great forefathers did,
> Bring the soul of man to God,
> Make him fill the cradles right.

For the battle of the pictures had moulded his 'vision of evil' and acted like a furnace to set his poetry into metallic hardness.

The connection is plain between the crudely direct command

> Make him fill the cradles right

and the earlier, relatively timid phrase about great art 'working in their veins like gentle blood'; but in tracing it we may follow several threads in the pattern of Yeats' thought. Great art; the ceremony of tradition; the inheritance of blood: these ideas grow more closely associated as time goes on.

He thought of two eternities, of the soul and of the race. The second hardly entered his poetry till middle age, then grew in importance as his sense of history deepened, but it was always complemented by the first which was there from the beginning. In

The King's Threshold of 1904, art and the soul were all but everything.
In that play the poet Seanchan, fasting to death for the rights of
poetry, saluted his loyal pupils as his true descendants:

> O more than kin, O more than children could be,
> For children are but born out of our blood
> And share our frailty.[9]

To the youngest pupil his master's death would bring greatness to
future generations:

> O silver trumpets, be you lifted up
> And cry to the great race that is to come.
> Long-throated swans upon the waves of time,
> Sing loudly, for beyond the wall of the world
> That race may hear our music and awake.[10]

This was the original ending; but in the final version, made after
Yeats had lost hope of the age, the eldest pupil answered:

> Not what it leaves behind it in the light
> But what it carries with it to the dark
> Exalts the soul; nor song nor trumpet-blast
> Can call up races from the worsening world
> To mend the wrong and mar the solitude
> Of the great shade we follow to the tomb.[10]

Here is that indifference to defeat, which was in him before
ever he began fighting but was never unlearnt whether he lost or
won his battles. But here also is a transcendental scorn of the world
which makes it easier for the imagination to accept defeat. As Yeats
grew in years and courage he gained faith in the reality of flesh and
blood and in embodiment in life as the end of dreaming. *Responsibilities* is dedicated to his ancestors: he is proud that they have passed
on to him the reckless blood of action, and apologizes for offering
them poetry instead of an heir:

> Pardon that for a barren passion's sake,
> Although I have come close on forty-nine,
> I have no child, I have nothing but a book,
> Nothing but that to prove your blood and mine.[11]

It was not long afterwards that he atoned to them by marriage and fatherhood.

This, of course, did not mean that the material world had value in itself. It was nothing except by virtue of what it embodied. In the last poem of *Responsibilities*[12] he turns gratefully from his growing success to find at *Kyle-na-No* (Coole Park)

> A sterner conscience and a friendlier home.

Success with the public is empty, even humiliating,

> Seeing that Fame has perished this long while
> Being but a part of ancient ceremony.

Chapman, in the third sestiad of his continuation of Marlowe's *Hero and Leander*, has a reverberating passage about 'all-states-ordering Ceremony'. For him she was a goddess who appeared

> with a crown
> Of all the stars, and heaven with her descended:

and

> all her body was
> Clear and transparent as the purest glass,
> For she was all transparent to the sense:
> Devotion, Order, State, and Reverence
> Her shadows were; Society; Memory;
> All which her sight made live, her absence die.

She beats back Barbarism and Avarice, and without her aid

> Fear fills the chamber, darkness decks the bride.*

It may be that these lines had echoed in Yeats' memory since boyhood, for his father loved the Jacobeans and used to read them aloud; or it may be that Coole Park had sent him back to the poetry of a pre-democratic age. At any rate, in his newly discovered social consciousness 'Ceremony' becomes a meaningful word. It recurs several times in the poems of the next seven years, always with the idea of the immaterial seeking its fulfilment in flesh and blood.

* Mr T. R. Henn has drawn my attention to the relevance of this passage, and to the borrowing from Marvell on p. 158.

In *The Phases of the Moon*, which summarizes the central doctrines of
A Vision, he declares that

> All dreams of the soul
> End in a beautiful man's or woman's body[13]

—filtered through life after life, till at last they take material form.
In *Michael Robartes and the Dancer* a few years later, arguing the
same theme in a lighter mood, he calls the painters to witness that
bodily beauty is the fulfilment of vision:

> *She:* And must no beautiful woman be
> Learned like a man?
> *He:*   Paul Veronese
> And all his sacred company
> Imagined bodies all their days
> By the lagoon you love so much,
> For proud, soft, ceremonious proof
> That all must come to sight and touch.[14]

I think the pictures are 'ceremonious' in the same sense that rituals
expound in ceremony the truth we aspire to in life, for he goes on:

> Did God in portioning wine and bread
> Give man His thought, or His mere body?

In the same book *The Second Coming* sums up the world's dis-
integration in three phrases:

> Mere anarchy is loosed upon the world,
> The blood-dimmed tide is loosed, and everywhere
> The ceremony of innocence is drowned.[15]

The last verse of the next poem, *A Prayer for My Daughter*, may
serve as a gloss to interpret this:

> And may her bridegroom bring her to a house
> Where all's accustomed, ceremonious;
> For arrogance and hatred are the wares
> Peddled in the thoroughfares.
> How but in custom and in ceremony
> Are innocence and beauty born?
> Ceremony's a name for the rich horn,
> And custom for the spreading laurel tree.[16]

'Ceremony' turns material things and actions into the embodiment of transcendental values. It guards those values and hands them on, keeping a field where human souls may grow up in the unconscious acceptance of them which is innocence.

For Plato, created nature was an imperfect image of immaterial reality. A boy's or woman's beauty was but an image which should lead the soul from temporal life to the contemplation of absolute beauty itself. Yeats was no Platonist in this sense, for to him the incarnate was the completion of the absolute. In his philosophy the soul was an aspect of infinity certainly, but its quest was for the fullest possible realization in the world rather than for disentanglement from matter; life meant more than the intervals between lives. The instrument of this embodiment is the artist's vision, reduced with all the exactitude of his craftsmanship to a concrete, imitable image. That was where Yeats parted company with his Brahmin teacher and where, as he saw it, the West had parted from the East. Not western force, but western art, everlastingly seeking an image of human perfection, had shaped European civilization: so he maintained explicitly in later years, both in prose and verse. In *On the Boiler* he wrote:

Europe was not born when Greek galleys defeated the Persian hordes at Salamis, but when the Doric studios sent out those broad-backed marble statues against the multiform, vague expressive Asiatic sea, they gave to the sexual instinct of Europe its goal, its fixed type.

And this is almost a paraphrase of lines in *The Statues*:

> for the men
> That with a mallet or a chisel modelled these
> Calculations that look but casual flesh, put down
> All Asiatic vague immensities,
> And not the banks of oars that swam upon
> The many-headed foam at Salamis.
> Europe put off that foam when Phidias
> Gave women dreams and dreams their looking-glass.[17]

That dreams which the artist invokes out of silence mould the imagination of the race was an old faith when Sidney and Spenser held it. Simple people have always had a more concrete belief, which survives unrecognized by science, that imagination takes part with the genes in moulding the body of man. A woman, brooding intently on some particular form of beauty, or it may be startled by a great horror of ugliness, may unconsciously mould her unborn children in its image. Yeats seems in old age to accept both beliefs:

> That girls at puberty may find
> The first Adam in their thought,
> Shut the door of the Pope's chapel,
> Keep those children out.
> There on that scaffolding reclines
> Michael Angelo.
> With no more sound than the mice make
> His hand moves to and fro.[18]

In this way the thought latent in *Responsibilities* becomes a literal interchange between the ideal and the physical—a kind of magic operating through art.

All this amounts to a defence of art, if the defence is needed; and in the modern world Yeats certainly thought it was. It is not so cogent a defence of aristocracy, for in spite of Coole Park it would be hard to show that privileged houses nowadays are in fact conspicuous as guardians of art and letters. In particular it is hard to claim that merit for the Irish landowning class as a whole, whatever they were like in the eighteenth century. Yeats' critics have reprimanded him for loving the 'big house' people beyond reason. Louis MacNeice, who clearly thinks them a good riddance from Eire, sums them up:

In most cases these houses contained no culture worth speaking of—nothing but an obsolete bravado, an insidious bonhomie, and a way with horses.

L. C. Knights quotes this with approval, and finds that some of their inhabitants' exploits which Yeats recalls affectionately in a prose essay had more silliness than heroism.[19]

It is true they had to go, because in modern times their place has vanished under them. The world's habit is to justify itself by disparaging a class it does not want, and then the fact of being unwanted makes the class itself go downhill. Still the 'nothing but' of Louis MacNeice's diagnosis is unfair. Broadly speaking they had the qualities he names: Yeats indeed saw them all. The 'insidious bonhomie' is a ruder name for what he deplored as loving too deeply 'those mortal arts which build up a gallant personality'. The bravado and the horsemanship struck him as survivals from an ancient sense of values which he admired though the modern world does not. It does not follow because they had these that their way of life left no room for other qualities. Perhaps there were none in particular which it still imposed on them, but its blessing was freedom. On the whole they lacked the money-reckoning prudence, the respect for externally imposed routine, the deference to respectable public opinion which belong to a middle-class business mentality, and had a life which could do without them. Not to have them, so long as it does not mean ruin, allows for the liberation of more wayward energies.

Yeats certainly loved them for themselves. He belonged to them in spirit, and being a poet not a statistician he let his imagination play on what he knew. In Lady Gregory and her son, in some of his ancestors of a generation back and some of his living relatives who were smaller fry of the same tradition, he saw a freedom of spirit, a reckless integrity and rich personality, a relation to the earth and the common life about them, which belonged to the same world that had conceived Cuchulain. Much of his best poetry is a celebration of them, individually and as types. They were out of key with the age, probably therefore doomed to worldly defeat. He wrote of Lady Gregory:

> For how can you compete,
> Being honour bred, with one
> Who, were it proved he lies,
> Were neither shamed in his own
> Nor in his neighbours' eyes?[20]

But this did not make his friends less real, it only reinforced his conviction that the values of the age were not the final word of time, or that even if they were they were still false. The poem goes on from bitterness into unassailable joy:

> Bred to a harder thing
> Than Triumph, turn away
> And like a laughing string
> Whereon mad fingers play
> Amid a place of stone,
> Be secret and exult,
> Because of all things known
> That is most difficult.

He did not think their qualities accidental. The tradition they belonged to came down from the eighteenth century, almost untouched by the commercialism of later times, but had its roots very much deeper. Alike in its follies and its virtues it kept the vestiges of a way of life that Homer would have understood.

> Beyond that ridge lived Mrs French, and once
> When every silver candlestick or sconce
> Lit up the dark mahogany and the wine,
> A serving-man, that could divine
> That most respected lady's every wish,
> Ran and with the garden shears
> Clipped an insolent farmer's ears
> And brought them in a little covered dish.[21]

'How idiotically lawless!' a sensible modern reader thinks. It is, but local legend would remember a just judgement in the courts much less affectionately. The roistering suitors who ate Penelope out of house and home belong to the same kind of world, though its scale then was more lordly, and so does Odysseus' handling of them. So too does the dignified

> Augusta Gregory seated at her great ormolu table,
> Her eightieth winter approaching: 'Yesterday he threatened my life.
> I told him that nightly from six to seven I sat at this table,
> The blinds drawn up'[22]

—and Yeats' recollection of his grandfather—

> Old merchant skipper that leaped overboard
> After a ragged hat in Biscay Bay.[23]

Much of its positive code is summed up in the advice given to the Japanese Samurai, which Yeats somewhere quotes admiringly, to be generous among the weak, truthful among one's friends, brave among one's enemies, and courteous at all times; and perhaps still more of its sense of values in a remark of John O'Leary's: 'Never has there been a cause so bad that it has not been defended by good men for good reasons.'[24] But it is too full of personal freedom to be contained in any code, and neither its violence nor its virtues sound probable in a world of public officials and equality beneath the law.

From early youth Yeats felt that in rural Ireland epic and folk-tale, and his own soul too, were at home as they were not in modern England. As he collected Irish lore and listened to the country people's stories and wrote about the men and women he admired, he seemed to be following the tracks of an ancient faith and an ancient way of life almost obliterated elsewhere in Europe. There was a subtle correspondence between its supernaturalism, which belonged neither to heaven nor hell but to the living earth, and its moral values which exalted generous personal relations and ardent living rather than abstract principles and universal brotherhood. It was the palimpsest of a world, scrawled over with the cash accounts of commercial civilization, but the faded writing was in the language of his own soul and this made his reading of it more than a piece of antiquarian research. He set himself to recover its image, and chose to belong to it, reconstructing the philosophy from traces within and without himself, clearing away alien accretions and, by an intense effort of dramatic imagination, walking the modern world with thoughts and feelings in harmony with the emergent pattern.

Had he lived before it was defaced, when its inhabitants were still lords of life, he might perhaps have been the epic poet he once dreamed of becoming. But they were stranded half-survivors, and epic is only possible when a great poet can express himself and his world in the same breath. Conceivably a West of Ireland peasant audience might have listened to the Odyssey, hardly aware that Homer was a singer of a vanished age, but for Yeats himself as for his social equals education made it impossible; his imagination would be with them but his consciousness of the surrounding alien world would separate him, so that he could neither listen altogether as they listened nor write as they thought. To write as he thought himself was undertaking enough. It meant living among contemporaries in a solitude of unshared values, deepening perpetually the more clear-sighted he became, without moral support from any growing thing in the world around him or in the foreseeable future of mankind. He needed a clear philosophy of history to fortify his poetic imagination.

This had been taking form in his mind, though not explicitly in his verse, long before he came to Coole Park. 'Unity of being' was his ideal—that integrated vitality which makes a man able to express every part of his nature in everything he says or does, so that the whole man seems always to respond to an impulse from within. He thought it possible only when men had an ordered sense of values, both inbred and acceptable to their reason, which enabled them to take the whole of their heritage for granted. He saw it in Homer's heroes and in the great figures of Irish mythology. In Europe it had come nearest to being an attainable ideal in the Renaissance; but the Renaissance had not touched Ireland till the landowning classes of the eighteenth century—the age of Swift and Berkeley and Grattan—had woken to its quickening power. In fact,

up to the eighteenth century western civilization felt its continuity
with Homer; even then men could still think of him as a guide to
life, bring up their children on him and quote him seriously in
Parliament. But about then a change came over men's whole outlook,
that reduced the mind to a kind of bureau for sorting and manipulating sense-impressions.

> Locke sank into a swoon;
> The Garden died;
> God took the spinning-jenny
> Out of his side[25]

—as he summed it up when he had read more philosophy. Thereafter
new science, new industry and a new ruling class made a break in
thought, and in modern democracy the very conception of unity of
being disappears.

What is wrong with democracy is that it makes the individual
accountable to the collective in man. Holding that authority is
derived from the common people and responsible to them, setting
up the service of man as a moral ideal, it sees human society as a
gigantic body roaring for ever to be fed and clothed and washed
and housed, for at that level men's needs are more or less common.
If it tolerates privilege at all it expects the privileged to account to
it in terms it can understand. It undervalues all that cannot be
generalized. But souls are not common, and the highest good of
each man is a different thing from the common good of all. In
following his own soul a man may feed the world or fight it or renounce
it as the case may be, but he can never hold himself accountable
to its judgement.

Democratic values may be those of common sense, but there is
a common imagination which is not impressed by them, if the legends
of three thousand years interpret it. The figures remembered round
cottage fires for generations are mostly reckless men, outstanding
in courage or strength or some eccentricity beyond the common
reach. Even the saint's charity is remembered less for its beneficence

than its spiritual grace or even its sheer extravagance. For that imagination a privileged class exists in order to breed heroes who let loose the whole strength of their nature and show to what wild lengths the spirit of man can fly. Such heroes do not defer to public opinion. Though they are not forgiven for tyranny or treachery they need not be benefactors of the people to be famous; but men who fail in greatness of personality are merely forgotten.

Yeats disdained the vocal ideals of democracy but believed that his poetry was in sympathy with the common imagination. *Coole and Ballylee*,[26] written in 1931, is a meditation interlacing two themes: the soul, whose symbol is a swan, and the glory of a great ancestral house. With the fall of the house and all it stands for in human thought three thousand years of ordered imagination are flickering into the dark, and the swan is homeless. It ends:

> We were the last romantics—chose for theme
> Traditional sanctity and loveliness;
> Whatever's written in what poets name
> The book of the people; whatever most can bless
> The mind of man or elevate a rhyme;
> But all is changed, that high horse riderless,
> Though mounted in that saddle Homer rode
> Where the swan drifts upon a darkening flood.

When his philosophy was codified in *A Vision* 'aristocratic' came to mean everything akin to his mind in life, history and thought, 'democratic' all that moved the other way. Aristocracy belonged to the pride of life, democracy to the life-rejecting thirst for universality. He knew, of course, that the tide was running against him, that civilization was moving towards democracy and universal levelling. But mankind is older than all remembered civilization and will outlast it, and move again towards creative joy; and in any case his philosophy was to be true to his beliefs, not to swim with the tide. Both in poetry and politics he went on praising an ordered hierarchical society with all the more zest because it was unpopular.

And yet it was a grace in him that in the thick of controversy he could withdraw, so to speak, to the solitude of eternity, aware that democracy could not kill the soul of man nor a social hierarchy of itself preserve it. At one extreme is a poem in *Responsibilities*: when he is most exasperated with the mean stupidities of the common man he hears a curlew's call:

> and suddenly thereupon I thought
> That on the lonely height where all are in God's eye,
> There cannot be, confusion of our sound forgot,
> A single soul that lacks a sweet crystalline cry.[27]

At the other is *Church and State*—possibly a comment on Fascism—in *A Full Moon in March*. For a moment it delights him to think of Church and State with reinforced authority, suppressing the ravings of the mob; but vulgarity can climb to high places, and there comes a grim afterthought:

> What if the Church and the State
> Are the mob that howls at the door!
> Wine shall run thick to the end,
> Bread taste sour.[28]

It is not easy to live in two worlds, watching the life of one with the eyes of the other, without a narrowing or darkening of vision. Yeats never sounds shallow or insincere, though sometimes his studied, aristocratic restraint makes him a little stiff, as I think it does in the series *Upon a Dying Lady*,[29] written about Aubrey Beardsley's sister. She was known to him: some of his letters show that her death moved him deeply. In the poems she is stylized into an impersonal abstract of courtly courage. One sees from outside, like a masque, the lady with the dull red tress over her shoulder, the friends with their assumed lightness of manner, bringing their frivolous gifts. One sees the defiant gallantry more clearly than the passion it masks.

It is subtly different when Ireland comes into the picture. No less than Mabel Beardsley, the airman in *An Irish Airman Foresees His Death*[30] is presented as a type: he is Robert Gregory, but also he

118

stands for the lonely aloofness which was part of Yeats' ideal.
But in his cold passion and measured recklessness and consciousness
of solitude he becomes intensely alive. And when he says:

> My country is Kiltartan Cross,
> My countrymen Kiltartan's poor,
> No likely end could bring them loss
> Or leave them happier than before

—place and people, though present in his thoughts only to be
disregarded, have actualized him in a definite context.

Shepherd and Goatherd,[31] again, is stiff because the conventional
pastoral form has taken it out of time and place, whereas the longer
poem *In Memory of Major Robert Gregory*[32] is the most genuinely
commemorative of all the great English elegies. *Thyrsis*, *Adonais*,
Lycidas: each is full of the poet's grief for his times or for the fate
of poets or for his own fate; the sorrow is real but the dead friend
dissolves into a symbol of sorrow. Yeats maintains his aristocratic
composure; he will not break down in public, only he laments that
such a man 'could share in that discourtesy of death'. But he recalls
three other friends individually in a few lines each, and then paints
Robert Gregory as he lived and moved in his own country, with such
a passion of admiration that all the sorrow is that such a man and
such a life should have passed from the world.

Even the purely imaginary figure of the Fisherman[33] in the same
book takes living personality from the countryside in which he is set.
Yeats conceived him, he says, when he was thoroughly disillusioned
with the Ireland of politics and petty squabbles:

> All day I'd looked in the face
> What I had hoped 'twould be
> To write for my own race
> And the reality.*

* Yeats' terse syntax allows many readers to construe this as 'to write for my
own race and [for] the reality'. But 'and' sets 'the reality' of writing for his race
against what he had hoped it would be—and the next twelve bitter lines reinforce the
contrast.

And then

> Suddenly I began,
> In scorn of this audience,
> Imagining a man,
> And his sun-freckled face,
> And grey Connemara cloth,
> Climbing up to a place
> Where stone is dark under froth,
> And the down-turn of his wrist
> When the flies drop in the stream;
> A man who does not exist,
> A man who is but a dream.

He is Yeats' ideal reader. He does not exist, but if he did he would be setting out on a grey morning from some dilapidated Irish country house. He is wise and simple, and he fishes a lonely stream in the far west. Certainly other kinds of men may be wise and simple, but for Yeats that scene, symbolically remote from the whole modern world, is two things in one—the nurse of the particular form of wisdom and simplicity that he conceives, and an actual place he knows.

For it is undeniable that he belonged in spirit not only to Ireland but to that maligned Protestant landowning minority of Southern Ireland, as surely as Wordsworth to the Lake Country or Rabindranath Tagore to the old ruling houses of Bengal. His homeland was the way of life of these disappearing 'big house' people, inseparable from the countryside and yet a distinctive thing in itself; and although his poetry, like his swan, leaps into the desolate heaven, it is at home nowhere else on earth. It is a general human habit to judge one's own country, one's own religion, even one's own political party, from an inner knowledge of its possibilities, and to judge all others from objective appearances. Yeats was no exception in that, but neither are his critics. To them it is an unpromising environment and a defeated world at best, and it is contrary to the order of things that greatness should come out of it; and yet so far as genius can be the product of its environment the genius of Yeats was born and nourished there.

In a sense, indeed, the vast sweep of his thought comes from the very fact that he belonged to a defeated world. A poet's imagination must start from where he stands, in the circle of his own experience, and if he has any philosophical bent must impose a symmetrical pattern on what he sees. If he stands at the hub of his own age he need not see beyond it; the accepted values and the commonplace assumptions will serve him very well. Tennyson was such a poet in his time, so perhaps was Walt Whitman. But if he is near the rim of the wheel his world will look asymmetrical: either he must shut his eyes to most of it or, to complete his pattern, take in realms beyond it, seeing it as a single movement in a vaster cycle. Milton did this in his old age after the defeat of his cause; Yeats' master Blake did it most notably of English poets, and Yeats did the same. At war with the contemporary democratic consciousness, he defeated it subjectively by extending his vision to a ghostly universe where two thousand years of recorded history are a transitory incident. A sociological critic who can make his judgements conform to his theories may label this 'escapism', but 'escapist', though a defensible adjective for his early work, will not stick to the poetry written after he had found his social bearings. It is not unrealistic, but is like a lonely torch from an unexpected angle, throwing disconcerting lights and shadows on all that moves within its range.

CHAPTER VIII

A VISION (I)

On 21 October 1917 Yeats married George Hyde-Lees. Four days later, it happened that his wife tried some experiments in automatic writing, with which they were both familiar. According to Dr Norman Jeffares' account[1] she began it more or less as a game to distract him from some worrying thoughts; but the sentences she wrote surprised herself and excited him. They took up ideas of which she knew nothing but which were working in his own mind, elaborated them in ways new to him, and suggested answers to problems he did not think he had solved. He was eager to go on with the experiment. Before they had been at it many days the writings brought him such a sense of revelation that he thought of devoting the rest of his life to expounding them; but they advised him not to, saying 'We have come to give you metaphors for poetry'.

They went on almost daily, however, for over three years. Yeats studied the teachings they contained and put them in order in the first edition of *A Vision*, published in 1925. He was not satisfied with this book, and further communications were coming; so in 1937 he brought out a new, very much revised edition.

In its final form *A Vision* amounts to a summing-up of Yeats' own sense of values in a system of thought about the soul in and beyond life, and also about the meaning of history, all worked out in a geometrical symbolism, based on the esoteric doctrines in which he and his wife had both become adepts. It is coherent but not simple. The general lines are easy enough to grasp, but innumerable details branch out from them and fly away in mazy patterns.

The unit of thought, so to speak, is an abstract idea of two movements, one towards perfect self-realization, the other towards perfect self-abnegation. Yeats says that any complex movement of life or thought may be seen in these terms: a single sustained action, a life, a series of incarnations, a cycle of civilizations, the universe itself so far as the mind can grasp it. Empedocles called them Strife and Love, the one separating all things into their several essences, the other fusing them in a homogeneous whole, and said that nothing could exist except by the interaction of these two. But Yeats, because the soul is his chief concern and the starting-point of his thought, expounds the process chiefly through the incarnations of a single soul.

Imagine the soul as a discarnate individual essence about to begin a series of incarnations. It has potentialities but no experience; it is, but as yet knows neither itself nor the universe. Its first aim is to know itself through incarnate existence as fully as possible, and through life after life it struggles to disengage its essential nature from everything accidental and external to it, until its form in the world becomes the perfect image of its unique being. All this time its true morality is self-expression; it seeks a law for itself, of which it can say, 'This is right perhaps for me only, but for me always'. But after this it begins to forget itself, and to know the world. Its aim now is to submit to circumstance, to thrust aside the subjective image of itself and to see the world as it actually is. Its morality is no longer self-expression but submission; it seeks a law of which it can say, 'This is right for all men in these circumstances'. In life after life it grows more detached, more self-denying, till at length it has learnt to will nothing for itself. Then, utterly plastic to the will of God, all its accumulated experience given back to the whole, it is 'kneaded up', and possibly its original essence emerges in some new form to begin a fresh cycle.

This history is summed up in the poem called *The Phases of the Moon*.[2] In his symbolism the moon governs human life and the nights of a lunar month stand for the successive incarnations.

When the soul achieves self-realization there is a moment of perfect poise, which is called 'Unity of Being'; it is also the moment of perfect beauty, for the soul actually is all that it wills to be. All that happens to it is identical with its ideal—chance and choice are one; and this is the fifteenth phase corresponding to the full moon. But there can be no such incarnation in the living world, for it is a phase without conflict, and life itself is a tension of conflicting forces. The fifteenth phase is therefore a phantom incarnation, a form of superhuman beauty such as visionaries may sometimes meet among the lonely hills.

Then the soul begins to spend itself in objective reality. Here too, it reaches a different moment of poise at the opposite pole of the cycle. There can be no bodily beauty, for there is no longer anything to express. But chance and choice are again at one because the soul now has no will except to take whatever comes to it from without, and conflict ceases. So this incarnation too, which corresponds to the moon's darkness, is beyond the world. But between these two all men's lives are moving towards one goal or the other.

The particular aims and fortunes in each life are products of past lives. They are shaped by the action of the soul's four 'Faculties' (not, of course, faculties as abstract philosophy uses the word), which Yeats calls 'Will', 'Mask', 'Creative Mind' and 'Body of Fate'. The Will is sheer vital energy, the drive towards self-realization. It sets before itself an image, shaped from moments of exaltation in past lives, of all it can conceive as most admirable, all that is most opposite to its actual incarnate self, and strives towards that. That image is the Mask; and thus through Will and Mask the soul moulds itself from within.

The Creative Mind is a kind of memory of ideas, or general principles, learnt in past lives, and is the power of thought which is inborn. Its purpose is to understand all circumstances that affect it from the outer world, and the sum of these is the Body of Fate. The living man sees his Body of Fate as something external to himself, but it is not really so; it has come to him by choice or rather by the very nature of his soul, from memories of the happenings of past lives. For ultimately it is his own bent, and the inherent limitations of which he is necessarily unaware, which determine how accidents shall mould his life.

Thus two processes are always at work: the Will is trying to assimilate itself to the Mask, the Creative Mind to understand the Body of Fate. Always these two confuse each other. The man wills to be his ideal self, but the circumstances surrounding him and his efforts to deal with them may confuse the image of his ideal or may change it for a factitious one. He tries to understand the world objectively, but his image of what he desires to be may distort what he sees.

Up to the fifteenth phase Will is the important force, for the soul's task is to hold to the integrity of its own ideal and realize all it has the power to become from within. It must use intelligence and experience merely to clarify this, not allowing what comes from outside to confuse it. It emerges from its fifteenth phase with a powerful personality, which thereafter, as the need for objectivity grows stronger, it must struggle to subdue. Creative Mind grows stronger as Will weakens, and vice versa. Yeats sees them as two gyres whirling in opposite directions, 'each one living the other's death, dying the other's life'.

They can be plotted on a flat surface as a wheel, with twenty-eight divisions for the phases of the moon, so that the fifteenth is opposite the first. This is shown in the diagram on p. 126, reproduced from the 1937 edition of *A Vision*. Treating Will, the dynamic factor, as determining the phase of a being, it depicts its movement through a lunar cycle of incarnations. Imagine the being standing on the threshold of embodiment at Phase One, which is hidden in the darkness of no-moon. Just then, Will and Creative Mind are at rest together, each contemplating its opposite, Mask and Body of Fate respectively, which likewise coincide at Phase Fifteen. Will, in pursuit of its ideal, the Mask, moves round anti-clockwise; but the

Mask, remaining opposite, moves to Phase Sixteen as Will enters Phase Two, and so on. Simultaneously Creative Mind moves round clockwise, keeping Body of Fate opposite to it. At Phase Fifteen, as at Phase One, Will and Creative Mind coincide, and so do Mask and Body of Fate opposite to them; that is why there can be no

conflict at these two phases. Everywhere else they fall in different positions and pull against each other. For instance, when Will reaches Phase Twenty the Mask towards which it strives is at Five; but Body of Fate, now at Twenty-four, is the objective of Creative Mind which is at Phase Ten and moving in the opposite direction. Thus a four-point tension is set up, changing as Will moves from phase to phase. These conflicting pulls are the key to the diversities of human personality: these, and the change of purpose as the being moves from darkness into full moonlight and again towards darkness.

Half of the wheel, from Phase Eight to Phase Twenty-two, belongs to the brightness of the moon; these are called the 'antithetical' phases, because in them the being is setting itself apart from the external world, finding in all things only what it can mirror in its ideal self.

In an antithetical phase, the being seeks by the help of the Creative Mind to deliver the Mask from the Body of Fate.[3]

That is, it sees circumstances frustrating its expression of the ideal and uses its powers of mind to subdue them.

The dark side, from Phase Twenty-two round to Eight, is called 'primary', because in them the being is seeking direct union with the external world.

In a primary phase the being seeks by the help of the Body of Fate to deliver the Creative Mind from the Mask.[4]

That is, its subjective ideal hinders it from full objectivity, therefore it tries to subdue self-will and to know, accept and serve the world as it actually is.

The purpose will naturally be most single-minded and clear round about the full moon and dark; elsewhere, as the pulls of the different forces are more or less in conflict, as the idea of the self and that of the world grow more or less powerful, the being passes gradually from the antithetical to the primary purpose. To live rightly 'in phase' is not to achieve any specific kind of success, but to keep the true balance of that phase without confusion. For there is a possibility of error, and if a life has been wrongly lived it may be necessary to go through the phase over again.

Yeats uses this scheme to set in order his understanding of people and their aims. His way of applying it may be seen from an example: I quote part of his account of the Twentieth Phase, in which he places both Shakespeare and Napoleon. It is, he says,

a phase of the breaking up and subdivision of the being....He no longer seeks to unify what is broken through conviction, by imposing those very convictions on himself and others (as the man of the preceding phase

127

did), but by projecting a dramatisation or many dramatisations. He can create, just in that degree in which he can see these dramatisations as separate from himself, and yet as an epitome of his whole nature.... Owing to the need of seeing the dramatic image, or images, as individuals, that is to say as set among concrete or fixed surroundings, he seeks some field of action, some mirror not of his own creation. Unlike Phase 19 he fails in situations not created wholly by himself, or in works of art where character or story has gained nothing from history.... There is a delight in concrete images that, unlike the impassioned images of Phase 17 and Phase 18, or the declamatory images of Phase 19, reveal through complex suffering the general destiny of man. He must, however, to express the suffering, personify rather than characterise, create not observe that multitude, which is but his *Mask* as in a multiplying mirror, for the *primary* is not yet strong enough to substitute for the lost Unity of Being that of the external world perceived as fact. In a man of action this multiplicity gives the greatest possible richness of resource when he is not thwarted by his horoscope ...but in the man of action a part of the nature must be crushed, one main dramatisation or group of images preferred to all others.

Napoleon sees himself as Alexander moving to the conquest of the East, *Mask* and Image must take an historical and not a mythological or dream form, a form found but not created; he is crowned in the dress of a Roman Emperor. Shakespeare, the other supreme figure of the phase, was—if we may judge by the few biographical facts, and by such adjectives as 'sweet' and 'gentle' applied to him by his contemporaries—a man whose actual personality seemed faint and passionless. Unlike Ben Jonson he fought no duels...but—through *Mask* and image reflected in a multiplying mirror—he created the most passionate art that exists. He was the greatest of modern poets, partly because entirely true to phase, creating always from *Mask* and *Creative Mind*, never from situation alone, never from *Body of Fate* alone....[5]

The standpoint is not that of a critic or philosopher or psychologist of any recognizable school, nevertheless it has its own clear perspective. For Yeats there is no one ideal, no single standard of judgement by which to measure all mankind. There is an inner vision symbolized by the full moon, seeking its realization in time and space, and there is the no-moon of an objective reality which, because no mind can comprehend it, must ultimately shatter the coherence of that inner vision, and each individual is at some point between the two.

The man of the Twentieth Phase still walks in 'antithetical' moonlight; that is, the inner vision is his guiding principle, but he has left behind the perfect poise where it was conterminous with his experience of objective reality. (Dante, in the Seventeenth Phase, was near this poise; his imaginative vision seems to find itself in heaven and earth rather than transforming them to its image.) To this extent Napoleon and Shakespeare are alike. Napoleon, the man of action, turns the world into a stage on which to dramatize himself, so that he may see himself as the figure he has it in him to be. But to do this in the actual world he has to concentrate himself wholly into conquest and government, as ruthless to his other potentialities as to the world itself. Shakespeare's medium is more plastic: he can take a hundred images from the outer world and project his vision, which is himself, into each, and the reality of his personal life is almost lost in that of his creations. He neither copies fact, nor creates independently of it. His characters are creative interpretations of figures already existing in history or fiction; they are not set in the Shadowy Waters of the mind, but in a world which though transformed is recognizably actual.

By the Twenty-second Phase the inner vision has become less insistent, more submissive to outer reality. It survives then as a craving for order, but the order must be impersonally valid; it has not to be imposed on the world but found in it by patient systematization of observed fact. To this phase belongs Charles Darwin. If Shakespeare had been more of a slave to realism, if Darwin had pressed his researches into the mould of his imagination, each would have missed his achievement by living out of phase.

Later still comes the self-effacing humility of the saint, who wills no synthesis of his own, seeking to be nothing himself that the total life of the world may flow through him. After this there is only the utter plasticity of the Fool, who has ceased to be anything but a channel of the universal.

All the twenty-eight phases are thus characterized, and to suit the two-dimensional page they are diagrammatized in the wheel. But Yeats' supernatural geometry is both solid and dynamic: his true symbol for all experience is those whirling, interlocking gyres, 'each one living the other's death, dying the other's life'. Reality, he says, is a phaseless sphere, timeless and all-inclusive, but the mind can only grasp it in a series of antinomies, or pairs of opposites. It is as if from one pole of an axis a point moved, tracing widening gyres till it took in the circumference of the sphere, and at the same time a point were gyring its way from the opposite end, unwinding the thread. As the one takes a wider circle in its sweep, contact with the axis which is the motionless centre of its circle weakens; but always from the plane of its widest and weakest circle the other gyre is beginning its opposing synthesis.

He expounds it as it operates through a cycle of incarnations, but says that the same gyre, or wheel, would serve with its interplay of Faculties to map the course of a single life from birth to death. Later he uses it to trace the rise and fall of civilizations. It is the abstract pattern repeating itself endlessly in everything under the moon.

'Under the moon' is the field of temporal being, with which all this part of *A Vision* is concerned. Incarnation and reincarnation are taken for granted as if they were the obvious way in which pure mind would choose to be spending its time. This is a true reflection of Yeats' inherent sense of values. There was much in eastern philosophy which attracted him, but not the longing for escape from the chain of births and deaths. Every life was a step in a dance rather than in a journey, for the goal of the steps was not a consummation which left life behind. He thought of living itself as an activity and a mode of knowledge which the soul desires.

But still the soul was more than any of its incarnations or than the sum of them, and the symbol was incomplete until it could include the rest. When he had written this part his ghostly instructors told him more, and he wrote the second and third books of *A Vision*, called *The Completed Symbol* and *The Soul in Judgment*.

These two books consider what is behind life. *The Completed Symbol* tries to fit the gyres of life into a wider scheme which includes the after-life, and is rather more difficult to grasp.

My instructors identify consciousness with conflict, not with knowledge, substitute for subject and object and their attendant knowledge a struggle towards harmony, towards Unity of Being. Logical and emotional conflict alike lead towards a reality which is concrete, sensuous, bodily.[6]

The key to the story seems to be here. Ultimate reality, as has been said, can best be described as a phaseless sphere, but the nature of consciousness is such that it can grasp reality only as a series of antinomies: the This, the That, the inner, the outer, and so forth. This is not merely a condition imposed by time and space; time and space themselves are modes in which the conflict is carried on.

The soul of a man, as it exists in eternity, is called his Daimon. It is a being which

contains within itself, co-existing in its eternal moment, all the events of our life, all that we have known of other lives, or that it can discover in itself of other Daimons.[7]

It is one of the Divine Ideas, a single aspect of the ultimate reality. It desires to know other Daimons. But if consciousness is conflict, it has to be conditioned by time and space; thus the Daimons must meet in incarnate form, as objects of sense to one another.

The Faculties are voluntarily acquired powers of the incarnate Daimon, constructed from life to life and operating between birth and death. Underneath them, a sort of ground from which they arise, are four 'Principles' inherent in the Daimon's eternal nature. They are called 'Spirit' and 'Celestial Body', or mind and its object, and 'Husk' and 'Passionate Body' or sense and its object.

The Daimon's hunger to know other Daimons is expressed in its 'Husk'; it might be described as a power of concentrating itself into embodied, temporal life. 'Passionate Body' is the sum of all the objectified Daimons with which, in the Husk, it surrounds itself. Perceived thus they are subject to time and space, cause and effect. But after meeting them in this way the Spirit knows them 'in their unity', as aspects of intellectual necessity. What Spirit knows has passed beyond embodiment and become part of itself, and is therefore independent of the Husk: this is the 'Celestial Body'. The Passionate Body exists 'that it may save the Celestial Body from solitude'.[8] If I have understood the idea rightly, it is that life is the self-consciousness of reality, the means by which it knows itself.

> What do we know but that we face
> One another in this place?[9]

Like the Faculties the four Principles have their whirling gyre, but its circle is wider. The gyre of the Faculties takes in only the time between birth and death; that of the Principles includes also the time between death and rebirth.

As in most ancient symbolic thought, the moon is the light of all changing and transitory life, the sun the intellectual light of the supersensory world. Or putting it otherwise, the sun is the light of nature in the old sense of nature as the fundamental laws by which all things exist, and the moon that of subjective perception. The moon at the full is most opposite to the sun, and the individual soul's fullest self-realization comes when it is furthest from being absorbed in the whole.

> She sings as the moon sings:
> 'I am I, am I;
> The greater grows my light
> The further that I fly.'
> All creation shivers
> With that sweet cry.[10]

The gyre of the Principles is, therefore, expressed as a solar day, in which life between birth and death is night, and daylight is from death to birth, or as a solar year in which incarnate life is winter. It is measured by the signs of the Zodiac. And as the relation is insoluble between the wheel of the moon's twenty-eight phases and that of the twelve months, there are some tricky calculations to reduce them to formal correspondence.

In the dark half of the wheel of the Principles Husk, with its gaze fixed on Passionate Body, predominates, and within this half the wheel of the Faculties completes its whole circle. The Will is related to Husk somewhat as the conscious ego is related to the unconscious, and Mask is imagined by Will out of the experience offered to it by Passionate Body, for there is nothing else conceivable by the incarnate soul. Thus through Will and Mask the soul chooses what shall matter to it for a lifetime, out of everything hypothetically possible for it to know and feel. The Principles exist in the background, but in the life of a man and in the cycles of human history they operate only as they are embodied in the Faculties.

All experience comes through the Faculties: by themselves the Principles have no power to gain fresh experience or to distinguish fact from idea. After death, the Spirit is working over and absorbing the knowledge which the Faculties brought to it in life. This process is described in *The Soul in Judgment* in stages named after the zodiacal signs from Aries to Scorpio—the summer of the Daimonic year.[11]

First comes a vision of all the impulses and images of the life just completed, simultaneously present. The illumination which people are said to experience at the point of death, seeing all their life before them in a flash, is part of this.

Second comes a reminiscent meditation over the whole of life's experience which may have to be very long drawn out. The Spirit lives over and over again, in order of their intensity, the events that have moved it most deeply, until they are a lesson thoroughly mastered; then it lives and relives them in the order of their happening. It must go on with this till it has understood them fully in all their causes and consequences and relations to each other, and made them a part of itself. It must further exhaust all uncompleted emotion, by living out in fantasy everything that was hoped and feared and imagined but not enacted. In this way the Spirit makes

Passionate Body fully intelligible to itself. When all this is done, Husk and Passionate Body fade away.

Third, when all the emotion of bodily life is over, comes the understanding of its good and evil. The Spirit must realize all that it did unknowingly in its relations with people: where it has inflicted suffering it must live through the act as victim, where it has been the victim it must live it as the tyrant. In this way, within the limits of its life experience, it comes to a perfect understanding of good and evil. Unlike the two earlier stages this is not a state of dream. Passionate Body has vanished, and the Spirit is no longer retracing the past but is subject to the law of necessity alone.

Fourth comes a moment of beatitude, passed in a trance of perfect equilibrium, which perhaps corresponds to the Full Moon of incarnate life. All that has existed is understood, good and evil vanish, and the soul is one with the universal soul. 'The Celestial Body is the divine cloak lent to all, it falls away at the consummation and Christ is revealed.'

The fifth stage is the first movement towards rebirth. Having seen the whole the Spirit finds its next particular aim, which belongs to its nature as all past lives have moulded it. It shapes for itself a new Husk and Passionate Body, though as yet it does not wear them, and waits for the conditions proper for its chosen rebirth. It may find them soon, or wait for centuries.

Last comes a phase of foreknowledge. Just as the whole of a life is recapitulated at death so it has to be foreseen and accepted before birth. Finally, during its sleep in the womb it accepts the future and acknowledges it as just.

Necessarily this part of the account is less of a synthesis of Yeats' remembered experience than the parts about the living world, but now and again he notes how it sets in order what he had gathered from studies in spiritualism and theosophy. The disembodied, he says, live in the human unconscious. As long as the traces of Husk and Passionate Body cling to them they remain 'the dead'; from such come hauntings, demonic possession and communication through mediums, and also much that puzzles living men in their dreams.

Have not old writers said
That dizzy dreams can spring
From the dry bones of the dead?[12]

Lacking bodies the dead have no direct access to the world of the senses, but they can tap the minds of living men for words and images to explain themselves to themselves; they may appear as phantoms, and sometimes ask the living to carry out for them some unfulfilled purpose. Sometimes also, to complete an unfinished experience of their own, they will live through the minds and nerves of living men. But after purification they are 'blessed spirits'. Ancient philosophy knew of a state of pure wakeful contemplation in which communion with them was possible, but the modern world has forgotten it.

Even then, however, in the fifth phase, there may still be some unfinished synthesis to complete for which they will need help from the living, since only the living can create. Those who taught him the script of *A Vision* must have belonged to this phase. They did it for their own sake, not for his, and not as a hangover from the past but to prepare for a coming life. There were others trying to interfere with the teaching, and he thinks of these 'frustrators' as sixth-phase spirits rebelling against something in their future destiny, though without final power to prevail.

For although somewhere behind it all there is an act of choice, the soul is irretrievably committed to its cycle of lives; there seems to be no way of stopping or changing it. It is only saved from mechanical determinism by an element which I have so far left out, called the Thirteenth Cone. This is a further extension of the pattern of opposing gyres. If the gyre of the Principles with its twelve revolutions is considered as an expanding cone, there is an opposing one, apex to base, cutting it at each round:

a being racing into the future passes a being racing into the past, two footprints perpetually obliterating each other, toe to heel, heel to toe.[12]

This is our deliverance from the cycle of time and space. It appears to us as a cone, but 'when the time for our deliverance has come' it is seen to be the phaseless sphere itself, which is reality.

Within it live all souls which have been set free, and every Daimon and Ghostly Self; our expanding cone seems to cut through its gyre; spiritual influx is from its circumference, animate life from its centre.[13]

It seems that a moment comes when we are no longer circumscribed in the gyre, but find ourselves at one with the all-inclusive phaseless sphere. And because the sphere alone is real, though all we ever see is the gyre, we are centred in that timeless moment though we sweep for ever round the predetermined wheel of time. From the very source of necessity the incalculable enters the chain of cause and effect.

This is not an illuminating statement and I do not believe that any scrutiny of the image will make it other than a rephrasing, in Yeatsian terms, of the universal double consciousness that the will is and is not free, that we live in time and also in the timeless. What is clear, however, from the whole drift of his symbolism is that in his thought 'deliverance' is not deliverance from experience but a full acceptance of experience.

My imagination was for a time haunted by figures that, muttering 'the great systems', held out to me the sun-dried skeletons of birds, and it seemed to me that this image was meant to turn my thoughts to the living bird. That bird signifies the truth when it eats, evacuates, builds its nest, engenders, feeds its young; do not all intelligible truths lie in this passage from egg to dust?[14]

—and he goes on to quote 'some Japanese monk's' account of Nirvana:

No more does the young man come from behind the embroidered curtains among the sweet clouds of incense; he goes among his friends, he goes among the flute-players; something very nice has happened to the young man, but he can only tell it to his sweetheart.[14]

A man may have to live through one phase twice, thrice or even four times before he has gathered from it what he must; also, according to the way he has lived, the schooling between death and birth may be brief or may last for centuries. The aim of living is not blamelessness as moralists usually understand it but fullness of experience, and to shirk the experience proper to one's phase is the failure that delays advance. But the normal time between death and birth is three generations, and a soul's full cycle of lives, completed with no major hitch, takes about two thousand years.

Even allowing that two of the incarnations are outside of time I find the ghostly instructors' arithmetic supernatural, or else their reckoning of the expectation of life is alarmingly short, but 'twere to consider too curiously, to consider so. The round figure of two thousand years is needed to correlate the gyres of men's lives with those of history, to which the rest of the book turns.

Ancient astronomers used to calculate the Great Year. By this they meant a period in which all the constellations would return to their original positions, so that a star-gazer, let us say at midnight of the vernal equinox, would see the map of heaven precisely as it had looked to some remote ancestor at that very hour and place. Surely, if human destiny is geared to the stars, this would mean that history had begun again. Such a date, could one mark it on a calendar, would be the starting and finishing point for the most enormous gyres the human mind could conceive; its ideal precision is all time returning back upon itself—the unity of all lesser unities in a stupendous work of art.

It is as though innumerable dials, some that recorded minutes alone, some seconds alone, some hours alone, some months alone, some years alone, were all to complete their circles when Big Ben struck twelve upon the last night of the century.[15]

Yeats goes over various philosophers' speculations upon this span of time, perhaps less to find the most accurate reckoning than to show what it stood for in their thoughts. He chooses to estimate it as about 26,000 years, so that the millennia of history, like the incarnations of the soul, may be ruled by the phases of the moon. Twenty-six, not twenty-eight—

> For there's no human life at the full or the dark.[16]

On this greater cycle he charts civilizations as he has already charted souls. On the Great Wheel of 26,000 years our present civilization began about the end of the eleventh century, in the sixteenth phase—which makes the 'Dark Ages' of Europe a reflection from the full moon of some nameless achievement of the spirit. We have now reached the seventeenth phase. But this is too vast a span for measuring history. There are wheels within wheels revolving, wheels primary and wheels antithetical, solar wheels of the Principles and lunar wheels of the Faculties, and every moment of time is part of the primary or antithetical phase of more than one such wheel. Every millennium is a wheel to itself, with its own full moon and its dark obliteration. But in two thousand years, more or less, a civilization sweeps round its phases. Four thousand years make a full wheel of the Principles, with its subjective lunar half, and a counterbalancing era of 'primary objectivity'. On this scale the pattern of recorded history may be seen.

In such a wheel Greek civilization was the antithetical and Christianity is the primary phase. Greek civilization began its course in history somewhere about 1000 B.C., but it must have begun to germinate centuries before that, in the womb of something earlier. The symbol of its Annunciation is the divine swan that impregnated Leda, 'bird and woman blotting out some corner of the Babylonian mathematical starlight',[17] which was the civilization of an earlier age. From Leda's eggs came the twins Castor and Pollux, and Helen of Troy and her twin Clytemnestra—Love and Strife. A third egg, never hatched, was according to Yeats once hung in a Spartan temple: when the time comes for the breaking of its shell something hidden in the remote past will emerge to shape the future.

The dove descended on the Virgin Mary at the mid-point between the birth and death of Greek civilization, when the Roman Empire had stabilized it over most of the world. Its death-point was about A.D. 1050, in the Dark Ages of Europe: the moon of this world was darkened but the solar light of Christianity lit the other world. Round about A.D. 2000 comes the mid-point between death and return. In the near future, therefore, the new revelation must come —the hatching of the third egg—to which the civilization of the future will look back as its source; and if it runs true to the time-chart it will possess men's minds and reach its zenith something over a thousand years hence.

Whatever shape it takes it will be what Christianity was to Greece, a focus of all that is most opposite to the predominating values of our era. Being 'antithetical' it will not exalt humility and self-sacrifice, nor the levelling doctrines that lose the uniqueness of men in the universal image of Man, nor look up to a remote transcendent God, but will restore to the individual man the pride of his personality, and seek the supernatural within the diversity of nature.

Something of what I have said it must be, the myth declares, for it must reverse our own era and resume past eras in itself; what else it must be no man can say, for always at the critical moment, the Thirteenth Cone, the sphere, the unique intervenes.[18]

This is his broad philosophy of history; but the four-thousand-year curve is still too wide to set in order all that he has in mind. *Dove or Swan*, the fifth book of *A Vision*, is mostly concerned with a view of history considered in lesser cycles of a thousand years.

History for Yeats is chiefly his understanding of art and thought, and above all of religion, not in any precise theological sense but as it expresses the general turn of men's minds to things natural and supernatural and to the outer and the inner world. He begins with the tribes of Greece, 'dominated each by its Daimon and oracle-driven', breaking up a great empire and establishing an intellectual anarchy. By Homer's time the idea of civil order is born; later comes the feeling for intellectual solitude, and this leads to the pre-Socratic philosophies and to the art of Phidias, all 'clarity, meaning, elegance, all things separated from one another in luminous space'. Periclean Athens is the full-moon phase of that era, when it comes nearest to perfect self-expression.

When he says that the spirit of Greek art, and also of Greek religion, is antithetical and makes for 'subjectivity', he is evidently not using the word in the ordinary sense. It is self-expressive in the sense that it seeks to realize all greatness and all beauty within human life, finding as many forms of possible greatness as there are men to live. Men are fragments of divinity and complement each other: heroes may have heroes to fight with, there is no need for the enemy to be evil in any absolute sense. The gods also are within the world and as multitudinous as nature itself. Life is a many-sided mirror of divinity, not a search for self- effacing unity with the transcendent One.

But the Greek secular intellect was primary. When Plato conceived his ideal absolutes as existing beyond nature, he was preparing the ground for the Christian rejection of the world. After its moment of achievement the creative spirit faded quickly from imaginative art. It passed into philosophy, to be exhausted there in Aristotle's systems. It found itself again for a moment in morals, when Stoics and Epicureans turned philosophy into a rule of life. But in the end, with no fresh inspiration from beyond itself, there was nothing left for it to take hold of. The impulse that had created Homer's heroes was petrified in an aristocratic social order, rank depending on rank, presided over by the Romanized gods of Greece, images of physical perfection from which the spirit of life had gone.

Earlier in *Dove or Swan* he said:

A civilization is a struggle to keep self-control, and in that is like some great tragic person, some Niobe who must display an almost superhuman will or the cry will not touch our sympathy. The loss of control over thought comes towards the end; first a sinking in upon the moral being, then the last surrender, the irrational cry, revelation—the scream of Juno's peacock.[19]

Christianity was that irrational cry, it was harsh and terrifying because it was the triumph of everything least comprehensible to the thought and science and religion predominant in the age. In ancient thought men had been fragments of the divine: the Emperor himself was the highest embodiment of God on earth. Now Christ gathered all divinity into Himself in human form, and as God in human form, He died. Henceforth God was to be everything and man nothing.

The mind that brought this change, if considered as man only, is a climax of whatever Greek and Roman thought was most a contradiction to its age; but considered as more than man He controlled what neo-Pythagorean and Stoic could not—irrational force. He could announce the new age, all that had not been thought of, or touched, or seen, because He could substitute for reason, miracle.[20]

To Yeats Christianity is less a fulfilment of the past of civilization than its Nemesis—though Nemesis itself is a kind of ironic fulfilment —changing every value into something most unlike itself.

We say of Him because His sacrifice was voluntary that He was love itself, and yet that part of Him which made Christendom was not love but pity, and not pity for intellectual despair, though the man in Him, being antithetical like His age, knew it in the Garden, but primary pity, that for the common lot, man's death, seeing that He raised Lazarus, sickness, seeing that He healed many, sin, seeing that He died.[20]*

Sexual love, that seeks its opposite and delights in possession, became evil. Love is changed into sacrifice and service—that of the Good Samaritan who 'discovers himself in the likeness of another, covered with sores and abandoned by thieves upon the roadside, and in that other serves himself'.

Early Christianity is transcendental. He finds it nearest to Unity of Being in the visionary art of Byzantium about the time of Justinian.

---

* Two plays elaborate these themes. In *Calvary* (1920) Christ's 'primary pity' is confronted with whatever rejects or is beyond its reach. In *The Resurrection* (1931) the risen Christ, humanity merged in God, is the reversal of an age of thought. His nearest analogy in Greek thought is Dionysus, whose worship is presented as something alien to the true Greek spirit, an orgiastic cult of the semi-barbarous, downtrodden elements of the population. Suddenly it has become the symbol of supernatural reality. For a full study, see Wilson, *W. B. Yeats and Tradition*, pp. 63–5.

Of all ages of history that fascinated him most, because he saw in it the most perfect expression of the unseen in visible form.

I think that in early Byzantium, maybe never before or since in recorded history, religious, aesthetic, and practical life were one; that architects and artificers—though not, it may be, poets, for language had been the instrument of controversy and must have grown abstract—spoke to the multitude and the few alike. The painter, the mosaic worker, the worker in gold and silver, the illuminator of sacred books, were almost impersonal, almost perhaps without the consciousness of individual design, absorbed in their subject matter and that the vision of a whole people.[21]

He does not know much about the end of the era. He looks for it in western Europe, not in the later history of Greek Christianity, and at the beginning of the eleventh century he finds a world where there is the utmost spiritual unity in Catholicism, and at the same time the utmost chaotic fragmentation in all things secular.

The spiritual life is alone overflowing, its cone expanded, and yet this life—secular intellect extinguished—has little effect upon men's conduct, is perhaps a dream which passes beyond the reach of conscious mind but for some rare miracle of vision.[22]

This, the last phase of a millennial wheel, is at the same time the full moon of a vaster era which he has delineated less carefully.

Then he traces the last millennium. In the dawn of Romance and the flowering of Gothic architecture, he finds a new impulse towards delight in life breaking in upon the otherworldly dreams of the Christian mystics. As yet it rested within the framework of religion. Inside that framework the expression of the solitary personality began: in Dante particularly, whose whole vast synthesis of the Divine Comedy was impersonally orthodox and yet was filled with his own spirit. Naturalism and curiosity about the living world were reborn in art and poetry. The Renaissance is the Unity of Being of the era, differently timed in different arts and regions, never quite fully expressed since the full-moon phase is never perfectly embodied in life; but nearest to perfection in the Italian painters of the fifteenth century.

He saw Byzantine art as absorption in a vision, with just enough of life inherited from ancient Greece to give it fineness and delicacy of expression. In contrast the art of Botticelli and Mantegna and Leonardo is full of intellectual curiosity and delight in the natural world, yet is lit up and harmonized from within by just enough of visionary insight to give it unity.

Intellect and emotion, primary curiosity and the antithetical dream, are for the moment one. Since the rebirth of the secular intellect in the eleventh century, faculty has been separating from faculty, poetry from music, the worshipper from the worshipped, but all have remained within a common fading circle—Christendom—and so within the human soul.[23]

Of course the synthesis swiftly fades. From visionary beauty the artist turns his attention to physical beauty and power; soon, as if his own ideals matter less to him, he paints the natural for its own sake, delighting in his technical facility but indifferent whether the thing he paints is beautiful or ugly in itself. This is the stage where Creative Mind pursuing the Body of Fate is beginning to take the place of Will and Mask.

In art and literature, in philosophy and science and administration, the objective spirit grows steadily. In art, everything creative now comes from the external world; all else is a conventional picturesqueness left over from the Renaissance. Among writers the greatest masters are the realists—Tolstoi for instance—and because they are most in harmony with their age their art is the most balanced and inclusive. In science, the greatest thinkers from Bacon onwards are growing more absorbed in the study of phenomena, more scrupulous not to confuse nature's laws with their own preconceptions. With this new awareness of nature the applied sciences develop rapidly, and men are able to organize the world as they never have before.

Yet even in the early eighteenth century, the soul hesitantly reappears, at first in small and seemingly trivial things. It is seen first in painting, then in poetry and last in prose. It is in the Romantic revival, and in everything most beautiful in English poetry from

Blake to Arnold. But it has remained the expression of a purely personal wisdom, without as yet finding a synthesis to capture the collective imagination of the world.

In the meantime the intellect seems to be exhausting itself, destroying its own foundations. By the mid-nineteenth century we had carried impersonality to the point of

synthesis for its own sake, organisation where there is no masterful director, books where the author has disappeared, paintings where some accomplished brush paints with equal pleasure, or with a bored impartiality, the human form or an old bottle, dirty weather or clean sunshine.[24]

In this, Yeats sees the beginning of that final surrender of the will which prepares once again for 'the scream of Juno's peacock'—the revelation of a new age.

I think of recent mathematical research; even the ignorant can compare it with that of Newton—so plainly of the Nineteenth Phase—with its objective world intelligible to intellect; I can recognise that the limit itself has become a new dimension, that the ever-hidden thing which makes us fold our hands has begun to press down upon multitudes. Having bruised their hands upon that limit, men, for the first time since the seventeenth century, see the world as an object of contemplation, not as something to be remade, and some few, meeting the limit in their special study, even doubt if there is any common experience, doubt the possibility of science.[25]

This was written in 1925. Nine years later he was still turning his gyres about, trying in vain to make them tell him something more specific about the future of mankind.

What discords will drive Europe to that artificial unity—only dry or drying sticks can be tied into a bundle—which is the decadence of every civilization? How work out upon the phases the gradual coming and increase of the counter movement, the antithetical and multiform influx:

> Should Jupiter and Saturn meet,
> What a crop of mummy wheat!

Then I understand, I have already said all that can be said. The particulars are the work of the *Thirteenth* sphere or cycle, which is in every man and called by every man his freedom.[26]

144

Yeats died before atomic science and hydrogen bombs had become the talk of the day. Had he not, it seems to me that they would have made little change in the forecasts of *A Vision*. To him the death of a civilization was as inevitable as the death of a man, and he was sure that the death of ours was near. He did not think of it as the final ruin of mankind; he was sure of the eternity alike of the soul and the race, and therefore could travel on in imagination to that remote future when, out of whatever remained, on a phase of the wheel more congenial to creative beauty a new civilization would emerge, a new moon grow towards the full.

Those,...
Lovers of horses and of women, shall,
From marble of a broken sepulchre,
Or dark betwixt the polecat and the owl,
Or any rich, dark nothing disinter
The workman, noble and saint, and all things run
On that unfashionable gyre again.[27]

CHAPTER IX

A VISION (II)

A Vision, with its doubtful origins, its bizarre terminology, and the unfashionable drift of its philosophy, is an awkward book to swallow. One naturally asks what Yeats himself thought about its sources and in what sense he believed in its contents. If the answer to neither question is quite simple it is not because Yeats was being needlessly obscure; but he was moving in an uncertain borderland for which ordinary language is not shaped. As he pointed out, 'belief' for the modern mind is not a word with precise, invariable meaning. Even people who accept a common creed may believe it in different ways with different implications, and it is almost impossible to tell the exact truth about one's own beliefs in language that cannot be mis-understood.

It would take an unusually dogmatic mind to be positive that telepathy, mediumship, automatic writing and the like can never happen, that every recorded instance is either pure chance or pure fraud or a mixture of the two; but to admit the phenomena is not to agree about the explanation or the value to be given to them. Their existence appears to imply something incompatible with a great body of assumptions valid for common life and for scientific reasoning, and this in itself fascinates one kind of mind and makes another kind prefer to leave them alone. Yeats had been fascinated by them since very early youth: he had set out by doubting most of the generally received notions of mind and matter, time and space, and was sure that much in his own experience justified his doubts. In the making of *A Vision*, it seems clear at least that in some way not usual in ordinary intercourse the separation between his own mind and his wife's had broken down. He was not, however, silly enough to make out on this account that the book ought to be accepted as a miraculously inspired gospel. To introduce the first edition he invented a story, which was not and fairly obviously was not intended to be convincing to the most childlike credulity, explaining how he came by the material. This, as he explained in the second edition, was because his wife did not wish to acknowledge her share in it, nor he himself to claim it as his creation in the same sense as his poems. In the second edition he gave a full account of its origin.

He gives the facts, and the construction he puts on them is implied in his phrases. He speaks of 'communicators' who are very clear about their doctrine, anxious to teach it to him, impatient of his ignorance and his mistakes, and still more impatient when he questions them in terms learnt from other philosophies. They appear to be bodiless minds, aware of minds and of thoughts, but unaware of the world of sense except as it is reflected in the minds of living men.

Once when they had given their signal in a restaurant, they explained that, because we had spoken of a garden, they thought we were in it.[1]

And yet the sensible world has meaning for them; at another time they call a halt in the work to listen to the hoot of an owl, because 'sounds like that give us great pleasure'. Sounds like that gave Yeats great pleasure too, for his poetry is full of them; they may well have listened through his ears.

They are hypersensitive to communicated thought, and afraid of being influenced by it:

They once told me not to speak of any part of the system, except of the incarnations which were almost fully expounded, because if I did that the people I talked to would talk to other people, and the communicators would mistake the misunderstanding for their own thought.[2]

They have a queer inner certainty of something which has to be communicated to the outer world, but this outer world is a confusion and a menace to them because they can only be aware of it through the intervention of embodied minds.

Besides the communicators there are 'frustrators' who slip in at times to confuse him with misleading teaching. But unless he himself is suspicious enough to ask point-blank, the communicators will not tell him when the frustrators have been at work. Only once, when some masquerading frustrator has been explaining 'a geometrical model of the soul's state after death, which could be turned upon a lathe', the communicators burst out with a reprimand as if goaded beyond endurance by seeing the symbols they have given him reduced to absurd mechanical toys.

The sudden indignant interruption suggested a mind under a dream constraint, which it could throw off if desire were strong enough, as we can sometimes throw off a nightmare.[3]

Throughout his writings, Yeats regarded the reasoning that systemizes mechanically for system's sake as a danger to the intuitive perception of truth. He was aware of his own bent for just such reasoning, and disapproved of it; it looks as if the communicators only anticipated what would have been his considered feeling about the ingenious gadget.

He tells us little more about the frustrators' actual messages. But if this hint is enough to go upon they were perhaps working with one side of his mind, the mechanically logical side, to the exclusion of the intuitive perception for which as a poet he must always be alert. In the completed structure of *A Vision* both obviously have their place, but its essence is in the second; logical coherence is only an instrument for expounding and ordering the intuitive perception and if it went beyond this would make nonsense of the whole.

He could not say positively why the frustrators desired to mislead or the communicators to instruct him. The teaching did not seem to be given out of regard for him. They were indifferent what else he did with it provided he put their meaning into a correct form; it was as if they needed his power of expression for some purpose not his. Nor would he say positively whether he took them to be separate beings, or separate parts of his own being, or different voices from a confused being other than himself; only, for the most part, treating them as separate beings was the clearest way to write about them.

In fact he could not easily have explained more. One thing Yeats certainly believed was that the source of all things is in mind, that human minds are in some way a part of that source and the world they look out on in some way an emanation or reflection of it. He believed in consequence that the mind, turned away from the phenomenal world, might have more direct access to ultimate reality and thence even a reinforced power over the phenomenal world itself. For this world, in its relation to reality, was what ultimately interested him: he was not disposed to cry 'Om! Om!' and let it go to blazes.

Many people, in Europe as well as Asia, may be ready to accept the theory in the abstract. But ordinary thinking for which ordinary language is framed begins from quite different assumptions, so habitual that they are used without even being consciously remembered, far less questioned. To throw them over is like passing from a known science to another with a totally different set of concepts, or learning a language with a different etymology and grammatical structure. Within the new terms you cannot talk about the same things in the same way, and though you can think about some things with a precision which was impossible before, the uninitiated cannot follow your process of thought. The old criteria for distinguishing between sensible and nonsensical statements do not apply. Not that the distinction ceases to exist, but to make it with confidence you must learn the appropriate discipline.

Yeats had done this in years of exacting occult studies, but few of his readers and critics find it worth while to follow him. Moving in a world of thought where matter is liable to dissolve into mind and the values normally given to subjective and objective perceptions break down, he could not give 'straight' answers to questions about whose mind is the source of what and in what sense minds are separate and in what sense one; but he did not therefore accept as authoritative any nonsense which purported to come from a super-natural source. He judged in terms of his own learning.

He compared the voices to dreams. He believed that dreams were not mere reflections from the actual, but projections from the reality underlying it, and at the same time they were plastic and deceitful. The two statements are not contradictory, and to accept them both perhaps brings us nearer to most people's experience of dreams than to deny either.

Sometimes the philosophic voices themselves have become vague and trivial or have in some other way reminded us of dreams. Furthermore their doctrine supports the resemblance, for one said in the first month of communication, 'We are often but created forms', and another, that spirits do not tell a man what is true but create such conditions, such a crisis of fate, that the man is compelled to listen to his Daimon. And again and again they have insisted that the whole system is the creation of my wife's Daimon and of mine and that it is as startling to them as to us. Mere 'spirits', my teachers say, are the objective, a reflection and distortion; reality itself is found by the Daimon in what they call, in commemoration of the Third Person of the Trinity, the Ghostly Self. The blessed spirits must be sought within the self which is common to all.

Much that has happened, much that has been said, suggests that the communicators are the personalities of a dream shared by my wife, myself, occasionally by others....In partly accepting and partly rejecting that explanation for reasons I cannot now discuss, in affirming a Communion of the Living and the Dead, I remember that Swedenborg has described all those between the celestial state and death as plastic, fantastic, and deceitful, the dramatis personae of our dreams; that Cornelius Agrippa attributed to Orpheus these words: 'The Gates of Death must not be unlocked, within is a people of dreams.'[4]

Readers may rephrase this for themselves and rationalize it according to the postulates of their own thinking, and in doing so will perhaps discover what they themselves think about the ghostly communicators. They are not likely to arrive at a more accurate statement of Yeats' own view.

But he did believe intensely in the teaching of *A Vision*, and if 'by their fruits shall ye know them' is sound logic he was right, for writing it increased his power as a poet enormously. Turning from *Responsibilities* to *The Tower*, it is impossible to think that he had been wasting his brains in the interval. He meant so much by it that he went on writing and revising it till within a year or two of his death, and wrote to Edmund Dulac in 1937:

I do not know what my book will be to others—nothing perhaps. To me it means a last act of defence against the chaos of the world, and I hope for ten years to write out of my renewed security.[5]*

The thinking which he put into it so ardently is neither metaphysical nor scientific, but mythological. His language about the soul begs all the questions which a metaphysician would be bound to reason out. In writing of history he does not try to investigate facts; he takes them from whatever authorities have appealed to him and interprets them by a thesis. But he creates and arranges images so as to express his sense of values, and this is the genius of mythology. A myth is a myth not because it is false to physical or historical fact but because, true or false, it offers just such an expressive image. If we believe absolutely in its values we accept it as true, in a sense to which mere factual accuracy can only be an endorsement. In this sense, without reference to their historical authenticity, the crucifixion of Christ and the meditation of Buddha and Demeter's search for Persephone are all alike myths. In this sense the evolution of man and the class struggle have perhaps taken shape as myths in our own time, but each of these expresses values which Yeats abhorred.

A Vision is his own myth, a statement of values completely true for himself, though, as his words to Dulac admit, possibly for no one else. The apparatus of Faculties and Principles and whirling gyres amounts to a complicated algebraical formula which arranges in intelligible order the whole of his knowledge and experience.

Hardly anything is set down 'as fact'. He assumes one concept— the soul, or Daimon, existing in eternity, and though he does not

---

* The words perhaps take on further meaning in the light of his description of a civilization as 'a struggle to keep self-control'.

define it very explicitly the meaning is clear enough for anyone but
a metaphysician. He conceives each individual Daimon as an aspect
of the all-inclusive One, the ground of all being. This underlying
One is acknowledged, but neither in *A Vision* nor in his poems as
a whole is it the thing chiefly emphasized. It is a knowledge on
which, at rare moments in his poetry, he sinks back restfully, but he
thinks of them as moments rather of exhaustion than of achievement.
One of the clearest is in the 1921 volume, in the middle of civil
war:

> For one throb of the artery,
> While on that old grey stone I sat
> Under the old wind-broken tree,
> I knew that One is animate,
> Mankind inanimate fantasy.[6]

But this knowledge is not what he seeks. The Daimon is man's link
with God, through which all souls are in some sense joined to one
another, and the bent of his mind made this belief a starting-point
for exploring magic and telepathy rather than for the beatitude of
contemplation. The mystic's ecstasy in merging himself with the
One is not his quest; more important, more exciting, is the uniqueness of the individual soul's experience. He does not think of life
in the world as a fall. The creative artist can hardly do so, for to him
the formless gains, not loses, by taking on form. It is the Daimon's
deliberate choice, for since time and space are necessary conditions
of consciousness the soul's experience is a part of the self-knowledge
of God.

Yeats' father, who was a rationalist, held that the greatest thing in
the world was human personality. In his own transcendental terms,
Yeats is not far from his father's position.

For a mind to which the soul's experience and its immortality are
so much more interesting than knowledge of the Absolute, reincarnation is almost a necessary idea. It appears to be a part of pagan
Irish tradition and may be latent in the Irish imagination, for it will
sometimes crop up like an irrepressible survival in the talk of quite

orthodox Christians. Yeats had accepted it naturally, and in his early
youth the Brahmin Mohini Chatterjee tried to make him think of it
as an exercise for the tranquillizing of desire.

Somebody asked him if we should pray, but even prayer was too full of
hope, of desire, of life, to have any part in that acquiescence that is the
beginning of wisdom, and he answered that one should say, before
sleeping, 'I have lived many lives. I have been a slave and a prince.
Many a beloved has sat upon my knees and I have sat upon the knees of
many a beloved. Everything that has been shall be again.'[7]

But though the doctrine itself was after Yeats' heart, his early
poem *Fergus and the Druid* shows that even then he was not satisfied
with this use of it. He was not at all sure that he wanted to lose the
active passion of life in contemplative serenity. In 1929, after writing
A Vision had cleared his thoughts, he recalled the Brahmin's words
with a gloss of his own:

> That he might set at rest
> A boy's turbulent days
> Mohini Chatterjee
> Spoke these, or words like these.
> I add in commentary,
> 'Old lovers yet may have
> All that time denied—
> Grave is heaped on grave
> That they be satisfied.'[8]

Ten years later he speaks of reincarnation in *Under Ben Bulben* as if
he had learnt it from Ireland, not India:

> Many times man lives and dies
> Between his two eternities,
> That of race and that of soul,
> And ancient Ireland knew it all.[9]

This poem ends in an epitaph, but in it, as in all his last poems, his
gaze is turned fiercely lifeward and he thinks of time as the incarnation of eternity. To return again and again to the flesh is not a
punishment as in Indian philosophy, but the soul's deliberate choice.

Long before, in his preface to Lady Gregory's *Gods and Fighting Men*, he had written:

It sometimes seems as if there were a kind of day and night of religion, and that a period where the influences are those that shape the world is followed by a period where the greater power is in influences that would lure the soul out of the world, out of the body.[10]

This is an earlier form of the thought which grew into *Dove or Swan*. It is the chief of the antinomies summed up in his symbolic gyres, a dual movement reflected in the magnifying glass of history. History for him was a partial interpretation of the human soul: men make it, not by planning, but inevitably as they make their shadows, by being where and what they are. In so far as prophesy was possible it was not by understanding the mechanistic forces which the Marxist uses as his key, but by understanding the complexity of the human soul and its rhythms. And because he took account of this complexity he could maintain a strange, detached tolerance side by side with fierce partisanship.

Within the soul the lifeward-turning impulse is what he calls the antithetical. It makes a man aspire to mirror in himself all that he can conceive of wisdom and beauty and power, and live to his utmost intensity. In history he sees it as dominant in the pagan ideal world, where the gods are within nature, where perfection is manifold and pride and passion and conflict are not evil; a world for heroes and poets, but harsh to the weak. The opposing primary movement is the soul's self-transcendence, the impulse to service and self-forgetfulness. It sees God beyond the world and sees man as nothing, unless he is the instrument of a power greater than himself. Pride is its deadly sin, but it shelters the weak under a canopy of brotherly love and teaches men to despise all that distinguishes themselves individually and to venerate only what is universal. In history its reign was heralded when the Virgin Mary sang, 'He hath put down the mighty from their seat, and hath exalted the humble and meek', and divinity took the form of the most helpless thing on earth.

But since these opposites are in the soul itself the world swings perpetually between them—in the lives of men, in religious and secular thought, in the greater and lesser cycles of civilization. Embodied in time the soul of man is not a simple essence, and while one part enjoys its carnival another part, feeding on scraps, grows quietly among the shadows till it steps forward and breaks up its opposite, reintegrating the dismembered pieces into an unimaginably new pattern of its own. An aristocratic age cracks when it has hardened into hierarchical forms, emptied of the indwelling divinity which once inspired them:

> What if the glory of escutcheoned doors,
> And buildings that a haughtier age designed....
> What if those things the greatest of mankind
> Consider most to magnify, or to bless,
> But take our greatness with our bitterness?[11]

A democratic age ends by losing its awareness of the God before whom all men are equally everything and nothing, and exalts equality for equality's sake in dead administrative efficiency. There is no evolution towards an all-inclusive perfection in his scheme, there is only the gyre, each circuit of which is the denial of another. And yet, with ages as with incarnations of men, the present builds out of the fragments of a superseded past, and for its new design it may draw much or little, according to its wisdom and vision, from the accumulated skill of the old builders. In interpreting history Yeats seems to have felt that he was preserving half-forgotten values from the far past, doomed to be still further obliterated before the far future tried to recreate them.

He was not religious, if religion is a striving for absorption out of the world into the universality of God. His father had told him this.

You can only pretend it. Your interest is in mundane things, and heaven to you is this world made better, whether beyond the stars or not.[12]

By contrast, and not with unqualified approval, he saw the genuine religious mystic in his son's friend and fellow-poet A. E.:

He has no love, no admiration for the individual man. He is too religious to care for really mortal things, or rather, for he does care, to admire and love them.[12]

The distinction was a true one. To A. E., visionary, democrat, and practical builder of the Irish co-operative movement, it was the common humanity in men that mattered: to Yeats it was the distinction of individual personality. In his wheel of incarnations Yeats puts A. E. with the saints and the great scientists and selfless workers for mankind in the primary phases where the celestial sun is king; for saint and scientist alike renounce the choices of the personal will to lay themselves open to a truth from beyond it. The great poets belong to the moon, with the passionate heroes they celebrate. But he might have answered his father that the moon also is religion, though of a different kind. In the doctrine as he formulated it there are elements from many sources, but the proportions of the complete design are neither Christian, Hindu nor Buddhist, but pagan; both the supernaturalism and the love of life are of a pagan kind. It is as if Oisin had lived on unconverted somewhere in Europe, and as the centuries passed had enlarged and adapted his original Druidic faith, taking into it whatever could be integrated of Greek or Christian or oriental thought. From the beginning Yeats had been on Oisin's side, and in old age he could still declare

Homer is my example and his unchristened heart.[13]*

In one passage of *A Vision* he relates his scheme to that of Plotinus, whose universe is arranged on levels of diminishing reality from the timeless One to the fleeting world of sense. It is necessary, he points out, that primary man who looks beyond himself should see it thus; it is equally necessary that gyres and not planes should express antithetical man's vision of a many-centred universe with the absolute at the heart of every circle. Plotted on a graph the phases of his gyres go round and round, so that there is no reason in logic or

---

* But cp. Virginia Moore's very different reading of this line in *The Unicorn*, chap. IX.

geometry, but only in emotion, to prefer the full moon to the dark. On his own showing indeed, Yeats too must enter a primary phase in some future incarnation. It is imaginable that by then the world will have come round to the antithetical and be pursuing such a vision of heroic anarchy as he longed for in his poems, while he slaves in patient humility in some hospital for the destitute, caring too much for the image of God in man to waste his energy on poetry. Or rather, of course, it will not be William Yeats who lives thus, but the timeless Daimon behind the transitory man who projects himself into life after life, foreseeing and choosing, between lives, what the next shall be, till he has taken in all experience. But here and now the writer of *A Vision* is antithetical man; he must pursue his own unity of being and admire all proud and lonely things, must set himself against the levelling spirit of his primary age. Through his symbol he acknowledges the right to exist, and even the necessity, of ideals he does not share, and at the same time fights for his personal ideal with the whole energy of his spirit; accepts the certainty of defeat, and makes defeat and victory equally unimportant in the endless cycle of change. This, though it is not listed in any register, is a religion both exhilarating and exacting.

The world's great myths and symbols are an attempt not so much to comprehend the directionlessness of infinity—if they were, the phaseless sphere would be enough for all—as to find a standpoint in it, and trace a pattern to which thought and experience may conform. The patterns differ but the fabric is the same for all: all have to take account of the fluid world, and of human action and passion, and of the consciousness of eternity which is behind these. But it is time rather than eternity that presses most heavily on the greater part of mankind for most of their lives. Throughout history, religion and philosophy have sought to tranquillize the passions by detaching men from their personal, temporal preoccupations. The great teachers and sages reach beyond the personal to a detachment which does not nullify joy and pain, but makes them indifferently

157

acceptable. There is a lower level on which religion is turned into a quest for immunity from the shocks of experience, in partial or complete withdrawal from passionate life. Not to love or hate much is not to be exposed to deep suffering, and so

> Lips that would kiss
> Form prayers to broken stone[14]

—and the serenity of emotions thus anaesthetized is a spurious copy of the serenity of a deeper insight.

Yeats was not in search of this kind of security. Poetry had admitted him to an eternal world before the actual world took hold of him, and he was more in danger of resting there than of losing sight of it. As a young man he knew and was troubled by this; in *The Man Who Dreamed of Faeryland*, one of the best of his early poems, he recognizes the power to withdraw from life as a gift not wholly blessed:

> He stood among a crowd at Drumahair;
> His heart hung all upon a silken dress,
> And he had known at last some tenderness,
> Before earth took him to her stony care;
> But when a man poured fish into a pile,
> It seemed they raised their little silver heads,
> And sang what gold morning or evening sheds
> Upon a woven world-forgotten isle
> Where people love beside the ravelled seas;
> That Time can never mar a lover's vows
> Under that woven changeless roof of boughs:
> That singing shook him out of his new ease.[15]

In some of his early letters to Katherine Tynan he is uneasy, both as man and poet, because he is too much wrapped up in his dreams; intensity of feeling for life is eluding him.

I have woven about me a web of thoughts. I wish to break through it, to see the world again.

Yesterday I went to see, in a city hotel, an acquaintance who has had sudden and great misfortunes, come in the last few days to a crisis....I saw his hands and eyes moving restlessly and that his face was more shrunken than when I saw him some months before. Of course all this pained me at the time but I know (now that he is out of my sight) that if I heard that he was dead I would not think twice about it. So thick has the web got.[16]

And when he was preparing *The Wanderings of Oisin* for press he wrote to her that his poetry so far was 'the cry of the heart against necessity', and that he hoped some day to write poetry of insight and knowledge. It is startling to find him, at twenty-three, so clearly aware of his limitations.

Evidently he was not content, even when he seemed to be so, to let the love of poetry beckon him out of the world as the love of God may beckon a saint. In middle age he wrote in an essay:

The imaginative writer differs from the saint in that he identifies himself —to the neglect of his own soul, alas!—with the soul of the world, and frees himself from all that is impermanent in that soul, an ascetic not of women and wine but of the newspapers. That which is permanent in the soul of the world, on the other hand, the great passions that trouble all and have but a brief recurring life of flower and seed in any man, is the renunciation of the saint, who seeks not an eternal art but his own eternity.[17]

And a poem in *The Winding Stair* sums it up succinctly:

> The intellect of man is forced to choose
> Perfection of the life, or of the work,
> And if it take the second must refuse
> A heavenly mansion, raging in the dark.[18]

The gyres make passionate experience as real and significant as the inescapable consciousness of eternity. Both are in his poetry, but the second was visible in it from the beginning: it is the first that grows in power and significance and freedom of expression. He needed and used his philosophy rather to drive him into life than to raise him above it, and this is where he chiefly differed from the contemplative mystics.

There are critics who write apologetically of *A Vision*, as if it were an embarrassment to admirers of Yeats' poetry. This seems to me needless; it is not only a storehouse but a great achievement in its own right. The claim that visionary revelations are valid, and are worth years of disciplined concentration to receive, will be called sense or nonsense according to different readers' prejudices, but this is not the main point. Dante and Milton would probably have made it, and that does not prevent their writings from being understood by sceptics. On the whole, however, the modern world clings to rationalist prejudices and prefers its own language for the medium of instruction. And it is hard to translate between the languages of supernaturalism and of modern rationalism, since few people are equally at home with both. Overtones of meaning are easily lost in translation, false implications easily slipped in; and like other language problems, this one raises passions over the language itself which obscure the importance of the things said in it, and thus estrange minds fundamentally akin. There are devout believers in the supernatural whose faith only extends into an inescapable eternity the dreary profit-and-loss mentality of a materialistic shopkeeper; there are also atheists and rationalists who transcend their egoism as completely as the most visionary of mystics.

Yeats at any rate believed that the whole man was needed to discover truth. He put himself through a discipline which welded together all his scattered perceptions and turned a dreamer's mind into hard crystal, and sought with intense, sustained concentration for a view of the universe which would hold his whole experience of life in one perspective with his whole sense of justice. In whatever form they came to him his conclusions could hardly be negligible. The judgements of *A Vision* are a tremendous intellectual summing-up of a view of life that is fearless and joyous, without blinking the fact of evil and the necessity of conflict. It includes the conception of eternity and the immortality of the soul, but unlike so many transcendental philosophies, it does not thin down the significance of flesh-and-blood experience. Perhaps its most striking quality is that, personal as it is, and full of combative energy, it recognizes diversity, and acknowledges for every man a vision, a quest and a salvation that are his alone. It also looks at history stretching into the far past and the far future, gives full value to civilization and tradition, and yet contemplates the destruction of both without losing faith in the creative energy of the spirit that has built and will build again. All this is harmonized in the intricate pattern of a cosmic dance, unity and multiplicity at once.

To recognize its moral and intellectual balance is not to treat the book as the sacred scripture of a revealed religion. Yeats himself, except perhaps in moments of dizzy exhilaration, did not think it would make converts or set the world to rights. It is what he called it, one man's defence against the chaos of the world, and this is its real strength.

It is a common complaint that the modern world lacks a coherent philosophy; that science has destroyed religious belief, and uncertain belief has destroyed the sureness of aim and proportion without which the greatest creative art is impossible. Mr T. S. Eliot has pointed out the strength that Aquinas gave to Dante, and suggests that even Shakespeare might have done greater work, not less passionate but more serene in its total effect, had his age been capable of a statement as inclusive as the *Summa Theologica*. It was not, nor is our own, and a philosophic synthesis cannot be faked and foisted on men whose actual values it does not fit. A poet is neither missionary nor philosopher; he cannot simultaneously reason out his principles and create from them; but he needs principles too self-evident to himself to be questionable, and an audience to whom he can make himself understood without stopping to expound them. Whether that audience is half the world or the fit few that Milton asked for, it is the only one that concerns him.

Yeats had dreamed in his youth of being a great popular poet, of writing epic and dramatic cycles to give back to Ireland, perhaps through Ireland to the world, an integrated vision of perfection; but he never dreamed of accommodating his sense of truth to the world's.

He discovered that art could not be popular unless it expressed a vision shared between artist and audience.

I did not see [he says] until Synge began to write, that we must renounce the deliberate creation of a kind of Holy City in the imagination, and express the individual.[19]

Even to do that in more than random flashes of insight, he had to work down to a 'Summa Theologica' hidden like a skeleton in the body of his own poetry, the frame which gave power to the wings. *A Vision* relates together ideas and images scattered through his previous writings, bringing out latent meanings which may sometimes have escaped him when he wrote them. In everything he wrote after it his thought moved with new swiftness and precision, as if he had a survey map of the country of his mind. To articulate it he drew on his life's experience, his reading of history, his Hermetic studies, and ten years of hard work at philosophy after the outline had been drawn, not 'constraining one by another', but unifying them in a new whole.

It is not an inviting book: as he truly observed, the symbols are harsh, like those of a dream that has not been worked over by the waking mind. They are also tediously repetitive:

Yet every symbol, except when it lies in vast periods of time and so beyond our experience, has evoked for me some form of human destiny, and that form, once evoked, has appeared everywhere, as if there were but one destiny, as my own form might appear in a roomful of mirrors.[20]

Just so a devout man will meditate on some text from his scriptures till it becomes a key to interpret things past, present and to come. He could dig poetry out of it as from a mine. Here, for instance, from an unpromising chapter entitled *Various Tabulations*, is

XVI. TABLE OF THE QUARTERS (ANTITHETICAL)

	Inward Contests	*Automatism*	*Condition of Will*
1st Quarter	with body	Instinctive	Instinctive
2nd Quarter	with heart	Imitative	Emotional
3rd Quarter	with mind	Creative	Intellectual
4th Quarter	with soul	Obedient	Moral

Such tabulations laid out one after another are dry, irritating, un-illuminating, anatomization in place of living discourse. But turn to the ninth *Supernatural Song* in *A Full Moon in March*, and see with how little change the dead matter springs to life:

> He with body waged a fight,
> But body won; it walks upright.
>
> Then he struggled with the heart;
> Innocence and peace depart.
>
> Then he struggled with the mind;
> His proud heart he left behind.
>
> Now his wars on God begin;
> At stroke of midnight God shall win.

If the text is thus alive with inspiration for Yeats himself, why should it not serve as spiritual food for a band of disciples, and become the scripture of a church? I think the answer is in the very structure of the teaching. It is based on a discipline of arduous submission, not to an authority beyond himself (which is what the book would be to a disciple) but to his own inmost self: a skeleton cannot be shared. Even the basic antinomy of 'primary' and 'antithetical', though it is a workable way of sorting out experience, is not the only way. Another man, less conscious than Yeats, or differently conscious, of divided aims and powers would probably need a different formula, and if he had Yeats' concentration of purpose would find his own, and see the world reflected in it. The constant presupposition is the Daimon, and the doctrine only makes sense to those who believe in their Daimon. 'For spirits', as the communicators told him, 'do not tell a man what is true, but create such conditions, such a crisis of fate, that the man is compelled to listen to his Daimon'—and if he listens his Daimon will say to him alone what no one else will perfectly understand.

This reinforces what I have said or implied already—that Yeats was no sort of Christian. The statement can be disputed and is hard to defend absolutely: there are many kinds of Christians, and he not only believed in supernatural power but acknowledged the divinity of Christ more unequivocally than some of them. Yet he could not be called a follower of Christ, for it was not in Christian teaching, whether scripturally or traditionally interpreted, that he sought the all-inclusive liberating truth. He sought it within rather than beyond the subjective self; life-giving sap drawn up through the roots rather than rain falling from heaven on the leaves. By pushing the metaphor further one might say that all the waters of life are from one primal fountain, or say in Yeats' own terms that in the phaseless sphere there is no distinction between primary and antithetical. But the distinction does exist in consciousness and alters values, and it seems to me to have a crucial bearing on the meaning of Christian humility. Yeats' own writing seldom echoes that emphasis on shared suffering and shared salvation which, if the ideals of one faith can be distinguished from those of another, is what marks out Christianity. In his play *Calvary*[21] there is a latent antagonism to the thought of Christ as universal redeemer. 'God has not died for the white heron'; and the heron's lonely self-sufficiency, though it wanes with the moon, consoles him more than the sacrifice of God.

This aloofness pervades the whole of his thought and sets him as far from Christianity, or indeed from any of the great religious folds, as from atheism or materialism. He demonstrates that a man can walk alone. In our age of collective security this is a portent all the more significant because so few desire to see it.

CHAPTER X

VIOLENCE AND PROPHECY

The Wild Swans at Coole, of which the London edition came out in 1919, shows how Yeats was not an English poet. It was his first book of poems since the outbreak of war in 1914. English poets had reacted variously to the war, but whether they welcomed it, as some did to begin with, or hated it, it was a tremendous, inescapable, collective experience. Yeats remained aloof. His elegy on Robert Gregory, mourning the man, says not a word about the war in which he died. In *An Irish Airman Foresees His Death*[1] the cold and measured appraisal—

> Those that I fight I do not hate,
> Those that I guard I do not love

—must have been singularly alien to English readers at the time.* When he was asked for a war poem his answer was:

> I think it better that in times like these
> A poet's mouth be silent, for in truth
> We have no gift to set a statesman right;
> He has had enough of meddling who can please
> A young girl in the indolence of her youth,
> Or an old man upon a winter's night.[2]

Responsibilities had shown full confidence in his gift to set a statesman right on things that stirred him. But the war did not; its issues were not his, and the sheer scale of it did not hypnotize him into thinking they were.

The Irish rising of Easter Week, 1916, was a very different matter. Apart from a few minds of uncommon detachment all England saw it as a piece of unspeakable treachery. It belonged to a mental world

---

* A poem called *Reprisals*, on the same theme, was more positively anti-English in tone but was not published till after Yeats' death. See the *Variorum Edition*, p. 791.

which they did not and could not afford to understand. To Yeats, who both was and had passionately willed himself to be Irish, it was a shock, but it was directly relevant to the thoughts and feelings and quarrels of a lifetime. In January 1916 he had written to his future biographer Joseph Hone:

I know that my work has been done in every detail with a deliberate Irish aim, but it is hard for those who know it in fragments to know that, especially if the most that they know of me is about some contest with Irish opinion.[3]

It was here, not in the world war, that he had to come to terms with the spirit of violence, and it was the pattern of events in Ireland, smaller and swifter but not less intense than that of post-war Europe, which coloured his philosophy of history and his interpretation of things to come. But for that very reason, what he had written about Easter Week was not published in England till two years after *The Wild Swans*. In 1919 hardly anyone would have listened.

The rebellion dismayed his judgement and at the same time, in a way, restored his faith. It came as a complete surprise; he was even indignant at the discovery that he, once the trusted friend of the Fenian John O'Leary, had been taken into no one's confidence. It is true that conspirators who mean business do not talk unnecessarily; all the same his astonishment measured the length of the distance which now divided him from the fighting rebels.

The course of his nationalism has been partly traced in an earlier chapter. At first it was a simple romantic devotion which saw in the soul of Ireland everything he idealized and ignored everything else. It seemed only right that his generation should live up to their ancestors' tradition of heroic rebellion, but he had not grown up in a world which knew what armed rebellion meant. *Cathleen ni Houlihan*, the simplest and most dynamic play he ever wrote, belongs to this phase. It was dynamic because of its simplicity: it argued nothing, promised nothing, but took the fight for freedom for granted as men take the gods they serve.

It is a hard service they take that help me. Many that are red-cheeked now will be pale-cheeked; many that have been free to walk the hills and the bogs and the rushes will be sent to walk hard streets in far countries; many a good plan will be broken; many that have gathered money will not stay to spend it; many a child will be born, and there will be no father at its christening to give it a name. They that have red cheeks will have pale cheeks for my sake, and for all that, they will think they are well paid.[4]

In the play this is enough to make the bridegroom leave his bride, because poet and audience are equally sure that it should be so. To a later generation such words seem a pale romanticization of sacrifice, dwelling on the least unendurable things as if they were all; but this was 1902, when violence was only a dream.

> Did that play of mine send out
> Certain men the English shot?[5]

It probably did. Not directly, but at least it helped to send them out with less misgiving because he had none when he wrote it. He set in motion a revival of the imagination that filtered through many channels; it put a spirit of confident nationality into books and poems and a lyrical emotion into countless fiery speeches, and shaped a vision of something to fight for which lasted better than resentment:

> Our courage breaks like an old tree in a black wind and dies,
> But we have hidden in our hearts the flame out of the eyes
> Of Cathleen, the daughter of Houlihan.[6]

But his own thought left the play behind. Except O'Leary the patriots he worked with were not legendary heroes and did not illustrate his vision of Ireland. In one of his essays he wrote:

When Mr O'Leary died I could not bring myself to go to his funeral, though I had been his close fellow-worker, for I shrank from meeting about his grave so many whose nationalism was so different from any-thing he had taught or that I could share.... I learnt much from him and much from Taylor, and that ideal Ireland, perhaps from this out an imaginary Ireland, in whose service I labour, will always be in many essentials their Ireland.[7]

He goes on to explain how his writings had aimed at kindling Irish patriotism into a blaze of hatred for everything despicable in the modern world, everything that Ruskin and Morris hated. Morris's socialism had made no deep impression on him, but Morris the man seems to have inspired him with the idea of a magnificent hatred, the other side of a powerful personality's conviction. The idea stayed with him for ever; it gave a keen edge to the poems of his old age and became the defiant doctrine of *Ribh Considers Christian Love Insufficient*:

> I study hatred with great diligence,
> For that's a passion in my own control,
> A sort of besom that can clear the sense
> Of everything that is not mind or sense.[8]

But in fact there was singularly little hatred in Yeats' poetry till the 1910 volume—which was later than the essay quoted—and then it was chiefly directed against the fellow-countrymen whom he could not induce to purge their souls by hating rightly. He had no use for the mean passions of mean minds. And work with Maud Gonne, who was not a mean mind, taught him that he did not share her restless craving for action for action's sake. Above all, loving heroic legend as he did, he distrusted the abstract fixations of politics, which prevent men from recognizing greatness intuitively and teach them to love and hate by thesis. No doubt his admiration for Lady Gregory, who shared his ideal of art and of Ireland but stood outside nationalist politics, deepened this feeling, and Maud Gonne's marriage to Sean MacBride instead of to himself embittered it, but it was a conviction born of more than private emotion. The lessons of three public controversies were summed up in his verdict:

Neither religion nor politics can of itself create minds with enough receptivity to become wise, or just and generous enough to make a nation.[9]

His own work was directed steadily to the refining of the imagination, along lines which, in practice at least, did not go with mass violence.

It was not his idea of heroism that he lost faith in, but the men of his generation, who seemed to him to be too small to write any heroic chapter of history, and perhaps some faith in himself went down with the rest. It was this that put bitterness, out of proportion to the controversy over the Lane pictures which evoked it, into *September 1913*.[10]

> What need you, being come to sense,
> But fumble in a greasy till
> And add the halfpence to the pence
> And prayer to shivering prayer, until
> You have dried the marrow from the bone?
> For men were born to pray and save:
> Romantic Ireland's dead and gone,
> It's with O'Leary in the grave.
>
> Yet they were of a different kind,
> The names that stilled your childish play,
> They have gone about the world like wind,
> But little time had they to pray
> For whom the hangman's rope was spun,
> And what, God help us, could they save?
> Romantic Ireland's dead and gone,
> It's with O'Leary in the grave.

Less than three years later, men such as this was addressed to went open-eyed to defeat and almost certain death to proclaim the Irish Republic.

The English naturally and necessarily saw the rising in the context of their war, and for the moment cared little about the background which every Irishman knew. Before the war Parliament had passed an Irish Home Rule Bill. Sir Edward Carson had armed and drilled his Ulster Volunteers to resist by force a separation from England, and it looked almost certain that the Government would give way to them, when the outbreak of war shelved the question. There was no certainty and little belief that the Bill would be implemented when the war was over. Outside Ulster the Irish as a whole claimed the moral right to freedom, so emphatically that when conscription was made law in England it could not be enforced in Ireland.

The men who made the rising did so with the clear expectation of defeat. They thought it useless to wait for the consent of England and died deliberately in the belief—justified by the event—that their death would commit the nation to fight on till freedom was won. Their courage could not be questioned: their judgement might, for it was conceivable that after the war the English might have consented to Home Rule. But the rising made that question unanswerable for ever.

Yeats was of course aware of all this, as well as of more personal feelings. Among the dead leaders one or two had been his friends; some he had disparaged or despised; one was Sean MacBride (long separated from Maud Gonne) whom he thought the type of all windy demagogues; among their followers were young enthusiasts whom his own work must have influenced. 'I keep going over the past in my mind', he wrote to a friend in America, 'and wondering if I could have done anything to turn those young men in some other direction.'[11] Victory was unforeseeable, but he saw that the deed must generate a turbulence that would thrust his own kind of labour into the background for years, if not undo it altogether. Who now was going to break his heart over Dublin's claim to an art gallery? But the clearest thing, however strange its implications, was that the men whom he had disregarded had changed the quality of life in his generation.

Maud Gonne was not in it herself, but she, who lived in deeds, was much less hesitant in her assessment. Before she knew of her husband's execution she wrote to Yeats from France, exulting characteristically that 'tragic dignity has returned again to Ireland'.[12] Yeats himself flung down his disconnected thoughts in a letter to Lady Gregory a few days after sentence on the captured leaders had been carried out. 'I am trying to write a poem on the men executed,' he said—'terrible beauty has been born again.'[12]

The poem,[13] which was not finished till September, is perhaps the most remarkable poem of our time upon a public event—remarkable alike for sincerity and complexity. Since the days of *Red Hanrahan's Song* fourteen years of lonely thought had isolated Yeats, and he could not now be simply the voice of a collective emotion. His individual wonder and trouble and uncertainty are in it, not banished but overruled and subdued to a new sense of proportion by the recurring theme:

> All changed, changed utterly:
> A terrible beauty is born.

He thinks of the men themselves, as he had known and disregarded them in their lives:

> Being certain that they and I
> But lived where motley is worn.

The casual 'and I' including himself in his verdict on his generation is an immense distance from the scathing, rather arrogant invective of *September 1913*. Then he thinks of them individually: Constance Markievicz, whose shrill political passion had seemed to him a denial of her beauty and breeding, Pearse and Macdonagh and his old enemy MacBride; and there is generosity in the way that Macbride is placed last so that he gets the full force of the recantation:

> He, too, has resigned his part
> In the casual comedy;
> He, too, has been changed in his turn,
> Transformed utterly;
> A terrible beauty is born.

And yet his own conviction remains; he had rejected their fanaticism because in his eyes it cramped the whole of life into a single thesis, atrophied emotion and perception and nullified all experience beyond itself. This had estranged him from the dead leaders. In the next paragraph, the kernel of the poem, he reaffirms his belief through the image of stone and stream:

> Hearts with one purpose alone
> That summer and winter seem
> Enchanted to a stone
> To trouble the living stream.

> The horse that comes from the road,
> The rider, the birds that range
> From cloud to tumbling cloud,
> Minute by minute they change;
> A shadow of cloud on the stream
> Changes minute by minute;
> A horse-hoof slides on the brim,
> And a horse plashes within it;
> The long-legged moor-hens dive,
> And hens to moor-cocks call;
> Minute by minute they live;
> The stone's in the midst of all.

There is no recantation here, but the image seems to grow as he writes, shedding over the whole troubled poem the quiet of its own world. At the end he no longer sees their petrifaction simply as the narrowness he had blamed, but as part of the nature of things; it is itself the very tragedy of the long battle for freedom in which men lay down so much more than their lives:

> Too long a sacrifice
> Can make a stone of the heart.
> O when may it suffice?
> That is Heaven's part, our part
> To murmur name upon name,
> As a mother names her child
> When sleep at last has come
> On limbs that had run wild.

But he rejects the euphemism of the simile and returns to the bare fact:

> No, no, not night, but death.

For the finality of their death had swept into irrelevance all the world of his doubts and objections, making their names as unanswerable as a legend:

> I write it out in a verse—
> MacDonagh and MacBride
> And Connolly and Pearse

> Now and in time to be,
> Wherever green is worn,
> Are changed, changed utterly:
> A terrible beauty is born.

The form of the poem, with its three-stress beat and loose rhymes which do not distract attention from the thought, was one he had used rarely before but would use again in reflective meditations. His first sustained use of it seems to be *The Fisherman*,[14] which must have been written not very long before Easter Week. There too he was trying to resolve the conflict between his devotion to Ireland and his feuds with Irishmen, and he went to the same place for the image which set his thoughts in order:

> a place
> Where stone is dark under froth.

The use of the image is totally different but the emotional logic is similar; it is as if his mind retreated there to find the serenity where opposites are reconciled.

Confronted with an unacceptable view of life, that has justified itself by heroism, a mean mind might deny or disparage the heroism to save its own righteousness; a shallow mind might be swept away, temporarily at least, to deny its own convictions. Yeats denied nothing: he held his belief but set beside it the heroic action, no less real, and prepared himself to meet the new world it had created.

Some of the complex threads woven into this summing-up are separated in two or three poems written soon afterwards. 'We make out of the quarrel with others, rhetoric', he has said,[15] 'but of the quarrel with ourselves, poetry.' But the difference is not so clear-cut: perhaps every fierce quarrel with the world is part of a campaign, or the aftermath of a pyrrhic victory, in the soul's everlasting quarrel with itself. If Yeats hated demagogues and agitators it was because he knew the sweet taste of their power, though he was too serious a poet ever to let it drug him. In *The Leaders of the Crowd* he is defining his chosen path:

> They must to keep their certainty accuse
> All that are different of a base intent....
> How can they know
> Truth flourishes where the student's lamp has shone,
> And there alone, that have no solitude?[16]

In an era of violence it took courage to say it. But his hatred is for the falseness of their false certitude and the cheapness of its rewards: neither here nor anywhere is he deeply moved by its cost in the sufferings of common humanity. The Christian virtue of compassion was not the strong point of his poetry. Sean O'Casey, who plunged into the rebellion, could express the splendour and sordidness and selfless heroism and petty selfishness of the common man's part in a revolution, and beside *Juno and the Paycock* and *The Plough and the Stars* all that Yeats wrote of those years is cold and self-enclosed.

One daughter of a 'big house', Constance Markievicz, had carried arms in Easter Week, and the troop she led was among the last to surrender. Because she was a woman the death-sentence passed on her was changed to life imprisonment. This, no doubt, was why Yeats left out her name from the roll of honour at the end of *Easter 1916*. His lines about her there are harsh:

> That woman's days were spent
> In ignorant good-will,
> Her nights in argument
> Until her voice grew shrill.

What impressed him was not the courage of her exploit but the ruin of a beauty that should have been sufficient to itself. In *On a Political Prisoner* [17] he thought of her, in the long emptiness of prison days, taming a seagull (she wrote of this in a letter to her sister), and remembered what she was like

> before her mind
> Became a bitter, an abstract thing,
> Her thought some popular enmity.

174

In those days she had seemed herself a bird

> Sea-borne, or balanced on the air
> When first it sprang out of the nest
> Upon some lofty rock to stare
> Upon the cloudy canopy,
> While under its storm-beaten breast
> Cried out the hollows of the sea.

The weird glory of that seabird is superficially as irrelevant, and by unanswerable poetic logic as deeply meaningful, as the perilous seas so improbably haunted by Keats' nightingale. It is all that the arguing intellect knows nothing of, all the intense life of spirit and instinct poised between unknown deeps above and below and around it, which Yeats' own poetry sought to realize.

It makes no difference to the poem that he was wrong about the Countess, if her letters from gaol reveal her. Whether in gaol or under arms, she lived more fully and freely in reckless adventure for a political idea than in the county society where Yeats had admired and preferred to think of her. Yeats could not see this because in his imagination she deputized for Maud Gonne; and it was an enduring legacy from his love that woman's beauty and the politician's rant stood for the extremes of good and evil. The perfection of beauty was life itself, possessed down to its minutest cell by spirit:

> All dreams of the soul
> End in a beautiful man's or woman's body.[18]

The other was the loud rattle of an intellectual machine.

But the dominant thought to which *Easter, 1916* had kept on returning was the world-changing finality of 'a terrible beauty is born', and this is echoed more matter-of-factly in *Sixteen Dead Men*:[19]

> O but we talked at large before
> The sixteen men were shot,
> But who can talk of give and take,
> What should be and what not
> While those dead men are loitering there
> To stir the boiling pot?

About ten years later, in a song from the play *The Resurrection*, come these lines:

> Odour of blood when Christ was slain
> Made all Platonic tolerance vain
> And vain all Doric discipline.[20]

It is the same thought reverberating in a wider context; the comparison shows how the Irish rising sank into his mind, to be merged with his whole philosophy of history.

Indirectly the rising had changed the course of his own life, for Sean MacBride's death set Maud Gonne free. He asked her again to marry him, and again and finally she refused. He asked her daughter Iseult, whom he loved with a mixture of protectiveness and passion, but she was too young to be happy with him and refused likewise. Then, with some misgivings, he made an end of that long story and married George Hyde-Lees, who brought him, besides happiness, her strange gift of the script of *A Vision*.

After 1917 he was gradually formulating the philosophy of *A Vision*, with Ireland as the background to his thoughts. These were years of general insurrection, of civil disobedience and guerilla fighting, which culminated in the British Government's 'Black and Tan' campaign of repression. Then came the Treaty of 1921. As plenipotentiaries for the insurgent government in Dublin, Michael Collins and Arthur Griffith accepted Dominion Status for Southern Ireland, leaving the six northern counties of Ulster under British rule. De Valera, who was head of the government, repudiated the agreement; some of his colleagues accepted it. Insurrection changed to civil war, which petered out gradually as the Free State Government established its authority. But ten years later De Valera came in by election, and then, by a peaceful revision of the Treaty, the Republic of Ireland came into being. Only Ulster remained a bone of contention, to be fought over intermittently.

There was romance in all this, especially at first, for young men and girls who campaigned up and down the country, burning police stations, derailing trains, robbing mails, setting up republican law courts and post offices in secret places in the hills, and carrying out the mandates of a ghostly government. There was also a swift degeneration into brutality, which never quite ceased to be tempered by a touch of romantic chivalry, except perhaps where religion embittered it between the Catholics of the South and the Ulster Protestants. Life grew cheap, leaders were murdered at the command of other leaders who had fought beside them a few months earlier, and the shiny surface of romance was cracked.

For non-combatants in the middle of it all day-to-day life went on, but with an edge of insecurity. People going about their shopping came to accept a burst of firing in the street as a momentary inter-ruption, or they listened to it in the fields at night and wondered, 'Is it a skirmish or is it the Irregulars out after duck?' Protestants in country houses would hear of neighbours who had lost everything overnight but their lives, with diminishing concern for the neigh-bours and growing unease for themselves. And although this was not the declared intention of either side, within a few years that whole class of the landed gentry which was Yeats' symbol of tradition and civilization was almost literally burnt out of the land.

Undoubtedly the European war, which hardly touched Ireland, was more demoralizing in many ways, as well as much vaster in its destructiveness, and a later war has made even that look small. But in a war of nations the ordinary man has no choice between ideas. The combatants are aligned automatically, the foreign enemy is only by a conscious effort to be realized as a human being and a potential neighbour. In a civil war, where men choose their sides and brothers may be in opposite camps, the issues come home with greater intimacy; the narrowing of sympathies, the cheapening of life, the sacrifice to ideas, are seen more clearly as acts of the will. Perhaps too the habit of humanity is suppressed with more difficulty and breaks through more often so that the tragedy of degeneration is less easy to ignore. Looked at from the chaotic post-war world this last episode in the Irish fight for freedom may appear—outside of Ireland—too negligible a portion of history, too circumscribed in its effects and too swiftly over, to be deeply significant. But it happened, as nothing can happen again, before men had grown used to the knowledge that civilization is a precarious possession. In most western minds the Russian Revolution was still a shadowy wonder in 1921, Fascism and total war had not been thought of, and 'ideology' was not yet a word in the common vocabulary. Yeats, whose imagination had remained cold to the war, was able to see in Ireland an epitome of things to come.

He was in and out of the country. He had bought and was repairing the dilapidated tower near Lady Gregory's house that he named Thoor Ballylee; he planned to settle there but hesitated on his wife's account till there were chances of a moderately quiet life. As he moved about he heard fresh reports of murders, saw traces of recent fighting here and there; he mentioned them in letters that, without losing a certain detachment, showed a deep concern for the country's future. He thought of Ireland as his home, no matter what uncongenial discords might be whirling through it, but he took no part in the civil war. Neither Free State nor Republic could have meant as much to him as the burning-out of the tradition Coole Park stood for, the way of life

> Where passion and precision had been one
> Time out of mind[21]

—though Coole Park itself was not burned, for Lady Gregory was loved in her own country. Long before the days of violence he had characterized the antagonist of his ideals as one

> Who, were it proved he lies,
> Were neither shamed in his own
> Nor in his neighbours' eyes.[22]

And while the violence went on his ghostly instructors were unfolding to him how civilizations rise and are swept away, and relating the process to the soul's adventures in eternity. He must have felt that

Ireland had become a crystal-gazer's mirror, focusing the whole of human history.

Much of this is contained in *Nineteen Hundred and Nineteen*.[23] It is a horror-stricken poem, or series of poems: Yeats seems to be realizing in his nerves things that brain and imagination had grasped already, and understanding deepens the horror at the same time that it just manages to control it. So intense is the feeling that he is carried out of himself; usually he writes in the singular, as himself or one of three or four dramatis personae who are voices of himself, but here for once he says 'we' as if he were the voice of humanity.

The first part is as masterly in its music, and compact intensity of thought, and seeming ease of utterance, as anything he had written yet. It begins as a lament for Athens:

> Many ingenious lovely things are gone
> That seemed sheer miracle to the multitude,
> Protected from the circle of the moon
> That pitches common things about. There stood
> Amid the ornamental bronze and stone
> An ancient image made of olive wood—
> And gone are Phidias' famous ivories
> And all the golden grasshoppers and bees.

—And our civilization too is going into the dark, with its different glories that seemed no less inviolable.

> We too had many pretty toys when young;
> A law indifferent to blame or praise,
> To bribe or threat....
>
> Now days are dragon-ridden, the nightmare
> Rides upon sleep: a drunken soldiery
> Can leave the mother, murdered at her door,*

* Cp. *Reprisals*:   Half-drunk or whole mad soldiery
        Are murdering your tenants there;
        Where may new-married women sit
        And suckle children now? Armed men
        May murder them in passing by....

Some of the incidents that provoked these lines are noted in Lady Gregory's *Journals*, ed. Lennox Robinson. For a clear picture of the times, with the misdeeds on both sides unexaggerated, the reader may consult *The Black and Tans* by Richard Bennett.

> To crawl in her own blood, and go scot-free;
> The night can sweat with terror as before
> We pieced our thoughts into philosophy,
> And planned to bring the world under a rule,
> Who are but weasels fighting in a hole.

The picture is drawn unmistakably from Ireland in the days of the Black and Tans, and to realize the bitterness of the disillusion one need only look back to the innocence of *Cathleen ni Houlihan* or to his speech at Wolfe Tone's centenary. In the face of Ireland he is reading the defeat of two thousand years of human endeavour.

> He who can read the signs nor sink unmanned
> Into the half-deceit of some intoxicant
> From shallow wits; who knows no work can stand,
> Whether health, wealth or peace of mind were spent
> On master-work of intellect or hand,
> No honour leave its mighty monument,
> Has but one comfort left: all triumph would
> But break upon his ghostly solitude.

His philosophy did not break down in the face of experience, nor prevaricate nor muffle the intensity of loss; only it gave him a kind of rooted steadfastness.

> But is there any comfort to be found?
> Man is in love and loves what vanishes,
> What more is there to say?

The unimaginable, that happened to Babylon and to Egypt and to Athens, is happening to us now; and it is no consolation, but a bleak fact, that the human spirit will survive it.

The next part expounds the Platonic Year.

> When Loie Fuller's Chinese dancers enwound
> A shining web, a floating ribbon of cloth,
> It seemed that a dragon of air
> Had fallen among dancers, had whirled them round
> Or hurried them off on its own furious path.

The symbol is subtle, for the dragon seems to control men, and is created by them; and yet again, since they are not free-stepping men but dancers, the dragon only makes visible the predetermined rhythm their feet obey. It is as if the poet retreated to a vast distance where particulars are obliterated and time congealed into a form, and the shape of all creation becomes visible. It has the force of sudden, absolute detachment, like death, severing the soul from its creations and flinging it upon its own solitude—the leap of the swan into the desolate heaven.

> Some Platonist affirms that in the station
> Where we should cast off body and trade
> The ancient habit sticks,
> And that if our works could
> But vanish with our breath
> That were a lucky death,
> For triumph can but mar our solitude.

Suddenly the awareness of solitude becomes an intense excitement, that is seen in a momentary flash to be in itself the impulse of destruction:

> The swan has leaped into the desolate heaven:
> That image can bring wildness, bring a rage
> To end all things.

The meaning of these lines is illuminated if one looks forward sixteen years to *Meru*:

> Civilisation is hooped together, brought
> Under a rule, under the semblance of peace
> By manifold illusion; but man's life is thought,
> And he, despite his terror, cannot cease
> Ravening through century after century,
> Ravening, raging, and uprooting that he may come
> Into the desolation of reality.[24]

But in 1919 it was too vast a solitude to sustain, and in the next two parts he returns to stare with tormented mockery at the fiasco of human life:

> We, who seven years ago
> Talked of honour and of truth,
> Shriek with pleasure if we show
> The weasel's twist, the weasel's tooth.

The last part is a whirl of violent images, beauty dissolving into delirium as the times worsen, and ending, as if to clamp the whole meditation down to Ireland, with 'an evil spirit much run after in Kilkenny at the start of the fourteenth century':

> There lurches past, his great eyes without thought
> Under the shadow of stupid straw-pale locks,
> That insolent fiend Robert Artisson
> To whom the love-lorn Lady Kyteler brought
> Bronzed peacock feathers, red combs of her cocks.

This is at the opposite pole from Mr T. S. Eliot's

> This is the way the world ends,
> Not with a bang but a whimper[25]

—but for all its energy it is as near to despair and to utter loss of control as the end of any poem Yeats ever wrote. Taken as a continuous meditation the six parts all but lose coherence. The first, perfect in itself, expresses a terrifying contradiction without denying either side:

> Man is in love and loves what vanishes,
> What more is there to say?

But one cannot rest in a contradiction, and in trying to resolve it he follows the two threads of the heart's and the mind's understanding, to find them moving further apart. He is like a baffled lover raging at the world, and taking a vow of celibacy: at one minute exulting in freedom, at the next furious over failure. But there is the courage of tragedy in refusing any false reconcilement. His poetry is what he said civilization was, a struggle for control; the passion must be powerful enough to wrestle with an angel and this is only the first round of the match.

In the political tension when it was written *Nineteen Hundred and Nineteen* could have met with little understanding in Ireland or England. It was published in both countries in 1921 in literary journals: after that it waited for *The Tower* volume of 1928 where it was printed with two other meditations, dated, but arranged in reverse chronological order so that one reads back to it from the achieved aloofness of *The Tower* (1926) through *Meditations in Time of Civil War*[26] (1923).

Meditations is an altogether more collected poem. It takes up the same theme of the ruined ancestral houses, but by this time ruin is no longer an impending horror but an accomplished fact. The first part is a noble and less rebellious lament. Birth, wealth, tradition: essentially his love for these was a worship of freedom, of the creative energy of life springing fountain-like for its own delight. He thought of the houses as founded by strong chieftains who asked no man's leave to spend life and wealth as they chose; and because the free spirit was at home in them poets of old time had found both themes and shelter there. And yet, what are they now?

> Mere dreams, mere dreams! Yet Homer had not sung
> Had he not found it certain beyond dreams
> That out of life's own self-delight had sprung
> The abounding glittering jet; though now it seems
> As if some marvellous empty sea-shell flung
> Out of the obscure dark of the rich streams,
> And not a fountain, were the symbol which
> Shadows the inherited glory of the rich.

The image itself, and the argument of the verses that follow, are a reluctant acquiescence in their doom, for he acknowledges that there was decay from within; the very sweetness and beauty of the aristocrat's court puts to sleep that furious energy that created and sustains it.

> O what if levelled walks and gravelled ways
> Where slippered Contemplation finds his ease
> And Childhood a delight for every sense,
> But take our greatness with our violence?

Against it he sets the enduring bareness of Thoor Ballylee, symbolic of the life he has chosen:

> An acre of stony ground,
> Where the symbolic rose can break in flower,
> . . . .
> A winding stair, a chamber arched with stone,

> A grey stone fireplace with an open hearth,
> A candle and written page.
> *Il Penseroso*'s Platonist toiled on
> In some like chamber, shadowing forth
> How the daemonic rage
> Imagined everything.

Here, if anywhere, his soul may remain a habitation for the daemonic rage, and his children inherit the vigour of his mind. When the tower means this no longer, let it be a nesting-place for owls. And from this stronghold he looks out with a sort of half-detachment, seeing the civil war as part of the everlasting flux.

> We had fed the heart on fantasies,
> The heart's grown brutal from the fare;
> More substance in our enmities
> Than in our loves...

is a devastatingly plain statement. But plain statement cannot convey all he sees: in the last section he is back among such visions as filled his early poems, and even the tune of the verse is remembered from twenty years ago. He is looking from the tower at phantoms, forming and dissolving in the wind-stirred mist that rolls under a sword-like moon, 'phantoms of hatred and of the heart's fullness and of the coming emptiness', images of alternating phases of the world's life. Last among them comes a vision of brazen hawks:

> Nothing but grip of claw, and the eye's complacency,
> The innumerable clanging wings that have put out the moon

—the spirit of a new age that cares only for the ruthless, organized efficiency of power.

Nineteen Hundred and Nineteen had ended in such dissolving visions, only more widely incoherent, but here the last words are a collected personal statement, finally if a little wistfully separating himself from what he sees:

> I turn away and shut the door, and on the stair
> Wonder how many times I could have proved my worth
> In something that all others understand or share;

But O! ambitious heart, had such a proof drawn forth
A company of friends, a conscience set at ease,
It had but made us pine the more. The abstract joy,
The half-read wisdom of daemonic images,
Suffice the ageing man as once the growing boy.

Fact and symbol, world and soul, history and eternity, are woven together in this poem with the utmost intricacy. He has found a standpoint to harmonize them, and the 'ghostly solitude' that exhilarated and appalled him in the earlier poem is now an accepted condition of life.

From this to the solitary meditation of *The Tower*[27] (1926) is a natural transition. The tower itself is more than ever the centre of his imagination, but the surrounding landscape is quiet now (for the war is over) and alive with its retention of a more ancient past. 'The world', in the sense of actions that make history, has receded to the background; his argument now is between the contemplative soul and the passionate heart that lives through experience. The soul wins this round, but only just, and perhaps only in theory, for the whole poem is crowded with experience both actual and imaginary: but at any rate it ends facing towards eternity:

Now shall I make my soul,
Compelling it to study
In a learned school
Till the wreck of body,
Slow decay of blood,
Testy delirium
Or dull decrepitude,
Or what worse evil come—
The death of friends, or death
Of every brilliant eye
That made a catch in the breath—
Seem but the clouds of the sky
When the horizon fades;
Or a bird's sleepy cry
Among the deepening shades.

Not that Yeats ever withdrew from the world, or even from public life; his poetry is a perpetual wrestling-match between the soul in time and the soul in eternity. While he was writing the two last of these three poems he was a conscientious senator in the new Irish Free State, and to the end of his life he took a fiery interest in Irish politics. The three, read in sequence, show a continuous movement from the turbulence of *Nineteen Hundred and Nineteen* to a detachment seven years later, which was very far from indifference. On the way, in 1921, he wrote that astonishing poem *The Second Coming*,[28] which sets his own age in the perspective of eternity.

The world that is ending is in the first eight lines. He still has in mind the flaming Irish country houses, but the description is less localized, though not less precisely worded, than in *Nineteen Hundred and Nineteen*.

> The blood-dimmed tide is loosed, and everywhere
> The ceremony of innocence is drowned;
> The best lack all conviction, while the worst
> Are full of passionate intensity.

This is not so much the description of a scene as a historian's verdict on it. The thought of Doomsday—the Second Coming—follows naturally from the description; and then there rises suddenly 'a great vision out of *Spiritus Mundi*', condensing a whole philosophy of history into itself so that it has the force of prophecy. At first it is the image, uncouth and ominous, that sinks into the reader's mind. But stare at it long enough, and the latent meaning begins to emerge even without help from *Dove or Swan*.

Now is the breakdown of our two-thousand-year-old civilization— something like this the implicit argument runs—and out of its ruins what is taking shape? What was Christianity to the Graeco-Roman world into which it came? (One may recall that Tacitus could make nothing of it; in an inquiry more puzzled than hostile he concluded that Christians were enemies of the human race.) It conquered at last in the sign of the cross, the emblem of a condemned criminal, that is, of everything rejected by the commonsense of two thousand years. Or again, what is summed up in the Sphinx, who survives from an age before those two thousand years began? To her blank gaze, which is neither Christ's nor Apollo's, would Notre Dame and the Acropolis seem equally false and frivolous in their design? No scheme of values can include the whole of reality; always something must be left out of its proportions, to gather strength in the womb of time till the inevitable hour for its assertion; and therefore the new civilization never appears as the outcome of the old, but always as its doom. The only thing we know of it for certain is that it will appear monstrous and terrifying to those whose traditions it supersedes.

This is a verbose way of putting what comes to life all at once in the image. What is being born was engendered from something neither Greek nor Christian but more primeval, overlooked by both; it is as remote from our understanding as Bethlehem from that of the ancient world:

> Now I know
> That twenty centuries of stony sleep
> Were vexed to nightmare by a rocking cradle,
> And what rough beast, its hour come round at last,
> Slouches towards Bethlehem to be born?

The Second Coming, with its vision of Christianity superseded, must have germinated in Yeats' mind for at least seven years, for in a short poem in *Responsibilities* he sees the Magi, still searching from the sky

> With all their ancient faces like rain-beaten stones,...
> Hoping to find once more,
> Being by Calvary's turbulence unsatisfied,
> The uncontrollable mystery on the bestial floor.[29]

The thought belongs to an argument that links it with *Leda*, and the two plays *Calvary* and *The Resurrection*, and some of the 'supernatural' poems of his last ten years; but to follow it further would take me far beyond the theme of this chapter. I wish only to point out how the urgency of present events, coming at the same time as the far-reaching synthesis and the store of coherent imagery which *A Vision* was bringing him, quickened his poetry into something very like prophecy.

Mr T. S. Eliot has also, in two poems, pictured the birth of Christianity disturbing the values of the ancient world: like Yeats, he sees it as birth and death in one. His Simeon in the Temple foresees the long martyrdom of the Church and prays for death with an emotion less simple than the 'Lord now lettest Thou Thy servant depart in peace' of the Gospel:

> I am tired with my own life and the lives of those after me,
> I am dying in my own death, and the deaths of those after me,
> Let thy servant depart,
> Having seen thy salvation.

The old men in his *Journey of the Magi* querulously want to know:

> Were we led all this way for
> Birth or death? There was a birth, certainly,
> We had evidence and no doubt. I had seen birth and death
> But had thought they were different; this birth was
> Hard and bitter agony for us, like death, our death.

They appear to return home without peace of mind, hardly more satisfied than Yeats' Magi by Calvary's turbulence, and yet no longer at ease in the old world, 'with an alien people clutching their gods'.

Yeats and Eliot, besides standing out among the poets of our century, have certain things in common. Both are intensely aware of man in history and of the soul in eternity, both at times see history as an image of the soul writ large. Both see an uncongenial world disintegrating and an unknowable future taking shape in the surrounding dark.

> What are the roots that clutch, what branches grow
> Out of this stony rubbish? Son of man
> You cannot know nor tell, for you know only
> A heap of broken images—[30]

Both call in eternity to redress the balance of time. Even their images touch, for Eliot's 'still centre of the turning world' and Yeats' gyres revolving round a timeless axis express a like relation of time to eternity.

And yet how different! Two minds looking at the same scene are worlds apart in themselves. Mr Eliot, within the circle of Christian revelation, sees it as ultimate and all-inclusive: history will not go forward to anything other than Christ. There is one world, whose values are the values of death, and one faith that is a rejection of the world and a surrender to eternal life; the surrender is always to be made and is the only answer to the troubles of the soul or of history. His wheel revolves about the Christian values of conviction of sin, humility and renunciation. Possibly the majority of English-speaking people of our day do not think long and deeply about salvation, but if there is another world they acknowledge that the way to it is the way of the Cross. Mr Eliot speaks the language they know, and this gives him a power over his generation that is not the same thing as his greatness as a poet, but is hard to disentangle from it.

In Yeats' supernatural order, as in Satan's, there is no surrender. Spirit, which is both one and many, is the source and centre of all things; its life is in the drama of the world that it creates and acts for ever. To live in eternity is to abandon oneself to the allotted part and still to remain aware that the play goes on and the actors outlive the scenes. And Christian civilization is only a two-thousand-year episode, like others that have preceded and will follow it, a true but partial expression of the eternal spirit. Contemplating a wrecked world, he does not learn to renounce life and passion, but detaches them from time, declares that they belong to eternity and will be rebuilt again and again in new forms. This is his answer to cataclysm, so unlike the orthodox answer that it makes eternity seem an unfamiliar place. Because it is unfamiliar, readers who grasp Yeats' meaning often wonder if he really meant it, whereas they do not doubt Mr Eliot's Christianity, whether or not they share it. Although one need not share a poet's beliefs to enjoy his poetry, the enjoyment is marred if the poet himself is suspected of shamming. But however unorthodox, it is no sham conviction that moulds the whole of Yeats' poetry; under the symbolism there is a faith deeply felt and coherently thought out, and closely integrated with his experience of life.*

* When I wrote this I had not yet read F. A. C. Wilson's *W. B. Yeats and Tradition*. With more learning in the relevant field than most of Yeats' critics can show, it establishes not only the intrinsic coherence of his thought but its ancient and honourable ancestry.

CHAPTER XI

THE SWORDSMAN

By clarity of conviction and mastery of technique Yeats had come to the height of his power in *The Tower* and *The Winding Stair*, and both style and thought had a strange, not always easy lucidity. *Meditations in Time of Civil War* shows much of its range. No modern poet has so mastered traditional stanza forms of the kind that Chaucer handed down through Spenser to the Romantics; perhaps none of any time has written stanzas at once so rich in music and so compact in thought and phrase. His language had lost the eclectic pre-Raphaelite decorativeness of his early days, had grown more trenchant and adaptable to a wider range of ideas. He was no longer afraid of abstract thought, nor on the other hand did his vocabulary exclude the actual world; when he chose he could put the starkest facts into the starkest words. But above all he thought naturally in symbols, and had learnt to manipulate them to convey swift transitions and intricate connections of thought. For instance, in the lines about the Japanese sword on his table they work at lightning speed:

> In Sato's house,
> Curved like new moon, moon-luminous,
> It lay five hundred years.
> Yet if no change appears
> No moon; only an aching heart
> Conceives a changeless work of art.

The new moon is a natural image for the beauty of the curved sword; but because the moon governs passionate life it reminds him that without passion, which is grief and change, no enduring beauty can be created; and he thinks what long-sustained passion must have kept alive the chivalry of Japan. A chord is touched and his whole philosophy vibrates in answer. And this is recalled in the last section, in the moon of phantoms:

> That seems unlike itself, that seems unchangeable,
> A glittering sword out of the east

—and so a cumulative meaning is given to the final vision of passion-less mechanical power, as

> The innumerable clanging wings that have put out the moon.

Or again in the sixth section, fact and argument and image are blended in a complex piece of symbolic thinking which keeps close to actual life.

A symbol is not a mere substitute for an abstract idea, and though every use of it has an immediate meaning there are always others latent, ready to come to the surface with a slight shift of emphasis. Think for instance of the Cross. A Christian may speak of 'the way of the Cross', thinking in his context simply of the acceptance of suffering, but somewhere behind it the idea of participation in Christ's atonement gives value to accepted suffering, and behind this again is the idea of ultimate triumph in the world of the spirit; potentially the phrase evokes the relation between God and man as Christian thought conceives it, and though only a fragment of this may be in the speaker's thought at the moment, and some of it he may never have understood, it cannot be completely cut off from the image.

Yeats' thoughts, as we have seen, are related together in ways that differ profoundly both from modern materialism and from orthodox religion. His symbols map them, but to follow them closely the reader needs to be alert. The more fully he understands an image in one poem the richer its meaning becomes in others.

> Some moralist or mythological poet
> Compares the solitary soul to a swan

he says in *Nineteen Hundred and Nineteen*. Some years earlier he had seen in the swans at Coole Park[1] the inviolable, unageing eternity of nature contrasted with time-ridden human experience.

> Unwearied still, lover by lover,
> They paddle in the cold
> Companionable streams or climb the air;
> Their hearts have not grown old;
> Passion or conquest, wander where they will,
> Attend upon them still;

and this timeless immunity entering into his conception of the soul
adds an overtone to

> The swan has leaped into the desolate heaven[2]

in the stormy nightfall of civilization. But this swan that sails out of
time is also Zeus, for the gods too are mirrors of the soul of man;
Zeus the swan, whose wayward impulse ravished Leda and brought
to birth the world Homer sang of:

> A shudder in the loins engenders there
> The broken wall, the burning roof and tower
> And Agamemnon dead.[3]

He ruled western thought for two thousand years, when divinity
was seen mirrored in nature rather than shining beyond it. And
echoes of these thoughts are gathered into *Coole Park and Ballylee*[4] in
the lines about the 'sudden thunder of the mounting swan':

> Another emblem there! That stormy white
> But seems a concentration of the sky;
> And, like the soul, it sails into the sight
> And in the morning's gone, no man knows why;
> And is so lovely that it sets to right
> What knowledge or its lack had set awry,
> So arrogantly pure, a child might think
> It can be murdered with a spot of ink

and in the last lines of the poem they re-echo, giving fuller meaning
to his lament for the passing of romantic poetry:

> But all is changed, that high horse riderless,
> Though mounted in that saddle Homer rode
> Where the swan drifts upon a darkening flood.

It is not a different swan standing for a different idea each time, nor yet a code-word for a fixed idea, but the same swan acting in different ways, much like a living bird; there is a cluster of thoughts which affect each other, and now one, now another is in front.

From the swan to Homer by way of these last lines is an easy transition, for where the swan led the poet followed. Homer is his ideal poetic self, as appears in a pregnant answer given by the heart to the soul in *Vacillation*:[5]

> *Soul:* Look on that fire, salvation walks within.
> *Heart:* What theme had Homer but original sin?

And he bids farewell to Von Hügel with

> Homer is my example and his unchristened heart.*

For by the standards of Christian asceticism all that glorying in passionate experience, summed up in the swan, is changed into the lust of the flesh and the lust of the eyes and the pride of life. From Homer to Helen; and Helen's beauty is inseparable in his thought from Maud Gonne's, and thus symbol is interwoven with living experience. The pattern of the tapestry is inexhaustible. It is partly this intricacy that gives Yeats' later poetry its intense power: it fills the simple words with deep, half discernible meaning.

But symbols are not all. If Yeats had desired only to expound an abstract faith, if eternity were all that mattered, he might have disregarded the surface facts of life and created a symbolical world in the rapt, almost disembodied language of his early manner. This later poetry is embodied faith, and is alive with things temporal, with his passing thoughts and the countryside and his tower, and above all with people, living and dead. Often a stray comment when his eye is on the object will light up both the object and the mind behind the eye. Sometimes his philosophy is brought into play deliberately, as in the portrait of Lady Gregory in *Coole Park*.[6] He sees her as

---

* Virginia Moore puts a different construction on this passage. I reached my view before reading her book, and having read it am unconvinced by the argument; but her chapter, 'Was Yeats a Christian?', should be read by anyone interested in the question.

a central personality, harmonizing, like the axis of one of his symbolic gyres, a group of creative minds in a design that makes each one greater than itself; and the living woman and the philosophical figure interpret one another:

> They came like swallows and like swallows went,
> And yet a woman's powerful character
> Could keep a swallow to its first intent;
> And half a dozen in formation there,
> That seemed to whirl upon a compass-point,
> Found certainty upon the dreaming air,
> The intellectual sweetness of those lines
> That cut through time or cross it withershins.

Or again, in *Blood and the Moon*,[7] his four beloved masters of the eighteenth century are presented in four word-pictures, each as it seems for his own sake, but so marshalled that they bear witness collectively to Yeats' scheme of thought:

Swift beating on his breast in sibylline frenzy blind
Because the heart in his blood-sodden breast had dragged him down into mankind,
Goldsmith deliberately sipping at the honey-pot of his mind,

And haughtier-headed Burke that proved the State a tree,
That this unconquerable labyrinth of the birds, century after century,
Cast but dead leaves to mathematical equality;

And God-appointed Berkeley that proved all things a dream,
That this pragmatical, preposterous pig of a world, its farrow that so solid seem,
Must vanish on the instant if the mind but change its theme;

Saeva Indignatio and the labourer's hire,
The strength that gives our blood and state magnanimity of its own desire;
Everything that is not God consumed with intellectual fire.

Sometimes it seems to come unselfconsciously to the surface, in a way more revealing than a planned statement. In *Among School Children*[8] the children at their desks make him think of Maud Gonne as she must have been in childhood; and of mothers' dreams for their children, and then how even the profoundest wisdom is

inadequate to compensate for that bodily perfection which is life's
natural ideal:

> Plato thought nature but a spume that plays
> Upon a ghostly paradigm of things;
> Solider Aristotle played the taws
> Upon the bottom of a king of kings;
> World-famous golden-thighed Pythagoras
> Fingered upon a fiddle-stick or strings
> What a star sang and careless Muses heard:
> Old clothes upon old sticks to scare a bird.

The language is light-hearted but not shallow; there is a depth of
admiration in the sketches of all three philosophers. There is also
irony in the punning play upon 'play' that carries him from Plato's
belittling of phenomena to the practical Aristotle's buttock-drum-
ming (presumptive but fair, since Aristotle was tutor to Alexander
the Great) and thence to the Pythagorean music of the spheres. It
prepares for their abrupt dismissal; and the sudden descent from
the romantic phrasing of the fifth, sixth and seventh lines to the racy,
earthly idiom of 'old clothes upon old sticks to scare a bird' is a
dramatic use of language, which delivers judgement by changing
the perspective.

A verse in *All Souls' Night*:

> Two thoughts were so mixed up I could not tell
> Whether of her or God he thought the most,
> But think that his mind's eye,
> When upward turned, on one sole image fell;
> And that a slight companionable ghost,
> Wild with divinity,
> Had so lit up the whole
> Immense miraculous house
> The Bible promised us,
> It seemed a gold-fish swimming in a bowl[9]

—is, first of all, an affectionate recollection of a friend. But on its
haphazard path from God to the goldfish it becomes much more.
'A slight companionable ghost, Wild with divinity' turning heaven

into a fish-bowl is superb hyperbole mingled with ironic mockery. Theology has changed its proportions, for the ghost is not mocked but heaven is, though unmaliciously. Alive with his own faith, Yeats reveals its contours in speaking of his friend's, and because he is not arguing a case but speaking his mind quietly all the subtle under-tones of thought and feeling find expression. It is like good talk where a man's whole soul comes into play in a casual repartee.

In February 1926, in a letter to Professor Grierson,[10] Yeats praises some lines from *Don Juan* as 'almost perfect personal speech', and goes on:

The over-childish or over-pretty or feminine element in some good Wordsworth and in much poetry up to our date comes from the lack of natural momentum in the syntax. This momentum underlies almost every Elizabethan and Jacobean lyric and is far more important than simplicity of vocabulary. If Wordsworth had found it he could have carried any amount of elaborate English.... Perhaps in our world only an amateur can seek it at all—unless he keep to the surface like Kipling—or somebody like myself who seeks it with an intense unnatural labour that reduces composition to four or five lines a day. In a less artificial age it would come with our baby talk. The amateur has the necessary ease of soul but only succeeds a few times in his life.

What he sought with such intensity may be seen in the passages already quoted. Take one, almost at random:

> though now it seems
> As if some marvellous empty sea-shell flung
> Out of the obscure dark of the rich streams,
> And not a fountain, were the symbol which
> Shadows the inherited glory of the rich.

He maintains the formal pattern without losing an apparent natural-ness of phrase. He gives full value to melodious words like 'marvel-lous' and 'inherited' casually, exploiting the riches of the language without forcing it. Shakespeare in his maturity uses words so, only far more exuberantly. Tennyson is more ostentatious. In such lines as

> Now thy forum roars no longer,
> fallen every purple Caesar's dome

musical resonance and the turning of sensations into sounds have become a sort of conjuring-trick; he is performing rather than speaking. Yeats' sentence is spoken thought developing as it moves. This part of it is an afterthought to the beginning of the verse, yet complete in itself, and the balance of the two phrases 'As if some marvellous empty sea-shell flung Out of the obscure dark of the rich streams, And not a fountain' has an unpremeditated ring; it would be top-heavy if the second had not a space cleared about it, so to speak, by its position at the beginning of the final couplet. The eager, springing syntax carries the whole thought across rhymes and line-endings like a jumping cat, kicking off from an almost imperceptible touch on the footholds and coming to rest with assured poise.

In a different key is

> An affable Irregular,
> A heavily-built Falstaffian man,
> Comes cracking jokes of civil war
> As though to die by gunshot were
> The finest play under the sun.[11]

Here is objective report with implied comment, and it would be impossible, by doing away with the metre, to put it in a sentence more concisely clear. It differs from conversational talk only by the absence of every unnecessary word; in talk one would perhaps say 'comes along' for 'comes', or turn the last clause round with 'as though it were the finest play—' and maybe add a few superfluous details, but none of this would make it better talk. The economy has not destroyed the movement of life.

Spoken syntax is expressed in time, not space. A voice can vary the length of its pauses, for which punctuation is a clumsy measurement, and its pace, which has no direct notation on paper, and its stress and tone, which can change the point of a sentence or the meaning of a word; with all these resources a speaker will often jump verbal links, leaving out pronouns, relatives and conjunctions

without loss of precision. Writing translates speech from the ear
to the eye, and a man writing to be read must put all this meaning
into the order of words and the accuracy of his connectives, so that
his sentences are bound to flow differently. Good talk is learnt from
good talkers: 'to speak like a book', the semi-literate man's ambition,
is to miss the most vital resources of speech in a stilted imitation of
an imitation. Living thought is a mind thinking, not an abstraction
from a mind; it is in motion, and since words are speech first of all,
speech syntax follows its movement more closely than written prose.
When the thought is most spontaneous and the relation between
speaker and hearers most unstudied, the speech is most alive.

Yeats rightly says that this is more important than a simple vocabulary. Studied simplicity can be as artificial as studied grandiloquence:
either falls short of poetic good manners by offering the reader
something other than the respect due to an equal, and either way
the unnatural vocabulary will make the phrasing move unnaturally
as surely as bodily movements are cramped by ill-fitting clothes.
'Ease of soul' only comes when the language is natural between
speaker and hearer, so that its reception may be taken for granted
and all that need be studied is its precision in relation to the moving
thought.

If the Jacobeans had this natural grace it was partly because with
all its formality their age was less convention-ridden. A gentleman's
ambition was not to be indistinguishable from other gentlemen;
eccentricity, provided that it had style and was not mere ineptitude,
could be accepted as a part of good breeding. But such diversity
would be impossible if an underlying unity of culture were not taken
for granted. Nowadays we live in a superficially coherent world,
where those who converse have no depth of understanding in common.
Instead they have clichés and conventions to simulate the easy swing
of freedom in surface communications, so that whatever depths
they have need not be sounded. But besides this, the Jacobean poet
had the advantage of listening more than he read, and listening to

speech that had not been flattened out by school reading-lessons. His ears could tell him how to vitalize his rhythms by natural stress and pause.

Whether or not these are the reasons, certainly most modern poets write something other than heightened speech. To throw off traditional metres may lead to greater precision of phrase, but it does not necessarily restore the sound of the voice. Whereas Yeats' later work always has the authentic ring of speech although he writes in metre. Sometimes his obscurities arise from this; a meaning ambiguous on paper can be cleared up, when the movement of thought is understood as a whole, by an inflection of the voice.

Musical speech, accompanied by a stringed instrument, had been one of his preoccupations from early days. It was part of his dramatic technique, of a piece with his desire to create through ritual art the 'ceremony' he dreamed of. He was not concerned with this in the poems of these two books; indeed they have so much nerve and movement that they seem to belong organically to actual life, and to set them to a psaltery would be like cutting them out to be framed; but undoubtedly the discipline of writing for the psaltery had sharpened his keen ear for stress and cadence. And this perhaps helped to give his lyrics their individual singing note: they are not actual songs, but there is a lilt in the words. For instance:

> When cradle and spool are past
> And I mere shade at last
> Coagulate of stuff
> Transparent like the wind,
> I think that I may find
> A faithful love, a faithful love.[12]

Or:

> A lonely ghost the ghost is
> That to God shall come;
> I—love's skein upon the ground,
> My body in the tomb—
> Shall leap into the light lost
> In my mother's womb.[13]

Few modern poets can sing, or care to except in rare snatches, mostly satiric; perhaps most of them would say that the simplicity of song excludes the complicated thoughts and emotions which burden our age. Yet the thought in both of these, and the vocabulary in the first, is abstruse, and the feeling though poignant is too equivocal to be given a name. They sing or chant themselves from sheer rightness of sound. The content is more intricate and the expression barer than that of the lyrics in *The Wind Among the Reeds*, and the lyrical tune is in no way imposed, but grows from the words themselves. The lightness of song comes not so much from simplicity as from a kind of assurance, when the tongue finds speech for what is believed in the bones, whether or not it echoes a common faith. This assurance distinguishes Yeats from nearly all his contemporaries; as he aged his thought grew lonelier and more recondite, but his power of song increased.

He was a laborious artist whose whole labour was to make the word transparent to the thought. He is thus the least imitable of masters. A young poet, lacking the Eliotic vision, might yet turn to account Mr Eliot's allusiveness, his contemporary imagery, his studied anticlimax like the trailing away of a well-bred English voice. From the later Yeats he could borrow hardly anything usable, not even the symbolism, for it would be heavily pretentious stuff if it did not express an integrated vision precisely. Yeats' style is stripped, and utterly dependent on the intense life of his mind, for which it has been moulded to a perfect instrument; without that it would have the negative virtues of direct, unaffected speech. When he is difficult it is because of the thought; and the thought is not confused, but too well-knit and too remote from most people's preconceptions to be followed easily.

I have described his continuous theme as a wrestling-match between the soul in eternity and the soul in time, or the self or the heart as he variously calls it, but the word is too narrow for the intricacy of their shifting relationship. For a formula to cover it one has to go back to *A Vision*. At any rate there is the embodied self that lives and dies and alone is capable of passionate experiences; this self is and is not the same as the enduring being who projects it into life after life. The poet is both, and now one is up, now the other. At the end of *The Tower* and in the two *Byzantium* poems eternity is winning after a fashion, for he writes as an ageing man preparing to leave the world of the senses.

Byzantium is beyond the world. In *A Vision*[14] he thought of it as the one moment in history when an inclusive idea had been almost perfectly embodied in a civilization; the nearest approach to the Full Moon of early Christianity.

The painter, the mosaic worker, the worker in gold and silver, the illuminator of sacred books, were almost impersonal, almost perhaps without the consciousness of individual design, absorbed in their subject matter and that the vision of a whole people.

Impersonal and changeless, such art is a truer image of the eternal soul than the artist is who makes it. He is tired of the flux of time and seeks to be purged of passion, but it is characteristic of him that he seeks the fixity of pure form, not dissolution into the formless infinite.

> Once out of nature I shall never take
> My bodily form from any natural thing,
> But such a form as Grecian goldsmiths make
> Of hammered gold and gold enamelling
> To keep a drowsy Emperor awake;
> Or set upon a golden bough to sing
> To lords and ladies of Byzantium
> Of what is past, or passing, or to come.[15]

Sailing to Byzantium explains itself, but *Byzantium*,[16] written three years later, is powerful before it is intelligible. It has an authentic but fragmentary quality like Cassandra's second sight in the *Agamemnon*, as if he has been to an unimaginable place and is speaking of it, but in words to which some of the clues are missing. The intensity with which it is seen and felt almost overwhelms the translatable meaning. It is night; the daylight revelry fades away, leaving the austere silence of a deserted pavement and a dome towering against the stars. Gradually the place is felt to be possessed by spirits and one from the dead, 'death-in-life and life-in-death', leads him to the bird on the golden bough; and then there breaks, in light and sound and movement, the vision of an unearthly purposeful activity.

The bird on the golden bough, in the earlier poem, was the form of the poet's own soul. It was the same golden bough that Aeneas carried to the underworld, and thus Byzantium is the world beyond life, described in the book of *A Vision* called *The Soul in Judgment*. There, it was made clear that Yeats' cosmography has no final Paradise. In life the soul seeks passionate experience; after death it assimilates, masters and finally discards the memory of its experience, until it is purified and ready for 'the Marriage', which is a trance of pure beatitude, a reunion with absolute Spirit; and then it enters life afresh. There is no judgement but its own upon itself, when all its life has passed before it.

I think of a girl in a Japanese play whose ghost tells a priest of a slight sin, if indeed it was a sin, which seems great because of her exaggerated conscience. She is surrounded by flames, and though the priest explains that if she but ceased to believe in these flames they would cease to exist, believe she must, and the play ends in an elaborate dance, the dance of her agony.[17]

And in another passage:

'We have no power', said an inhabitant of that state,[18] 'except to purify our intention.' 'Of what?' 'Of complexity.'

'That state', anatomized in the prose book, is actually witnessed in the poem:

> At midnight on the Emperor's pavement flit
> Flames that no faggot feeds, nor steel has lit,
> Nor storm disturbs, flames begotten of flame,
> Where blood-begotten spirits come
> And all complexities of fury leave,
> Dying into a dance,
> An agony of trance,
> An agony of flame that cannot singe a sleeve.

The dolphins with their mire and blood in the last verse are the living bodies on which spirits ride to Byzantium across the sea of time. They come with all the confusion of sense and passion on them to be purged and stilled in the dance of pure mind; this is made clear in *The Soul in Judgment*. And the smithies against which the sea breaks in vain must be where the golden bird is hammered into its eternal form.

'A starlit or a moonlit dome—' The alternative lighting suggests to me that Yeats himself was not sure whether the vision he had seen belonged to the full or the dark of the moon, the moment of realization of self or of its absorption into the changeless universal being. But among those complex gyres and counter-gyres, 'each one living the other's death, dying the other's life', the illumination of one form of being is always the darkness of another. In his own terminology, he was 'antithetical' man, who could only seek death as a clearing of the ground for intenser life, and that is why the energy of the smithies is the poem's keynote, rather than the serenity of the dome. In *Sailing to Byzantium* it seemed that one had only to touch that shore to attain deliverance from passionate life, and that the 'sages standing in God's holy fire' were at rest, but now that he is there this furious imagery of purgation tells a different story.*

Although between death and birth the senses are withdrawn, he conceives of this state no less than bodily existence as related to the spirit's life in time. Within and around it, however, there is a timeless darkness, 'Everything that is not God consumed with intellectual fire'. Absorption in that darkness is the mystic's goal, the ultimate truth which delivers from birth and death. It is different from Byzantium and Yeats was not seeking it, but from early youth he had acknowledged its reality. In *A Dialogue of Self and Soul*[19] the Soul summons the Self towards it:

---

* Jeffares (*W. B. Yeats, Man and Poet*, pp. 261–2) points out one reason for the difference: Yeats wrote *Byzantium* after an illness that had brought him very near to death. The prospect no longer has the serenity of far-off cliffs.

> Fix every wandering thought upon
> That quarter where all thought is done:
> Who can distinguish darkness from the soul?

The Self counters with Sato's sword, 'consecrated', the emblem of a will to action outlasting life after life. He is old and has no illusions about life; what matter

> The ignominy of boyhood; the distress
> Of boyhood changing into man;
> The unfinished man and his pain
> Brought face to face with his own clumsiness;
> The finished man among his enemies?

And still, knowing it all, he rejects the summons:

> I am content to live it all again
> And yet again....
> I am content to follow to its source
> Every event in action or in thought;
> Measure the lot; forgive myself the lot!
> When such as I cast out remorse
> So great a sweetness flows into the breast
> We must laugh and we must sing,
> We are blest by everything,
> Everything we look upon is blest.

What the Self rejects is the mystic's deliverance from life through absorption in the timeless absolute. He stares at life's reality with its necessary suffering and necessary retribution, and like a boy who decides that the apples are worth the thrashing, makes the hero's or the artist's choice of life after life, experience for itself.

A great artist can hardly will the mystic's renunciation: his works, created out of the passion of life, refute him. Even if they are symbols of eternity the symbols must be lived, if they are to have more than mathematical meaning. Yeats never denied this. But self and soul are not always at variance. The deliverance called in *A Vision* the 'Thirteenth Cone' is a realization of eternity, not where the saint seeks it beyond the circumference of experience but in the

very rhythm of time's pulse; a consciousness of time and eternity
co-existing in the moment. The great mystery religions of the
ancients may have been initiations into some such double consciousness, and he implies as much in some lines in *Vacillation*.

> A tree there is that from its topmost bough
> Is half all glittering flame and half all green
> Abounding foliage moistened with the dew;
> And half is half and yet is all the scene;
> And half and half consume what they renew,
> And he that Attis' image hangs between
> That staring fury and the blind lush leaf
> May know not what he knows, but knows not grief.*

The whole series called *Vacillation* wavers 'between extremities',
between temporal life and eternal mind whose surface it is. At one
moment he is ablaze with a universal ecstasy, at another the whole
of his past isolates and weighs him down. The tree is eternity but is
also time and death, and

> From man's blood-sodden heart are sprung
> Those branches of the night and day
> Where the gaudy moon is hung.
> What's the meaning of all song?
> 'Let all things pass away.'

At the end he bids farewell to saintliness, in the person of the
Christian mystic Von Hügel, to live in the pride of his finite strength;
but he never denies that beatitude is in surrender to the infinite,
which can only be through humility. At rare moments he even feels
it. In the last poem of *The Winding Stair*, he suddenly sees his own
struggle for self-sufficiency as the cause of all his torment:

* He had found the tree half a lifetime earlier in the story of Sir Peredur, in Lady
Guest's version of the Mabinogion. He referred to it in 1897, in discussing 'The Ancient
Religion' in *The Celtic Element in Literature*. In *The Happiest of the Poets* (1902) he wrote
of William Morris: 'The early Christians were of the kin of the Wilderness and of the
Dry Tree, and they saw an unearthly Paradise, but he was of the kin of the Well and of
the Green Tree and he saw an earthly Paradise.' From Welsh myth to Attis' image is by
way of the early Christians. It is a good example of his symbolic thinking and of the
accumulation of meaning in a symbol.

> Repentance keeps my heart impure;
> But what am I that dare
> Fancy that I can
> Better conduct myself or have more
> Sense than a common man?[20]

—and in swift answer, infinite peace flows through him.

But he was not seeking infinite peace except as a rare respite from tension. His most powerful poetry is proud and defiant and full of the joy of conflict. When his friend Kevin O'Higgins was assassinated he wrote:

> A great man in his pride
> Confronting murderous men
> Casts derision upon
> Supersession of breath[21]

—and that last phrase, so bare and functional, is like a level stare into death's eyes. Its certainty that life is more ultimate than death is the ground rather than the consequence of his faith in reincarnation.

In religion and temperament Yeats was not very like Donne, but one thing they shared was the need to find spiritual reality embodied in sense. But Donne, beginning as a profligate, made sure of the senses first and then found through sex a reassurance of something beyond them. Yeats began from ascetic idealism, absolute certainty of the spirit, and love poetry that was almost disembodied, and learnt in late manhood to understand with his senses how spirit becomes incarnate in sex. When he did, it set the keystone on the arch of his philosophy and he wrote of love in a new way.

> I offer to love's play
> My dark declivities[22]

is sheer impersonal passion, the physical intensified into the supernatural. And in *Words for Music Perhaps*, more especially in the mouth of Crazy Jane, he puts his profoundest metaphysical vision into snatches of song. To put a philosophy in homely terms and sing it light-heartedly takes completer understanding than any

other way of expounding it; Crazy Jane is the final test of Yeats'
faith. It could hardly be stripped barer or emerge more triumphant.

> I had wild Jack for a lover;
> Though like a road
> That men pass over
> My body makes no moan
> But sings on:
> *All things remain in God.*[23]

The human race was also a being to Yeats, and the interplay of
time and eternity filled him with the same excitement in history as
in the life of the individual soul. The rules of the play are expounded
in *Dove or Swan*. A few poems concentrate his whole sweeping
conception of history into a gigantic myth that is a creation of his
own; for though the figures come from ancient chronicle and legend
and are seen in the light of esoteric tradition, the pattern they are
set in gives them fresh significance.

God and woman mate: eternity engenders on time. In *Leda and the
Swan*[24] his theme is the birth of Homeric Greece, which is where
his imaginative understanding of history begins, but the sonnet does
not borrow its power from the significance of the theme. It was perhaps suggested by Michelangelo's picture in the National Gallery,
but it has more than Michelangelo's demonic energy. In the first
four lines the picture is drawn with strong economy:

> A sudden blow: the great wings beating still
> Above the staggering girl, her thighs caressed
> By the dark webs, her nape caught in his bill,
> He holds her helpless breast upon his breast.

In the next four it is not so much seen as felt through Leda's body:

> How can those terrified vague fingers push
> The feathered glory from her loosening thighs?
> Or how can body, laid in that white rush,
> But feel the strange heart beating where it lies?

Only when the deed has made its own impression of power does he
allow his consciousness of history to enter the poem:

> A shudder in the loins engenders there
> The broken wall, the burning roof and tower
> And Agamemnon dead.

The siege of Troy and all the radiant and stormy Hellenic civilization that followed it are not too much to have sprung from that mating. The poem ends with a wondering question:

> Being so caught up,
> So mastered by the brute blood of the air,
> Did she put on his knowledge with his power
> Before the indifferent beak could let her drop?

It happened for passion's sake, not history's. The woman had no choice, the god passed on a lonely flight, aware of what would come but indifferent; but men inherited his life. 'The brute blood of the air' sums up the spirit, at once animal and ethereal, which Yeats saw as the pagan genius that possessed Europe till Christianity superseded it.

A. E. refused to publish the sonnet in the *Irish Statesman*, of which he was the editor, saying that it would not be understood, but the real obstacle was that it could not be misunderstood. It is alive with Yeats' conviction that the reality of the spirit is in the body, and this is what a certain timid kind of occultist, for whom the supernatural is a refuge from the natural, would wish to evade.

Then there are two wild songs from *The Resurrection*,[25] where Dionysus, himself a son of Zeus by a mortal woman, is linked with Christ. The first begins:

> I saw a staring virgin stand
> Where holy Dionysus died,
> And tear the heart out of his side,
> And lay the heart upon her hand
> And bear that beating heart away.

In the next verse the heart has become a star and the virgin, another or the same, reappears in the decline of Rome:

> The Roman Empire stood appalled:
> It dropped the reins of peace and war
> When that fierce virgin and her Star
> Out of the fabulous darkness called.

And in the second song the god dies again, but this time on the cross, and another era of history has begun.

In *The Winding Stair* a gentler poem called *The Mother of God*[26] belongs to the same meditation. 'Did she put on his knowledge with his power?' had perhaps brought to mind Botticelli's madonnas, loaded as Pater describes them with a sense of 'intolerable honour'. This time the terror of conception is less overwhelming in itself, but is made greater by the terror of partial foreknowledge:

> What is this flesh I purchased with my pains,
> This fallen star my milk sustains,
> This love that makes my heart's blood stop
> Or strikes a sudden chill into my bones
> And bids my hair stand up?

In *The Trembling of the Veil*[27] Yeats had written much about a dream of a naked woman shooting an arrow at a star, and how it was related to a country rite in Devonshire where the star was a boy in an apple tree, and to the cult of a Cretan Mother Goddess where the star became a heart: but originally, he says, it was neither heart nor single star but the starry heavens themselves drawn down into a woman's womb (for 'where there is nothing there is God'; but to be born in the world God must be concentrated into a form). His explanation was cryptic but the whole mystery had obviously excited him intensely; he hoped he had seen a vision of a divine event 'in some world where myth was reality'; in fact, that it heralded a fresh divine incarnation and a new era for mankind.

But that was before 1916. In those days it had not fully dawned on him that this is the world where myth is reality, that as he put it later

> Whatever flames upon the night
> Man's own resinous heart has fed.

His visions had not yet taken colour from the times, but came to him in idyllic loveliness as if an era of civilization could be inaugurated with courteous ceremony like a new festival of the church. This one had returned in a very different form in *The Second Coming*, already discussed, and reappears brought down to earth more savagely in *Parnell's Funeral*, which belongs to the next chapter. As with Byzantium, the coastline that was serenely beautiful in the distance changes as it draws near to a scene of merciless fury.

No modern poet, unless perhaps Rainer Maria Rilke, has so much of the ancient mythopoeic gift as Yeats. From the first, because he understood the logic of images, myth and legend had a deep significance for him. But the shock of his own times, breaking on him when his mind was mature, made him aware that actual life was as much the stuff of legend today as in the ancient world. It energized his images, and at the same time the formulations of *A Vision* saved them from incoherence.

Myth, history, politics, art, philosophy, friendship, love: in proportion to the bulk of Yeats' poetry the range of his subject-matter is immense. Yet his singlemindedness is more striking than his range, for he touched on nothing till he could see it in the light of a vision that was fundamentally simple. He himself knew this. When he was preparing for press the last collected edition of his poems made in his lifetime, including all his poetry up to 1932, he wrote to Olivia Shakespear:

I have just finished the first volume, all my lyric poetry, and am greatly astonished at myself. As it is all speech rather than writing, I keep saying what man is this who in the course of two or three weeks—the improvisation suggests the tune—says the same thing in so many different ways. My first denunciation of old age I made in *The Wanderings of Usheen*... and the same denunciation comes in the last pages of the book. The swordsman throughout repudiates the saint, but not without vacillation. Is that perhaps the sole theme—Usheen and Patrick—'so get you gone Von Hügel though with blessings on your head'?[28]

CHAPTER XII

THE LAST PHASE

Yeats was growing old in peace. He was free from want, famous, happy in his marriage, and had thought his way through to his own final understanding of life; and this troubled him. In February 1933 he was writing to his friend Olivia Shakespear:

I have of late I think come to a coherent grasping of reality and whether that will make me write or cease to write I do not know.[1]

More than once in the next year or two his letters say that he seems to have exhausted his capacity for personal experience. In *Fergus and the Druid*,[2] written in his twenties, Fergus had attained the Druid's vision and lamented

> But now I have grown nothing, knowing all

and he himself must have felt rather like that, deprived by the very inclusiveness of his philosophy of a focal standpoint for the passionate excitement of lyric. Of all things he dreaded settling down into the professional sage, the patriarch who, having outlived his passions and found an answer for every question he has the brains to ask, grows year by year more serene, more benevolent, and less capable of fresh understanding.

> O what am I that I should not seem
> For the song's sake a fool?

he cried in *A Prayer for Old Age*,[3] and

> I pray—for fashion's word is out
> And prayer comes round again—
> That I may seem, though I die old,
> A foolish, passionate man.

The prayer is repeated more gravely in *An Acre of Grass* and is implicit in *What Then?* and *Are You Content?* among his last poems.[4] He prayed it so earnestly that it kept his mind active to the last days of his life and made him, of all poets who have written of old age, the least tranquillizing and the most exhilarating.

It seems that anger was the first personal emotion to return with full force, for taken as a whole the poems of his next book, *A Full Moon in March*, are as angry as those of *The Green Helmet* a quarter of a century earlier. The anger rages over things natural and super-natural, and much of it is set to swinging, irresponsible tunes, suggesting not so much anger as a delighted realization that he could still be angry.

For anyone who prays to make a fool of himself there is always a chance in politics, and it so happened that in the middle 1930's Eire had an embryonic Fascist movement called the Blueshirts, led by General O'Duffy. Yeats liked them because he thought for a while that they were the enemies of his own enemy, the levelling common mind, and he wrote them marching songs with a fine tune and catchy refrains and words of reckless bravado. For all their verve, however, it seems unlikely that the Blueshirts took them to their hearts. For good political propaganda they are too complex, not in the ideas expressed but in the feeling, and a shade too sardonic, balancing perilously on the edge of burlesque. A rousing song about Ireland's past heroes—

> Justify all those renowned generations;
> They left their bodies to fatten the wolves,
> They left their homesteads to fatten the foxes,
> Fled to far countries, or sheltered themselves
> In cavern, crevice, hole,
> Defending Ireland's soul[5]

—has a refrain that, though suitably militant, keeps it well clear of bombast:

> '*Drown all the dogs,*' *said the fierce young woman,*
> '*They killed my goose and a cat.*
> *Drown, drown in the water-butt,*
> '*Drown all the dogs,*' *said the fierce young woman.**

* The refrain appears to have been inspired by a neighbourly dispute between the Blueshirts and Mrs Yeats, who did not share his admiration of them. Cp. *Letters*, p. 798.

A few years later, as if he repented of putting words in other people's mouths, he rewrote them, changing little but the refrains but thereby changing the whole mood and feeling. This refrain is replaced by

> Be still, be still, what can be said?
> My father sang that song,
> But time amends old wrong,
> And all that's finished, let it fade[6]

—and the wistfulness of it alternating with the fiery verses makes a new, curiously personal harmony. In fact, the chasm between his own ideals and those of any movement of his age was too unbridgeable to allow him a political cause to fight for, and he soon dropped the Blueshirts.

Parnell's Funeral[7] is much more serious. It is the bitterest political poem he ever wrote, but to recognize its full force needs a little knowledge of Irish history. In Yeats' youth Parnell had been the national leader of his dreams, arrogant and aloof, holding himself accountable only to his own spirit, equally indifferent, at least outwardly, to the worship of his Irish followers and the hatred of the House of Commons. His tactics had almost disorganized Parliament, almost brought about an agrarian rising in Ireland, and in the end the Irish people turned against him, not for anything he had done or failed to do for them but because of the public scandal when he was cited as co-respondent in a divorce. The priests raised the cry and the people responded with a moral uproar. Yeats, who was old enough to see for himself, had seen in it not moral idealism but the unreasoning hatred of mean minds for one incomparably greater than themselves. In a note to *Responsibilities*,[8] he said it was the first of three public controversies—the second was over *The Playboy of the Western World* and the third over the Hugh Lane pictures—that excited his imagination and taught him the meanness of popular passions. It excited the whole country so much that although press and pulpit have long ago let the story drop it is still, after two generations, capable of generating heat at public bars or family dinner tables.

At Parnell's funeral a star was seen falling in daylight, as if the heavens themselves blazed forth the death of princes. Yeats begins by recalling funeral and star in quiet, objective language; then in 'What is this sacrifice?' he hints a meaning more sinister than that of the Shakespearean tag. Then he recalls another scene:

> A woman, and an arrow on a string;
> A pierced boy, image of a star laid low.
> That woman, the Great Mother imaging,
> Cut out his heart.

It is his own myth of the Cretan Mother Goddess, changed since first he dreamed about it into a barbaric rite of human sacrifice. Parnell's fate gives him insight into its meaning.

> *Hysterica passio* dragged this quarry down.
> None shared our guilt; nor did we play a part
> Upon a painted stage when we devoured his heart.

Hysterica passio is that fury of passion ungoverned by the intellect, known to King Lear as 'the Mother'; and *mater*, the Mother—whose name is cognate with matter—is at once the womb of all forms and the grave where they return to dissolution. In a flash the association sets all the images in order. The Mother—the Goddess—the sacrifice of a life—the fall of a star—the end of an era. Is fact an image of myth or myth of fact? Mankind has never been sure, but here are two things that mean one another: the Mother brought down a god from heaven and mob-fury has brought an era to an end in Ireland. For though patriots had died before, it was not their followers who destroyed them; the soul of the nation was unstained by their fall. But when the people themselves can do this to their leaders the legends have lost their meaning:

> An age is the reversal of an age

—and an age of heroes has given place to the tyranny of the mindless mob.

All that was sung,
All that was said in Ireland is a lie
Bred out of the contagion of the throng,
Saving the rhyme rats hear before they die.
Leave nothing but the nothings that belong
To this bare soul, let all men judge that can
Whether it be an animal or a man.

But Yeats was not satisfied with abstract invective; it had to be pointed at particulars, and he added an ironical correction. They might drag down Parnell, but not a leader among them was great enough to eat his heart. Not De Valera, not Cosgrave—

Had even O'Duffy—but I name no more—
Their school a crowd, his master solitude;
Through Jonathan Swift's dark grove he passed, and there
Plucked bitter wisdom that enriched his blood.

The postscript that set out to be a climax of cold anger had turned to the praise of a hero. Yeats would willingly have written satire as bitter as Swift's, but his imagination was not so deeply embittered: it could not stray far from the heroic, and in spite of himself his cursing brought him round to contemplation of the solitary greatness he loved.

And yet the images of the poem were recreated by fury. That Cretan Archer, who had been in Yeats' imagination for years, had stood there as a radiant figure signifying creation rather than destruction, for she drew down the starry heavens to be born as a god from her womb. And anyone in a less sombre mood would have been content to take the shooting star simply as the tribute of heaven to a great man's passing. It was a rage of disillusionment with Ireland that made the two stars coalesce into one lurid flame to light up the atavism he saw around him. 'When we devoured his heart' brings out the sinister implications of the rite, and throws the emphasis not on the birth of a new order but on the chaos of dark passions that destroys the old. When he thought of the whole world lapsing into barbarism he could keep his equanimity, remembering that time returns upon itself and hero and artist come again. But Ireland was less abstract than the whole world; Ireland was his own dream shattered in waking, and he felt the tragedy in his nerves.

Apart from this, the most powerful poetry of *A Full Moon in March* is in the impersonally passionate *Supernatural Songs*[9] where in the person of Ribh, a defiantly heretical Irish monk, he sets forth his philosophy of heaven.* On one side Ribh is a fury of rejection raised to a kind of transcendental purity. He is impatient of the universal tolerance of Christian love and denounces all formulated thoughts of God as fiercely as any puritan denouncing image-worship:

> Thought is a garment and the soul's a bride
> That cannot in that trash and tinsel hide:
> Hatred of God may bring the soul to God.
>
> At stroke of midnight soul cannot endure
> A bodily or mental furniture.
> What can she take until her Master give!
> Where can she look until He make the show!
> What can she know until He bid her know!
> How can she live till in her blood He live![10]

Yeats was at home with the seventeenth-century Metaphysicals, and he seems to have borrowed and transformed his 'furniture' from Andrew Marvell's *The Gallery*:

> the great *Arras*-hangings, made
> Of various faces, by are laid;
> That, for all Furniture, you'll find
> Only your Picture in my Mind.

At first hearing, however, one is reminded less of Marvell than of Donne: there is the same religious passion, the same violence of sexual imagery. But instead of the struggle for faith that makes

---

* For Ribh's general outlook, cp. Yeats' preface to *A Full Moon in March*: 'His Christianity, come perhaps from Egypt like much early Irish Christianity, echoes pre-Christian thought.'

Donne's religious verse so poignant there is triumphant certainty. Ribh stares at the utter blankness of the dark without trembling, and his words ring exultantly:

> Egypt and Greece, goodbye, and goodbye, Rome!
> Hermits upon Mount Meru or Everest
> Caverned in night under the drifted snow,
> Or where that snow and winter's dreadful blast
> Beat down upon their naked bodies, know
> That day brings round the night, that before dawn
> His glory and his monuments are gone.[11]

'Where there is nothing there is God' was the name of one of Yeats' early stories, and then of a play. Ribh in ecstasy hears

> Those amorous cries that out of quiet come[12]

—knowing that emptiness itself is creative. And on the other hand, for that very reason, he protests against the religious ascetic's severance of body from spirit and asserts that man becomes the image of God through intensity of passion, not denial of it:

> Eternity is passion, girl or boy
> Cry at the onset of their sexual joy
> 'For ever and for ever'; then awake
> Ignorant what Dramatis Personae spake.[13]

He denounces Saint Patrick for preaching an all-masculine Trinity, as if sexual love were no part of the divine essence

> Man, woman, child (a daughter or a son)
> That's how all natural or supernatural stories run.
> Natural and supernatural with the self-same ring are wed.
> As man, as beast, as the ephemeral fly begets, Godhead begets Godhead,
> For things below are copies, the Great Smaragdine Tablet said.[14]

Passion is a copy of divine love, imperfect only because the conditions of bodily life dull it. Sex is a partial union of bodies, but lovers freed by death from their gross bodies may attain to absolute fusion while the moment of passion lasts:

> when such bodies join
> There is no touching here, nor touching there,
> Nor straining joy, but whole is joined to whole;
> For the intercourse of angels is a light
> Where for its moment both seem lost, consumed[15]

—and by that light Ribh can see to read his holy book.

Yeats says that he learnt about this angelic intercourse from Swedenborg; he might equally well have found it in *Paradise Lost*. It goes back to a pre-Cartesian idea of continuity between the mental and the physical. All life is matter informed by spirit: the celestial differs from the fleshly being in that greater subtlety and plasticity of matter enables the spirit to possess it more fully. As Yeats takes hold of the idea, sexual union becomes the most perfect attainable copy of the divine ecstasy.

Ribh's philosophy is closely based on *A Vision*. There is the inexpressible, all-consuming One, with its multiple reflection in nature, 'the mirror-scaled serpent'.[16] The soul is balanced between desire for submergence in the One:

> There all the gyres converge in one,
> There all the planets drop in the Sun[17]

—and desire for realization of its separate identity; and the inter-action of these two sets nature spinning.

> She sings, as the moon sings:
> 'I am I, am I;
> The greater grows my light
> The further that I fly.'
> All creation shivers
> With that sweet cry.[18]

His mood is as heretical as his doctrine. Renunciation, compassion, humility in the world of men, all these Christian virtues are irrelevant to his vision, intrusions on the fierce loneliness of the soul in ecstasy; but he has a blazing faith in the eternity of the spirit, and in life as its creative power made manifest, which almost fuses the two worlds in one. Almost but not quite; Ribh is always conscious of the fragmentariness of time against the wholeness of eternity. In this he is one side of Yeats himself; he is Yeats preparing to leave the world. If, as for a while he thought possible, he had outlived experience, if the embodied soul was exhausted, there was still his Daimon to be faced in eternity.

But it was not the end. He had more to say, and quite possibly the rejuvenating operation that he underwent gave him energy enough for it. At any rate *Last Poems*, written in the last four years of his life and published posthumously, is a magnificent return, full of the sense of life, and greater in range, intensity of feeling and variety of style than any book he had written yet.

It is true that his most violent personal experience was all in the past. He would never know again the self-abandonment of his worship of Maud Gonne, nor such utter allegiance as he had felt to Lady Gregory and Coole Park, nor grieve for anything in human history as he had grieved for the burning of the old Irish country houses. But all this past was alive in his mind turning the present into clear sea water with a world living and moving underneath it. He was still capable of fresh friendships though they took some of their depth and colour from the past. While there were old houses still standing with owners who cared for the arts the vanishing world of his allegiance survived, and this was partly why he loved to visit Dorothy Wellesley at Penns in the Rocks in Kent. But it was a living feeling, not a memory of his admiration for Lady Gregory, that inspired his poem to her:

> What climbs the stair?
> Nothing that common women ponder on
> If you are worth my hope! Neither Content
> Nor satisfied Conscience, but that great family
> Some ancient famous authors misrepresent,
> The Proud Furies each with her torch on high.[19]

Several, and some of the best of these last poems are written out of his brooding over history. They are often difficult for a reader unfamiliar with Yeats, but the difficulty is not in vagueness of thought, which is sharp and clear as ever, nor in obscure allusions that need vast learning to follow, nor in a symbolism that has to be known before it can be interpreted. The elaborate symbolic system of *The Tower* and *The Winding Stair* has disappeared, as the Rose vanished from his earlier poetry. Neither in *A Full Moon in March* nor in this last book is a swan once mentioned; perhaps it was inseparable from Coole, and ceased to live when his days there were over. Now he picks up symbols as they come to hand, from legend or history or common life, and everything he touches is a lens through which to focus the supernatural. The difficulty is partly in his condensed language—usually simple in vocabulary but packed with meaning—and the abrupt transitions, often, as in excited talk with friends, left without pointers, and chiefly in the sheer concentration into his phrases of years of passionate and lonely thought, and these are the same qualities that make the book exciting. The poems grow clear as one looks at them, and the clearer they grow, the vaster appear the thoughts they uncover.

It is hard already to recall what those years from 1936 to 1939 were like. It was a time of deepening frustration and the foreknowledge of war; in Europe the circle of terror and violence was widening, in England people seemed to be sitting hypnotized, waiting to be sucked in. They were waiting for air raids and incendiary bombs, with enough knowledge to imagine them. In a way the waiting was more tense than the reality, because the one thing unimaginable was the discovery of courage to face what was to come—and this to Yeats was a symptom of breakdown.

The younger poets of the 'New Signatures' group were reiterating their warnings, bracing themselves for a prospective revolution and trying hard to fall in love with it. W. H. Auden's 'possible dream'

> preparing to lay on our talk and kindness
> Its military silence, its surgeon's idea of pain[20]

was a fine euphemism for revolutionary violence, containing the
veiled callousness of all euphemism. Yeats had seen a possible dream
—different from Auden's certainly—translate itself into

> a drunken soldiery
> Can leave the mother, murdered at her door,
> To crawl in her own blood, and go scot-free.[21]

If he had waited till now to write *The Second Coming* it would still
have seemed a trenchant though unpopular comment on the times:
spoken from fifteen years earlier it had the eerie force of prophecy
visibly coming to fulfilment. What he wrote now might have been
a voice from outside time.

In *The Gyres*[22] he forsees the end of civilization, and invokes
a presence impassive behind it:

> The gyres! the gyres! Old Rocky Face, look forth.

Who is Old Rocky Face? He is, in the first place, not an abstraction
but a sculptured stone head, set in the side of Yeats' Tower facing
Coole—staring, therefore, on the symbol of the glory that a turbulent
age is sweeping away. The rest of his meaning, whatever it is, he
gathers from the poem that invokes him. Miss Vivienne Koch[23]
regards him as the poet's inner consciousness; I should be more
inclined to answer 'the prophetic soul of the wide world dreaming
on things to come'. The difference is less wide than it looks, for in
Yeats' philosophy the soul that dreams is a being of which all minds
are parts. He is, at any rate, a stillness in the centre of time's flux
rather than beyond it, and a being whose impassive gaze the poet
can share.

Yeats stands aloof, not out of contempt for what is ending, for his
words link it with three thousand years of tradition:

> Irrational streams of blood are staining earth;
> Empedocles has thrown all things about;
> Hector is dead, and there's a light in Troy:
> We that look on but laugh in tragic joy.

He sees physical and moral downfall:

> What matter though numb nightmare ride on top,
> And blood and mire the sensitive body stain?

and

> Conduct and work grow coarse, and coarse the soul.

And still the poem's reiterated keynote is 'What matter?'

> What matter? Out of cavern comes a voice,
> And all it knows is that one word 'Rejoice!'

Out of cavern: out of the nothing that is the source and end of all things. In the face of all reason and all history and all experience Yeats comes down to the unshakeable basis of his philosophy. Aware of a central joy in the heart of emptiness, he cannot help his certainty that the values he loves will spring again from an inexhaustible fountain.

> What matter? Those that Rocky Face holds dear,
> Lovers of horses and of women, shall,
> From marble of a broken sepulchre,
> Or dark betwixt the polecat and the owl,
> Or any rich, dark nothing disinter
> The workman, noble and saint, and all things run
> On that unfashionable gyre again.

In the poetry of his twenties everything had led him back to Faeryland, 'the cry of the heart against necessity' as he called it in a moment of insight. Now, everything leads him to the acceptance of necessity on so vast a scale that necessity itself becomes a kind of faeryland. In *Lapis Lazuli*,[24] a piece of Chinese carved stone sets his thoughts moving. Here is art, like Rocky Face aware of human suffering and still rejoicing, and all around him are people so panic-stricken because their world is ending that art says nothing to them. The aggressive crudity of the verse in the first lines expresses his impatience:

> I have heard that hysterical women say
> They are sick of the palette and fiddle-bow,
> Of poets that are always gay,
> For everybody knows or else should know

> That if nothing drastic is done
> Aeroplane and Zeppelin will come out,
> Pitch like King Billy bomb-balls in
> Until the town lie beaten flat.

The world is tragic drama and great actors, if it is their luck to be in the last scene, play it through without breaking down:

> They know that Hamlet and Lear are gay;
> Gaiety transfiguring all that dread.

'In all the great tragedies, tragedy is a joy to the man who dies', he had said in his introduction to *The Oxford Book of Modern Verse*; 'in Greece the tragic chorus danced'. Nor is tragedy increased by the size of the theatre or the number of the cast. The verse takes on resonance as the theme deepens:

> All men have aimed at, found and lost;
> Black out; Heaven blazing into the head;
> Tragedy wrought to its uttermost.
> Though Hamlet rambles and Lear rages,
> And all the drop-scenes drop at once
> Upon a hundred thousand stages,
> It cannot grow by an inch or an ounce.

As in *Nineteen Hundred and Nineteen*, he recalls the memory of civilizations destroyed, and how the world's life has nevertheless gone on:

> All things fall and are built again,
> And those that build them again are gay.

Then abruptly he switches over to the bit of lapis lazuli so delicately carved. There are two old men and a third with a musical instrument, climbing towards some little mountain rest-house:

> and I
> Delight to imagine them seated there;
> On all the tragic scene they stare.
> One asks for mournful melodies;
> Accomplished fingers begin to play.
> Their eyes mid many wrinkles, their eyes,
> Their ancient, glittering eyes, are gay.

To many English readers these still appear cold-blooded poems. 'We that look on but laugh in tragic joy' is hard to swallow for those who do not count themselves lookers-on, and one may ask whether gaiety is the full response to tragedy. Yeats, however, cared intensely for civilization; but he had already seen its end epitomized in Ireland where his English readers had perhaps seen nothing, and the sheer scale of events could not increase their significance for him. The terror of realization had been put finally in *Nineteen Hundred and Nineteen*:

> He who can read the signs, nor sink unmanned...
> Has but one comfort left: all triumph would
> But break upon his ghostly solitude.

These later poems are written from the far side of a crisis, and

> Things thought too long can be no longer thought;
> For beauty dies of beauty, worth of worth

is a brief synopsis of *Ancestral Houses*.

His political standpoint was neither Communism, Fascism nor Democracy, for he did not see civilization embodied in any of these. It could be found only in an inherited traditional order, accepted in the blood so that acceptance was a part of one's freedom; and it was dying and could only grow again slowly out of centuries of chaos. But since unlike the Marxists he thought of souls, not systems, as the eternal verities, to be on the losing side was neither a crime nor a meaningless calamity. Civilization cannot be reborn except from creative joy, and to maintain faith in the gaiety and glory of life through dark times is to prepare a cradle for its nativity.

Nevertheless there is a certain hardness: the spirit of Yeats' poetry is not compassionate. Neither is it cold, but the warmth of his feeling was for no abstract multitudes but for Ireland, and for men and women he had loved for the greatness he found in them. When he thought of them in *Beautiful Lofty Things*[25] and *The Municipal Gallery Revisited*,[26] his verse was full of poignant regret for the irrecoverable. 'Civilization' was then embodied in

> O'Leary's noble head;...
>   Maud Gonne at Howth station waiting for a train,
> Pallas Athene in that straight back and arrogant head;
> All the Olympians; a thing never known again.

It was

>   Kevin O'Higgins' countenance that wears
> A gentle questioning look that cannot hide
> A soul incapable of remorse or rest;

and

>   John Synge himself, that rooted man,
> 'Forgetting human words,' a grave deep face

and most of all it was Lady Gregory:

> But where is the brush that could show anything
> Of all that pride and that humility?
> And I am in despair that time may bring
> Approved patterns of women or of men
> But not that selfsame excellence again.

With these portraits round him, pride in the life of which he had been part overcame detachment, and he forgot to stand outside of time:

> You that would judge me, do not judge alone
> This book or that, come to this hallowed place
> Where my friends' portraits hang and look thereon;
> Think where man's glory most begins and ends,
> And say my glory was I had such friends.

In such personal, particularized generosity of feeling no modern poet stands anywhere near Yeats. It is different from the compassion for common suffering humanity that our modern sensibility fosters.

In the coming war he foresaw that the tradition of nobility would be smothered in vulgarity, because on either side only vulgarity commanded force. In terms of his personal experience it was the Ireland of Coole Park going down before the Ireland of *Parnell's Funeral*. And in *The Curse of Cromwell*[27] his dirge for his own past and the past of Ireland and of Europe, and his knowledge of the abiding reality of it all, are blended with uncanny pathos in a lyric which, being dramatic, is less restrained than *The Municipal Gallery Revisited*:

> I came on a great house in the middle of the night,
> Its open lighted doorway and its windows all alight;
> And all my friends were there and made me welcome too;
> But I woke in an old ruin that the winds howled through;
> And when I pay attention I must out and walk
> Among the dogs and horses that understand my talk.
> *O what of that, O what of that,*
> *What is there left to say?**

Ireland was his life, and in these last years he left behind the bitterness of *Parnell's Funeral*: the Ireland he had loved grew more real than the Ireland he had fought. He returns to it, not only in these poems but in rhymes about Parnell and Casement and the O'Rahilly.

In early youth he had written hopefully:

> And still the thoughts of Ireland brood
> Upon a holy quietude.

History would hardly bear that out, and in a later revision it became:

> And may the thoughts of Ireland brood
> Upon a measured quietude.

Measurement in his final philosophy is as significant an idea as ceremony had been a few years earlier. It means the concentration of vision into a finite form, whether in art or life, through precision and proportion. In *The Statues*[28] he asserts that this, not the command of physical force, is the distinguishing genius of Europe, and contrasts it with the Asian brooding on formless infinity.† The meaning of the first two stanzas is clear enough and has been discussed in an earlier chapter; he says that Greek sculptors made Europe

---

* But cp. also his letter on this poem to Dorothy Wellesley (*Letters on Poetry*, p. 131): 'I am expressing my rage against the intelligentsia by writing about Oliver Cromwell who was the Lennin [*sic*] of his day.'

† For a closer discussion see Wilson, *op. cit.*

when they shaped abstract thought into stone images of ideal perfection. Then come some rather cryptic lines:

> One image crossed the many-headed, sat
> Under the tropic shade, grew round and slow,
> No Hamlet thin from eating flies, a fat
> Dreamer of the Middle Ages. Empty eyeballs know
> That knowledge increases unreality, that
> Mirror on mirror mirrored is all the show.
> When gong and conch declare the hour to bless
> Grimalkin crawls to Buddha's emptiness.

Clearly the image crossed the many-headed foam from Europe to the tropic shade of Asia, not the other way. Greek sculpture went to India with Alexander, and the sculptured image of the Buddha is Greek in origin; in earlier times he had been represented symbolically, by the print of a foot. It is powerful because it expresses an oriental understanding of the formless infinity, in the measured terms of ideal human personality that belong to the European genius.

As for Grimalkin, the clue to her unexpected entry on the scene is in a letter to Olivia Shakespear, to whom Yeats' thoughts could always flow most freely. Here he packs a great deal into a transition from contemporary prudery about sex into the Witches' Sabbath:*

Yet why not take Swedenborg literally and think we attain, in a partial contact, what the spirits know throughout their being. He somewhere describes two spirits meeting, and as they touch they become a single conflagration. His vision may be true, Newton's cannot be. When I saw at Mrs Crandon's objects moved and words spoken from some aerial centre, where there was nothing human, I rejected England and France and accepted Europe. Europe belongs to Dante and the Witches' Sabbath, not to Newton.[29]

'Dante and the Witches' Sabbath' are a pregnant conjunction. He sees the earthiest and the sublimest sides of medieval thought as products of the same forgotten faith in spirit, operating directly on and through matter, and he contrasts it with modern thought—that

---

* Cp. also the theme of *Ribh at the Tomb of Baille and Aillinn*, CP, p. 317.

of Newton, or 'England and France'—that sees matter obeying mechanical laws and finds no place within the structure for spirit. This is enough to show that Grimalkin, the witch's cat, is not an image used in contempt of medieval magic. Nor do 'Buddha's emptiness' and his 'empty eyeballs' imply contempt for the Buddha. Yeats does not usually, and certainly not here, mean vapidness by emptiness. 'Where there is nothing there is God', and all creation is the circumscribing in measured forms of that infinity which, until we have thus embodied it, we can only apprehend as nothing.

The human eye cannot be carved naturalistically in stone, and the sculptor's choice of convention changes the whole effect of the figure. In the eyes of their statues Yeats read the essence of a people's characteristic vision. It was the Romans, he noted in *Dove or Swan*, who first drilled a small hole in the pupil, thus giving the figure a look of alert attention, the whole mind concentrated in the glance.

When I think of Rome I see always those heads with their world-considering eyes, and those bodies as conventional as the metaphors in a leading article, and compare in my imagination vague Grecian eyes gazing at nothing, Byzantine eyes of drilled ivory staring upon a vision, and those eyelids of China and of India, those veiled or half-veiled eyes weary of world and vision alike.[30]

He had studied for years in occult societies where medieval magic interlocked with oriental mysticism. Their doctrine that the one reality is spiritual, formless, eternal and infinite, and that all phenomena are illusions somehow generated and controlled by it, might inspire the true contemplative to turn from illusion and seek to be united with reality, or it might equally well inspire magician and artist to work their will on the illusions. For himself, Yeats chose the world of image and illusion; but he respected the contemplative vision and knew that the beginning and end of all was the 'fabulous, formless darkness'. This seems to me to be the meaning of:

When gong and conch declare the hour to bless
Grimalkin crawls to Buddha's emptiness.

And this throws light on the last verse of the poem:

> When Pearse summoned Cuchulain to his side,
> What stalked through the Post Office? What intellect,
> What calculation, number, measurement, replied?
> We Irish, born into that ancient sect
> But thrown upon the filthy modern tide
> And by its formless spawning fury wrecked,
> Climb to our proper dark, that we may trace
> The lineaments of a plummet-measured face.

The hero-figure of Cuchulain was one of those images, 'calculations that look but casual flesh', and are really the form and proportions of an ideal; powers brought down from the unknown infinite when the poetic imagination gives them precise definition. The Irish, for whom the materialism of the modern world is a chaos, inherit that ancient European understanding and 'climb to their proper dark' to bring them to life by passionate belief.

There may be other ways of interpreting this poem;* there certainly are overtones of feeling hard to paraphrase; but this seems to me the most coherent and the closest to the trend of Yeats' thought. It is difficult, not because the central thought is recondite, for that after all is the ancient doctrine elaborated by the Renaissance out of Aristotle, and well known to Sir Philip Sidney, that the artist looks into the mind of God and sets down what he has seen to be a light for mankind. But into his images Yeats has concentrated a vast range of lonely thought and feeling. To the ordinary mind darkness and emptiness are symbols of terror and negation, or else, as for some mystics, they imply a total renunciation of life. But for Yeats the finite does not deny the infinite. The spirit of God moved upon the face of the waters when darkness was upon the deep.

---

* Cp. Wilson, *op. cit.* Miss Vivienne Koch (*W. B. Yeats, The Tragic Phase*) has also examined the poem. She finds other suggestive links between phrases in it and in Yeats' prose writings. It seems to me, however, that to make the Buddha image travel *westward* is against the plain words of the poem and causes confusion. While this was in press I read Wilson's *Yeats's Iconography*. His close analysis (pp. 290–303) must modify mine—though I think him slightly less than fair to Grimalkin.

That civilisation may not sink,
Its great battle lost,
Quiet the dog, tether the pony
To a distant post;
Our master Caesar is in the tent
Where the maps are spread,
His eyes fixed upon nothing,
A hand under his head.
Like a long-legged fly upon the stream
His mind moves upon silence.[31]

Here too silence and emptiness are dynamic. In the opening lines
of each verse are three powers that make and unmake history: the
strength that imposes its ordered vision; the passion that destroys;
the dream that sustains and renews. There are three figures:
a commander of armies lost in reverie; a girl at the daybreak of
great beauty, dancing alone in idle delight; a sculptor whose hands
meditatively explore the uncarved stone. Their minds are on nothing,
and within that nothing is the destiny of the world; they are imaged
in the long-legged fly, moving quietly to and fro across waters
where no foothold is.

As Yeats observed,[32] a thought which begins as philosophy becomes
in the end 'life, biography and drama'. Before it has ceased to be
a philosophical abstraction it makes laboured and difficult poetry,
as in *The Statues*. Later it is domiciled, passes into the nerves and
senses; and then the words move with lyric ease, the images are
limpid and natural, the abstraction vanishes into them so completely
that one wonders how it had ever seemed obscure; and yet in gaining
clarity it loses nothing of its depth. This is the fulfilment of Yeats'
early axiom that nothing in philosophy is valid except what can be
embodied in poetry.

Often when Yeats wrote of Maud Gonne his father's gift of
portrait-painting seemed to get into his words. *A Bronze Head*,[33]
inspired by a sculptor's study of her in old age, is both a portrait and
a reinterpretation, in the light of his fuller understanding, of all

that she had stood for. Her face is withered now but the same eyes look out from it, indomitably alive; and in a grimly magnificent metaphor he likens the look to a lone bird in a graveyard:

> What great tomb-haunter sweeps the distant sky
> (Something may linger there though all else die;)
> And finds there nothing to make its terror less
> *Hysterica passio* of its own emptiness?

The last line inevitably recalls *Parnell's Funeral.* Her beauty had symbolized the lost ideal world he dreamed of, her actions had linked her in his thought with the mindless, destructive fury of the mob. This was the deepest cleavage in his life, from which he struggled to a coherent philosophy. He had tried to explain her revolutionary violence by blaming an unworthy age:

> Why, what could she have done, being what she is?
> Was there another Troy for her to burn?[34]

Even then she had seemed to be manipulated by a superhuman destiny. Now he remembers how that same glance of the eye, in the full bloom of her beauty, had filled him with forebodings not for himself but for her:

> But even at the starting-post, all sleek and new,
> I saw the wildness in her and I thought
> A vision of terror that it must live through
> Had shattered her soul

and the same thought returns, 'What could she have done, being what she is?' But now it is charged with all his reading of destiny and history, and he translates the meaning he had dimly understood in that 'tomb-haunting' eye:

> Or else I thought her supernatural;
> As though a sterner eye looked through her eye
> On this foul world in its decline and fall;
> On gangling stocks grown great, great stocks run dry,
> Ancestral pearls all pitched into a sty,
> Heroic reverie mocked by clown and knave,
> And wondered what was left for massacre to save.

But there is no need to chase this theme of the gyre of history through further metamorphoses. The mood changes, but always he writes like a man living in a vanished age, and knowing because he lives in it that it is as real as the present; so that his poetry is both inside and outside time. In the last poem of all, *The Black Tower*,[35] he is a band of outlaws faithful to a lost cause that no human power can bring back. The lyric tune has no regret in it, the outlawed life is made vividly and joyously real to the senses, the steady beat of the refrain is confident and carries the hint of a threat. Time is against them, eternity is for them:

> The tower's old cook that must climb and clamber
> Catching small birds in the dew of the morn
> While we hale men lie stretched in slumber
> Swears that he hears the king's great horn.
> But he's a lying hound:
> Stand we on guard oath-bound!
> *There in the tomb the dark grows blacker,*
> *But wind comes up from the shore:*
> *They shake when the winds roar,*
> *Old bones upon the mountain shake.*

In his poems on sexual passion there is a similar fusion of the natural with the supernatural. Ribh had put his thesis as:

> Natural and supernatural with the self-same ring are wed

but his eye was on eternity rather than on time. Yeats now returns to it with new lyrical zest, finding the animal and the divine to be shadows of one another.

The Wild Old Wicked Man[36] rejected by a religious girl, accepts the rebuff with an old sinner's dignity:

> Go your ways, O go your ways,
> I choose another mark,
> Girls down on the seashore
> Who understand the dark;
> Bawdy talk for the fishermen;
> A dance for the fisher-lads;

> When dark hangs upon the water
> They turn down their beds.
> *Daybreak and a candle-end.*

That is not the last word. A hint in the refrain of the next morning's disillusion is deepened into a verse beginning

> All men live in suffering

and he ends with an acknowledgement:

> That some stream of lightning
> From the old man in the skies
> Can burn out that suffering
> No right-taught man denies.
> But a coarse old man am I,
> I choose the second-best,
> I forget it all awhile
> Upon a woman's breast.
> *Daybreak and a candle-end.*

From verse to verse the refrain gathers an intensity of meaning that takes it to the break of eternity. All the same the word-music of the verse first quoted, at once wild and solemn and gay, calls the soul back from eternity: it is still the old pagan Oisin who speaks.

The ballad-and-lyric sequence called *The Three Bushes*[37] has a like duality. It tells the story of a lady, in love both with her knight and with her own virginity, who sent her chambermaid to take her place in his bed. The lover was deceived and all went well for a year. But on the first anniversary, riding too furiously to his tryst, his horse caught a foot in a rabbit-hole and he fell and broke his neck. The lady died of a broken heart, and was buried beside him. The chambermaid planted a rosebush on each grave and kept the secret till her own deathbed confession to a priest; and

> He bade them take and bury her
> Beside her lady's man,
> And set a rose-tree on her grave,
> And now none living can,
> When they have plucked a rose there,
> Know where its roots began.

Considered as a love-story it has that shade of prevarication that tinges the whole medieval cult of love. Dorothy Wellesley objected, justly from this point of view, that the lady's deception was unforgivable: if she loved with her soul she should have surrendered her body or else let him go.* But to Yeats it was an allegory of the body and the soul of love, and the lover, not either of the women, was the central figure. He told the story with all the skill of the anonymous ballad-singers of old times, barely and tersely, yet leaving out no detail needed to make it live as he saw it. The knight was a minstrel, and it was for his song's sake that the lady promised to sleep with him; the first verse as it rushes into action presents the whole situation:

> Said lady once to lover,
> 'None can rely upon
> A love that lacks its proper food;
> And if your love were gone
> How could you sing those songs of love?
> I should be blamed, young man.'

Likewise it was for song's sake he died, for before his breakneck gallop home he had lingered in some tavern to sing one more:

> 'A laughing, crying, sacred song,
> A leching song,' they said.
> Did ever man hear such a song?
> No, but that day they did.
> Did ever man ride such a race?
> No, not until he rode.

That was the kind of song, 'a laughing, crying, sacred song, a leching song', all in one breath, that Yeats himself was trying to sing,[38] and *The Wild Old Wicked Man* and *News for the Delphic Oracle* come as near it as anything in English poetry: the lover is thus the poet himself. The lady's and the chambermaid's songs interpret the body and the soul of love. For the lover they are not

* See her letter to Yeats, p. 88 of *Letters on Poetry*. (Both were making ballads on the same story.)

different, and *The Lover's Song* reaches the greatest intensity of impersonal lyric passion:

> Bird sighs for the air,
> Thought for I know not where,
> For the womb the seed sighs.
> Now sinks the same rest
> On mind, on nest,
> On straining thighs.

'I must leave my myths and images to explain themselves', he had once written, 'as the years go by and one poem lights up another.' To anyone who has followed the track of Yeats' symbols 'Bird sighs for the air' must recall 'The swan has leapt into the desolate heaven' and all the cluster of thoughts gathered round it; and thus the rest that sinks on consummated love is one with the void that is the beginning and the end of all things. This is how the lifelong concentration of thought in a few images creates an effect of unified, instantaneous vision.

The final, most carefully explicit confession of faith is *Under Ben Bulben*.[39] Substantially it is not a very different faith from the youth's who wrote *To Ireland in the Coming Times*, except that the otherworldly asceticism has given place to a fierce insistence on passionate experience; but the temper of the poem measures the change in the man. The language is racier, the rhythm is quicker, the verse is doggerel, rising carelessly to grandeur as the spirit moves it; he no longer veils his certainty in hesitant terms but asserts it article by article defiantly. He believes in the Immortals, and in man's two eternities of race and soul, and in the integrity that is achieved only by battle. He believes that we live on earth to realize, through both eternities, 'profane perfection of mankind', and that art translates the vision of celestial perfection into a palpable model for the embodied soul. He believes that our civilization is running down, and calls on Irish poets and artists to recreate it from the most ancient elements of their life.

Sing the peasantry, and then
Hard-riding country gentlemen,
The holiness of monks, and after
Porter-drinkers' randy laughter.

And then, as if his last words are spoken, he lays himself down
beside an ancestor in Drumcliff churchyard:

No marble, nor conventional phrase;
On limestone quarried near the spot
By his command these words are cut:
Cast a cold eye
On life, on death.
Horseman, pass by!

There is no surrender in his chosen epitaph and no longing for
everlasting peace, only a proud confidence in the sufficiency of his
soul to meet whatever may come to it from eternity.

To call Yeats a great poet is no longer daring, but the word needs
explanation when it is used of a near-contemporary who has not yet
had his chance of oblivion. Greatness is not measurable on a scale,
for in every great poet it is something different, but neither is it
a mere subjective expression of approval. Most of us take it on trust
to begin with that Homer, Dante and Shakespeare are great poets;
most of us agree with the judgement by conviction as our understanding of them deepens. This is so, even if we spend more of our
spare time with other writers, for to recognize greatness is not the
same as feeling at home with it.

It certainly goes beyond mastery of language, indispensable though
that is. Language enters poetry as paint enters pictures: the poet
must command it, as ordinary men do not, so as both to convey
everything he means and to mean everything he conveys. His
arrangement of words is all we have; he is judged by what he has
written, not by what he tried and failed to write, but in some
sense it was there before he wrote it, for

as imagination bodies forth
The forms of things unknown, the poet's tongue
Turns them to shapes.

The oldest idea of a poet is a 'maker'. His instrument of thought is the creative imagination; it has a different kind of insight from the abstract intellect and must not be subservient to it. By means of this he creates a world of passionate action, whose very structure is an evaluation of human experience, whether or not it is re-expounded in comment and aphorism. His vision of good and evil and of whatever lies beyond them is made clear through the intensity of his conceptions, and if he is great enough it is not only powerful and coherent, but is felt to be morally valid even beyond his created world. Thus Homer, Dante and Shakespeare have each defined in their art the vision of an age or a people, and we, who may not accept it as our own in practical life, yet acknowledge in reading any of them that life by those lights was a worthwhile adventure.

Yeats took the poet's creative responsibility seriously. It is useless to wonder what he might have become in a more propitious age; he certainly intended to follow the great tradition of epic and tragedy. He set out to create images embodying whatever was permanent and exalted in the Irish imagination, to bring about a renaissance of vision that would restore 'unity of being' to Ireland and perhaps spread from Ireland through Europe. He had the creative gift and the inward conviction, but he lacked what Homer and Dante and Shakespeare undoubtedly had, what Milton could at least look back upon at the end of his life—comrades to write for, to whom the values embodied in his images were as self-evident as they were to himself. To give full liberty to the epic imagination some kind of harmony is necessary between the poet and his world. And he was in a world where almost every common assumption was alien to his intuitive conviction and the solitary spirit was accorded no rights at all.

He took a long time to realize this isolation. Even after half of himself had seen through his hopes the other half was still urged into action by them, in secret brotherhoods and open societies, trying to build a world where he could create freely. Long after he had given up all practical hope his need for a fellowship of the imagination was expressed in nostalgia for 'Byzantium', where all the craftsmen were unconscious of individual style, absorbed in their subject-matter, 'and that the vision of a whole people'.

At the same time he never thought of exchanging his own vision for what the outer world would have imposed on him. He held the view of art he had learnt from his father:

Art is solitary man, the man as he is behind the innermost, the utmost veils. With the true poet we do not care what are his persuasions, opinions, ideas, religions, moralities; through all these we can pierce to the voice of the essential man, if we have the discerning senses. These are no more than the leafy wood out of which the nightingale sings.

But although the song itself is all that matters the nightingale must have a wood to sing from; how can he sing the Lord's song in a strange land? Yeats was not a blinded bird: he had to know his own persuasions, opinions, ideas, religions, moralities, not because he mistook them for the poetry that came out of them, but because he knew that great poetry had to be rooted in conviction. His convictions were as deeply held as Milton's, more coherent than Blake's who was his master, and he knew they were more than a private whim; they belonged authentically to the European tradition, though not to its present or immediate past. They were not explicit in any sacred scriptures other than his own, but they were inherent in his writings long before he formulated them in *A Vision*. It was as if they had been illustrated in the carvings of some incredibly ancient temple where he grew up, and his maturing mind instead of shaping had been shaped by them. *A Vision* was not conversion but confirmation in a faith to which he had belonged from birth.

It was indeed an incredibly ancient temple, and traces of still older ruins were mingled with its foundations. Few poets have brooded more deeply over the traditions of art and civilization. But everything in his background—the agnostic upbringing that cut him off from any church, his faith in the supernatural that alienated him from the rationalists, his inheritance of the culture of a small nation and of a minority group within it—all this joined with his innate creative energy to isolate him from any orthodox interpretation of them. He read the carvings with his own eyes, picking out what moved him to love or admiration or anger and ignoring the rest. In doing so he rejected most things that the modern world agrees to value, but found and synthesized what answered to certain enduring qualities in himself: joy in heroic greatness, indifference to mere sublunary defeat; faith in eternity and love of passionate life, not at war with each other but inseparable as two sides of a penny; love of his own ancestral roots, a deep conviction that mind is the source of all things. He discovered and rediscovered, expressed and re-expressed all this at deeper and deeper levels, working down to a focal point in himself where they were all one, and striving always for the utmost concentration of thought in the most transparent words. In the process he did not define the vision of an age, but the world he created is, like an epic world, an evaluation of human experience and a great world to live in. In creating it he found himself more completely, in a greater solitude of thought, than any poet of the past.

His beliefs have upset some of his admirers. In our day there is on the one hand a revival of Christian transcendentalism, and they do not fit in with it; the supernatural order they acknowledge is reared on a pagan foundation, as Yeats clearly saw. On the other hand there is a school of rationalism to which any kind of religious belief is a weakness that needs curing, either by psychoanalysis or by absorption in revolutionary politics. The great majority of readers belong to one side or the other, and when Yeats' poetry casts a spell on them they try to excuse the beliefs, or explain them away in terms of Maud Gonne, or make out that they really do not matter to the poetry.

They do not matter, only in the sense that the reader need not mistake Yeats' faith for his own. The poetry would be impossible without them, and in themselves they are neither incoherent nor ignoble nor weak nor indifferent to the heritage of the race. They are the form of a mind with courage to stand alone in its generation and words to make its stand clear, and only a generation in which collective values have all but drowned the voice of the solitary spirit could have evoked such defiant self-knowledge. In this backhanded sense alone, Yeats may be called a child of his age.

REFERENCES

CHAPTER I
1 *CP*, p. 265.

CHAPTER II
1 *CP*, p. 7.
2 Spenser, *The Ruines of Time*, lines 400–6.
3 *CP*, p. 101.   4 *CP*, p. 15.
5 *CP*, p. 304.   6 *CP*, p. 23.
7 *CP*, p. 27.   8 *CP*, p. 23.
9 *CP*, p. 167.   10 *CP*, p. 22.
11 See *Poems*, ed. of 1899: note, p. 312.
12 Quoted by Ellmann, *Yeats, The Man and the Masks*, p. 70.
13 *CP*, p. 17.   14 *CP*, p. 275.
15 *CP*, p. 20.
16 Allingham's poem, see *The Oxford Book of Irish Verse*, pp. 82–4.
17 *CP*, p. 71.   18 *CP*, p. 409.
19 Lady Gregory, *Gods and Fighting Men*, p. 431.
20 *CP*, p. 409.
21 Lady Gregory, *op. cit.* Preface, p. xvi.
22 *Ibid.* p. xxii.   23 *Ibid.* p. xviii.
24 *CP*, p. 223.   25 *Letters*, p. 63.
26 *CP*, p. 232.

CHAPTER III
1 *Plays*, p. 3.   2 *Autobiographies*, p. 417.
3 *Poems* (Fisher Unwin, 1899), pp. 307 ff.
4 P. xi.   5 Pp. xi–xii.
6 *Estrangement* (*Autobiographies*, p. 468).
7 *CP*, p. 391.   8 *Plays*, p. 53.

CHAPTER IV
1 *CP*, p. 42.   2 *CP*, p. 77.
3 *CP*, p. 65.   4 *CP*, p. 68.
5 *CP*, p. 73.   6 *CP*, p. 56.
7 *CP*, p. 265.   8 *CP*, p. 393.
9 *CP*, p. 41.   10 *CP*, p. 41.

11   *CP*, p. 42.   12   *CP*, p. 81.

13   *CP*, p. 62.   14   *CP*, p. 77.

15   *CP*, p. 77.   16   *CP*, p. 69.

17   *CP*, p. 70.   18   *CP*, p. 68.

19   *CP*, p. 439.   20   Pp. 190–1 (italics mine).

21   *CP*, p. 62.   22   *CP*, p. 332.

23   *CP*, p. 49.   24   *CP*, p. 75.

25   *CP*, p. 41.   26   *CP*, p. 35.

27   *CP*, p. 71.   28   *CP*, p. 66.

29   *CP*, p. 401.

30   *Letters to the New Island*, Preface, pp. xii–xiii.

CHAPTER V

1   *If I Were Four and Twenty*, 1940 (quoted by Ellmann, *op. cit.* p. 241).

2   J. B. Yeats, *Letters*, p. 48.   3   *Ibid.* p. 193.

4   *Ibid.* p. 144.   5   *Ibid.* p. 179.

6   *Autobiographies*, p. 65.   7   *Ibid.* pp. 102–3.

8   *Ibid.* p. 188.   9   *Ibid.* p. 171.

10   *CP*, p. 319.   11   *Autobiographies*, p. 96.

12   Quoted from Ellmann, *op. cit.* p. 115.

13   *Ibid.* p. 116.

14   *The Celtic Element in Literature* (*Collected Works*, VI, p. 225).

15   *Autobiographies*, p. 194.   16   *CP* (note), p. 530.

17   *Letters to the New Island*, p. 107.

18   *Autobiographies*, p. 204.

19   See Ellmann, *op. cit.* p. 151.

20   *Autobiographies*, pp. 493–4.

21   *Discoveries* (*Collected Works*, vol. VIII).

22   *CP*, p. 118.   23   *CP*, p. 232.

24   From a newspaper article of October 1892: quoted by Ellmann, *op. cit.* p. 144.

25   *Autobiographies* (*The Trembling of the Veil*, Book IV).

26   See *W. B. Yeats, 1865–1939*, p. 48.

27   *The Tree of Life* (*Discoveries, Collected Works*, vol. VIII).

28   *Collected Works*, VI, p. 23.

29   *Poetry and Tradition* (*Collected Works*, vol. VIII).

30   See *Autobiographies*, p. 255 and p. 270.

31   *Florence Farr, Bernard Shaw, W. B. Yeats: Letters*, pp. 55–6.

32   *The Holy Places* (*Discoveries, Collected Works*, vol. VIII).

33   *CP*, pp. 218 ff.

CHAPTER VI

1 *CP*, p. 91.   2 *CP*, p. 87.
3 *CP*, p. 70.   4 *CP*, p. 95.
5 *CP*, pp. 93–4.   6 *CP*, p. 90.
7 *CP*, p. 85.   8 *CP*, p. 41.
9 *CP*, p. 86.   10 *CP*, p. 88.
11 *CP*, p. 75.   12 *CP*, p. 93.
13 *CP*, p. 139.
14 *Collected Works*, VIII, pp. 16–17.
15 *Autobiographies*, p. 146.   16 *Letters*, p. 434.
17 *CP*, p. 101.   18 *CP*, p. 100.
19 *CP*, p. 102.   20 *CP*, p. 35.
21 *CP*, p. 105.   22 *CP*, p. 109.
23 *CP*, p. 106.
24 See *The Poetry of W. B. Yeats* (1941).
25 *CP*, p. 105.

CHAPTER VII

1 *CP*, p. 101.   2 *CP*, p. 107.
3 *CP*, p. 106.   4 *CP*, p. 108.
5 Cp. *Letters*, pp. 573–4 (Yeats to Lady Gregory).
6 *CP*, p. 123.   7 *CP*, p. 120.
8 *CP*, p. 398.   9 *Plays*, p. 141.
10 *Plays*, p. 143.   11 *CP*, p. 113.
12 *CP*, p. 143.   13 *CP*, p. 186.
14 *CP*, p. 198.   15 *CP*, p. 211.
16 *CP*, p. 214.   17 *CP*, p. 375.
18 *CP*, p. 382.
19 *The Poetry of W. B. Yeats*, pp. 104–5.
20 *CP*, p. 122.   21 *CP*, p. 219.
22 *CP*, p. 348.   23 *CP*, p. 113.
24 *Autobiographies*, p. 95.   25 *CP*, p. 240.
26 *CP*, p. 275.   27 *CP*, p. 122.
28 *CP*, p. 327.   29 *CP*, pp. 177–80.
30 *CP*, p. 152.   31 *CP*, p. 159.
32 *CP*, p. 148.   33 *CP*, p. 166.

CHAPTER VIII

1 *W. B. Yeats, Man and Poet*, p. 191.
2 *CP*, p. 183.

3 *A Vision* (1937), p. 91. All following references are to the edition of
   1937.   4 *Ibid.* p. 91.
5 *Ibid.* pp. 151–4.   6 *Ibid.* p. 214.
7 *Ibid.* p. 191.   8 *Ibid.* p. 188.
9 *CP*, p. 394.   10 *CP*, p. 331.
11 *A Vision*, pp. 223–37.
12 *The Dreaming of the Bones* (*Plays*, p. 433).
13 *A Vision*, p. 209.   14 *Ibid.* pp. 214–15.
15 *Ibid.* p. 248.   16 *CP*, p. 185.
17 *A Vision*, p. 278.   18 *Ibid.* p. 262.
19 *Ibid.* p. 267.   20 *Ibid.* p. 274.
21 *Ibid.* p. 279.   22 *Ibid.* p. 283.
23 *Ibid.* p. 292.   24 *Ibid.* p. 302.
25 *Ibid.* p. 300.
26 *Ibid.* p. 302. The verses are from the tenth *Supernatural Song*,
   CP, p. 333.   27 *CP*, p. 337.

CHAPTER IX

1 *A Vision*, p. 10.   2 *Ibid.* p. 11.
3 *Ibid.* p. 14.   4 *Ibid.* pp. 22–3.
5 From Ellmann, *Yeats, The Man and the Masks*, p. 294.
6 *CP*, p. 214.
7 *The Pathway* (*Collected Works*, vol. VIII).
8 *CP*, p. 279.   9 *CP*, p. 398.
10 P. xix.   11 *CP*, p. 226.
12 See Joseph Hone, *op. cit.* pp. 46–7.
13 *CP*, p. 286.   14 T. S. Eliot, *The Hollow Men*.
15 *CP*, p. 49.   16 *Letters*, p. 58.
17 *The Two Kinds of Asceticism* (*Collected Works*, vol. VIII).
18 *CP*, p. 278.   19 *Autobiographies*, pp. 493–4.
20 *A Vision*, p. 213.   21 *Plays*, p. 447.

CHAPTER X

1 *CP*, p. 152.   2 *CP*, p. 175.
3 *Letters*, p. 605.   4 *Plays*, p. 86.
5 *CP*, p. 393.   6 *CP*, p. 90.
7 *Poetry and Tradition* (*Collected Works*, vol. VIII).
8 *CP*, p. 330.   9 *CP*, p. 444 (note by W. B. Y.).
10 *CP*, p. 120.   11 *Letters*, p. 614 (to John Quinn).

12 *Letters*, p. 613.
13 *CP*, pp. 202–5.
14 *CP*, p. 166.
15 *Per Amica Silentia Lunae*, p. 21.
16 *CP*, p. 207.
17 *CP*, p. 207.
18 *CP*, p. 186.
19 *CP*, p. 205.
20 *CP*, p. 240.
21 *CP*, p. 106.
22 *CP*, p. 122.
23 *CP*, pp. 232–7.
24 *CP*, p. 333.
25 *The Hollow Men*.
26 *CP*, pp. 225–31.
27 *CP*, pp. 218–25.
28 *CP*, pp. 210–11.
29 *CP*, p. 141.
30 T. S. Eliot, *The Waste Land*.

CHAPTER XI

1 *CP*, p. 147.
2 *CP*, p. 235.
3 *CP*, p. 241.
4 *CP*, pp. 275–6.
5 *CP*, pp. 282–6.
6 *CP*, pp. 273–4.
7 *CP*, pp. 267–70.
8 *CP*, pp. 242–5.
9 *CP*, pp. 257.
10 *Letters*, p. 710.
11 *CP*, p. 229.
12 *CP*, p. 247.
13 *CP*, p. 293.
14 Pp. 279–80.
15 *CP*, pp. 218.
16 *CP*, pp. 280–1.
17 *A Vision*, p. 231.
18 *Ibid.* p. 233.
19 *CP*, pp. 265–7.
20 *CP*, pp. 288–9.
21 *CP*, p. 264.
22 *CP*, p. 312.
23 *CP*, p. 294.
24 *CP*, p. 241.
25 *CP*, pp. 239–40.
26 *CP*, pp. 281–2.
27 *Autobiographies*, pp. 372 ff. and note, pp. 576–9.
28 *Letters*, p. 798.

CHAPTER XII

1 *Letters*, p. 806.
2 *CP*, pp. 36–7.
3 *CP*, p. 326.
4 *CP*, pp. 346, 347, 370.
5 *CP*, p. 322.
6 *CP*, p. 378.
7 *CP*, p. 319.
8 *CP*, p. 530 (note).
9 *CP*, pp. 317–34.
10 *CP*, p. 330.
11 *CP*, pp. 333–4.
12 *CP*, p. 329.
13 *CP*, p. 332.
14 *CP*, pp. 328–9.
15 *CP*, p. 328.
16 *CP*, p. 329.
17 *CP*, p. 329.
18 *CP*, p. 331.
19 *CP*, p. 349.
20 Auden, 'O love the interest itself in thoughtless heaven'.

21 *CP*, p. 233.   22 *CP*, p. 337.
23 See *W. B. Yeats, The Tragic Phase.*
24 *CP*, p. 338.   25 *CP*, p. 348.
26 *CP*, p. 368.   27 *CP*, p. 350.
28 *CP*, p. 375.   29 *Letters*, p. 807.
30 *A Vision*, p. 275.   31 *CP*, p. 381.
32 Cp. above, chap. III, p. 32.   33 *CP*, p. 382.
34 *CP*, p. 101.   35 *CP*, p. 396.
36 *CP*, p. 356.   37 *CP*, pp. 341–6.
38 *CP*, p. 376.   39 *CP*, p. 397.

BIBLIOGRAPHY

I. WORKS BY W. B. YEATS

Poems (T. Fisher Unwin, 1899).

Collected Works in Verse and Prose, 8 vols. (Chapman and Hall, 1908).

A Vision (Warner Laurie, 1925).

A Vision (Macmillan, 1937).

Letters to the New Island (Harvard University Press, 1934).

Letters on Poetry from W. B. Yeats to Dorothy Wellesley (Oxford University Press, 1940).

Florence Farr, Bernard Shaw, W. B. Yeats: Letters, ed. Clifford Bax (Home and Van Thal, 1946).

Collected Poems (Macmillan, 1950).

Collected Plays (Macmillan, 1952).

Letters, ed. Allan Wade (Hart-Davis, 1954).

Autobiographies (Macmillan, 1955).

The Variorum Edition of Yeats' Poetry (Macmillan, New York, 1957).

II. OTHER BOOKS

BOWRA, C. M. *The Heritage of Symbolism* (Macmillan, 1952).

ELLMANN, R. *Yeats, The Man and the Masks* (Macmillan, 1949).

—— *The Identity of Yeats* (1954).

LADY GREGORY *Cuchulain of Muirthemne* (Murray, 1902).

—— *Gods and Fighting Men* (Murray, 1904).

—— *Journals*, ed. Lennox Robinson (1946).

HENN, T. R. *The Lonely Tower* (1950).

—— *The Permanence of Yeats* (Macmillan, 1950).

HONE, JOSEPH *W. B. Yeats, 1865–1939* (Macmillan, 1942).

JEFFARES, A. N. *W. B. Yeats, Man and Poet* (Routledge and Kegan Paul, 1949).

KNIGHTS, L. C. *Explorations* (Chatto and Windus, 1946).

KOCH, VIVIENNE *W. B. Yeats, The Tragic Phase* (Routledge and Kegan Paul, 1951).

MacNeice, Louis *The Poetry of W. B. Yeats* (Oxford University Press, 1941).

Menon, V. K. *The Development of William Butler Yeats* (Oliver and Boyd, 1942).

Moore, Virginia *The Unicorn* (Macmillan, New York, 1954).

Reid, Forrest *W. B. Yeats, A Critical Study* (Secker and Warburg, 1915).

Ure, Peter *Towards a Mythology* (Hodder and Stoughton, 1946).

Wilson, F. A. C. *W. B. Yeats and Tradition* (Gollancz, 1958).

Yeats, J. B. *Letters to His Son and Others* (Faber and Faber, 1944).

INDEX